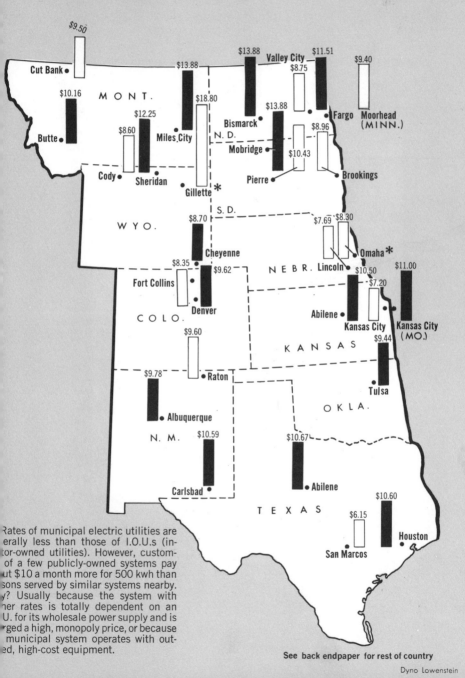

Rates of municipal electric utilities are ...erally less than those of I.O.U.s (in... ...tor-owned utilities). However, custom-... ...of a few publicly-owned systems pay ...ut $10 a month more for 500 kwh than ...sons served by similar systems nearby. ...y? Usually because the system with ...her rates is totally dependent on an ...U. for its wholesale power supply and is ...rged a high, monopoly price, or because ... municipal system operates with out-...ed, high-cost equipment.

See back endpaper for rest of country

Dyno Lowenstein

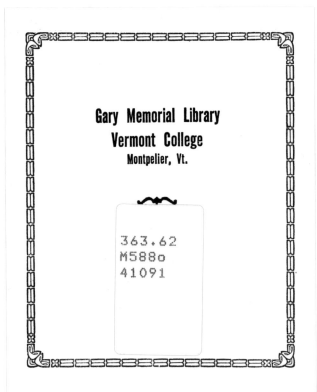

OVERCHARGE

OVERCHARGE

by
U.S. SENATOR LEE METCALF
and
VIC REINEMER

With best wishes and fondest regards from
Lee Metcalf + Vic Reinemer

DAVID McKAY COMPANY, INC.
New York

OVERCHARGE

Library of Congress Catalog Card Number: 66-25147

MANUFACTURED IN THE UNITED STATES OF AMERICA

VAN REES PRESS   •   NEW YORK

Acknowledgments

Many persons contributed toward this book. They work for the American Public Power Association, Congress, Consumers Information Committee on Resources and Energy (formerly Electric Consumers Information Committee), Edison Electric Institute, Federal Power Commission, Group Research, Department of Interior, Library of Congress, National Association of Railroad and Utilities Commissioners, National Rural Electric Cooperative Association, Northwest Public Power Association, Rural Electrification Administration, or Securities and Exchange Commission.

A six-month Congressional Staff Fellowship from the American Political Science Association and a grant from the Philip M. Stern Family Fund facilitated our basic research.

Special thanks are due Dr. Clay Cochran and his wife, Anne; Wayne Darrow; Dr. Laurence S. Knappen; Gus Norwood; Dr. Lawrence K. Pettit; Charles A. Robinson, Jr.; our wives, Donna Metcalf and Lois Reinemer; Mrs. Henry Reinemer; and, especially, Richard D. Warden, for their comments on the manuscript.

We also acknowledge the excellent deciphering and typing of Mesdames Vi Carmona, Judy Downer, Donna Mares, and Pauline Tooker, who put husbands, children, and utility bills aside to grind out succeeding drafts of the manuscript and notes. Any errors are chargeable to the authors, who will appreciate correction.

CONTENTS

Contents

PART IV. WHAT TO DO ABOUT IT

OVERCHARGE

PART I

THE OVERCHARGE IN THE LIGHT BILL

Introduction

On the evening of May 6, 1966, the wife of an assistant professor at the University of Illinois in Urbana reached the last two bills in the pile on her desk, and shook her head. The balance in the checkbook was too low to pay both. One bill, for $11, was from *Parents' Magazine,* for a four-year renewal. The other, for $13.51, was the monthly light bill from the Illinois Power Company.

Electricity was a necessity, of course. She and her family simply could not do without it. Magazines, like so many other things, were not really essential. She could borrow magazines at the library—if there were only time to go there. Regretfully she threw away the bill from *Parents'.* She wrote the check to Illinois Power, without questioning it or looking to see how much electricity—it was 500 kilowatt-hours in this instance— her family had purchased for $13.51.

Less than a hundred miles away her younger sister, a stenographer in the state capital at Springfield, was also paying her family's bills that evening. She was writing a check to the Springfield Water, Light and Power Department for only $7.70—for the same amount of electricity, 500 kilowatt-hours.

In Boston that day a barber was paying $13.41 to Boston

Edison, while his brother was writing a check to Seattle City
Light for $5. Each of them was paying for 500 kilowatt-hours,
too.[1]

The $8.41 a month—more than $100 a year—extra paid
for electricity by the Bostonian was only a fraction of the ex-
tras he paid. He and his brother each earned approximately
$10,000 a year. Each had two children; their homes and cars
were comparable. Yet the Bostonian paid $1,050 a year in state
and local taxes—more than twice the $513 paid by his brother
in Seattle, whose city-owned electric plant pumped millions of
dollars into the municipal treasury each year, despite the low
electric rates.[2]

The month before, in April 1966, a young clerk had paid
his light bill in Tennessee to the Knoxville Utilities Board—
$6.90 for 500 kilowatt-hours—before leaving for New York
and a new job. He and his wife had worked out their budget
carefully, including $20 to be set aside for savings each month.
Upon arriving in New York, however, they were dismayed to
learn that they had to pay Consolidated Edison $14.76 for the
same amount of electricity. That knocked almost $8 a month
off their savings plan.

Late last spring, an assistant shift boss in the Berkeley Pit
in Butte, Montana, paid his monthly electricity bill to Montana Power. He smiled wryly as he wrote "Ten and 16/hun-
dredths" dollars. Electricity was not quite as expensive as it
had been down in Superior, Arizona, where he had worked
in the Copper Queen. There, Arizona Public Service had
charged $13.78 for 500 kilowatt-hours—the same amount he
was getting for $3.62 less in Montana.

What was electricity really costing him, though? The young
mining engineer had been pondering that question ever since
he had spent an evening analyzing statistics of utilities and
other industries that had been printed in the August issue of
Fortune.[3]

He had learned that more than 20¢ of every dollar paid by electric consumers was kept as net profit by some of the largest power companies in Texas, Ohio, Oregon, Indiana, and Virginia. He knew that the 34 biggest power companies in the country—which together account for about two thirds of the profits of the private-power industry—net an average of 16¢ for each dollar of revenue. And he knew that even some smaller power companies, including the one he was now paying, netted about 25%, and collected as much as $7 a month more from each residential customer than was necessary for the company to provide good service and a 9% return on common stock.

How much, he wondered, would an overcharge of $5 in the monthly electricity bill amount to in a working man's life, from age 20 to 65?

He got out his slide rule. If that $5 went into a savings and loan account each month, drawing 4¼% interest compounded quarterly, it would amount in 45 years to $8,106.88!

He made another quick calculation on his rule. If a $5 overcharge would cost him more than $8,000, how much would it cost all of the local company's 134,000 residential customers during their working life? More than a billion dollars!

The engineer grew somber. The men on his shift made $24.70 a day—$6,422 a year. If they were laid off, they got $132 a month unemployment compensation. Some families would have to choose between meat and electricity. After six months, the unemployment compensation would stop. The butcher might give credit, but the power company would cut off the lights.

The engineer knew that the use of electricity will probably treble by 1980 and that the cost of producing it is dropping sharply, although rates charged are not. At stake by 1980, the Federal Power Commission had said, are possible savings of

$11 billion a year to the American consumer.[4] He quickly calculated that that could mean $150 a year for each of the nation's 73 million households in 1980. If the $150 is passed on to the customer and invested in savings, that will mean $20,000 to the average family during the breadwinner's working life.

Why is there so much difference in electricity rates? Why the growing spread between the cost of electricity and the rates? What can be done about it? This book will attempt to give some of the answers.

Chapter 1.

WHAT'S WHAT AND WHO'S WHO

In 10 hours a 100-watt bulb uses 1,000 watt-hours of electricity. Put another way, the bulb consumes one kilowatt-hour (1 kwh). That one kwh costs the customer about a penny in Seattle, about two cents in San Francisco, Chicago, and Miami, closer to three cents in Boston and New York City. That is the price paid by families who use about 500 kwh a month, which is typical of millions of homes. The price per kwh generally increases when less is used, and decreases when more is used.

In talking about the average consumer, the authors have reference to a household using 500 kilowatt-hours of electricity each month. This would be a rough average for a lower-middle-income family with normal electric lighting and appliances— refrigerator, electric stove, and hot water heater. Electric heating, air conditioning, and multiple TV sets will, of course, boost usage appreciably.

Where electricity is expensive, people do not use as much. In Detroit the annual household consumption averages about 2,750 kwh; in Boston it is about 2,000 kwh. However, in Eugene, Oregon, where rates are low, annual household consumption averages about 17,000 kwh—six times as much as in Detroit, eight times as much as in Boston. Yet the average annual electricity bill in Eugene—$147.76—is less than double the $86.13 bill paid by an auto worker in Detroit or the $90.12 paid by the Boston barber.[1]

If steak sold for 50¢ a pound in the Northwest and $1.50 in the Midwest, smart businessmen would ship prime Montana sirloins to Detroit, undersell the Michigan market, and make a good profit. The price would be reduced by normal competition. This doesn't happen in the sale of electricity. Its price is not determined in the marketplace, as many prices are. People cannot shop for Super Krunchy Kilowatts, or an Anniversary Special Rate, or go to an Electricity Clearance Sale.

One power company has all the business in its service area, for a simple reason. Normal competition is not practical or economical among companies that furnish electricity or other public utilities such as water, gas, sewerage, and telephone service. Duplicate wires, pipes, and other expensive equipment would increase the price paid by the consumer—and mess up the yard.

So most consumers have no choice. They can buy electricity from only one company. This does not mean that all electric distribution systems are the same. There are three main kinds, and they are significantly different in ways that affect the size of the light bill.

Most Americans buy their power from one of about 480 "investor-owned utilities"—the "I.O.U.s," if one wishes to abbreviate the phrase. These private power companies serve 79% of the customers.

The second group is the publicly owned local systems, which

serve 13.5% of the consumers. This group includes principally some 2,000 municipal (city-owned) systems, plus a few dozen public-utility districts, which are municipal corporations.

The third group, serving the remaining 7.5% of the customers, is made up of approximately 1,000 privately owned rural electric cooperatives.

The federal government does not sell electricity to residential customers, except in a few isolated instances. It sells power at wholesale only, principally through five agencies: the Tennessee Valley Authority, Bonneville Power Administration, Southwestern Power Administration, Southeastern Power Administration, and Bureau of Reclamation.[2]

The I.O.U.s—the investor-owned utilities—generate as well as distribute more than three times as much electricity as all the other power systems—76% of the total, or almost six times as much as the 13% generated by the federal government. The local publicly owned systems generate 10%, the cooperatives 1%. The electricity produced by the various power systems is frequently pooled, interconnected, and exchanged; 97% of the entire electric industry's generating capacity is interconnected in five large networks, one of which extends from Florida to Montana. The rural electric cooperatives buy as much power from the I.O.U.s as they buy from the federal government. The federal government sells twice as much power to private companies—industries and power companies—as it does to cooperatives. The biggest portion of federally generated power, one third of it, goes to other U.S. agencies, principally defense-related, such as the Atomic Energy Commission. Private companies and municipal power systems each buy about 22% of the federal power output; cooperatives, state power systems, and public-utility districts purchase the rest.[3]

Electricity is produced commercially by nuclear reaction, by falling water, and by burning coal, natural gas, and oil. It may be produced a few blocks away or transmitted instantly hundreds of miles. Regardless, the product is the same, like aspirin or salt, when it reaches the consumer—efficient, clean, essential, and marvelous.

Because of the superiority and necessity of electrical energy upon which modern civilization depends, the growth of the electric-power industry is unmatched. Use of electricity has doubled every decade during the power industry's 80-year history, increasing at about twice the rate of overall industrial production. Electric power is the nation's largest industry by far, unless one considers agriculture to be a single industry. The capital assets of electric power are 60% larger than those of the next largest industry—petroleum refining—and equal to the combined investment of the third- and fourth-ranking industries, railroads and communications. The power industry uses more than half of all the bituminous coal mined in this country and by 1980 will triple its 1960 fuel demand, requiring annually some 500 million tons of coal, four trillion cubic feet of natural gas, 100 million barrels of residual oil, and 20,000 to 30,000 tons of uranium for nuclear generation.

With few exceptions, and regardless of whether a power distributor is investor-owned, city-owned, or cooperative, the price of electricity should be decreasing steadily. Electric power is a classic example of an industry in which mass production and distribution are decreasing the cost per unit.

Technological improvements have steadily reduced costs. Steam power is being generated in larger and larger units at higher and higher pressures, permitting more efficiency. The amount of energy obtained from a ton of coal has doubled since the end of World War II. Quadrillions of gallons of water tumbling from the Rockies to the Pacific generate billions of kilowatt-hours of electricity at dam after dam. At some dams, multiple use of water is achieved by pumping water back into a reservoir, after it has flowed through the powerhouse. By use of this "pump-back" system the same water can be used over and over again to spin the turbines. Nuclear-generated power has moved from the experimental to the practical stage and by 1980 will be generating about one eighth of the nation's power needs. Each kilowatt-hour of electricity sold in 1950 cost, on the average, about half a cent—five mills—to produce. By 1964 the average was down to about four mills. In mid-1966 the Tennessee Valley Authority awarded General Electric a contract for two nuclear generators that will produce electricity at an estimated 2.37 mills per kwh—less than half the cost in 1950. Scientists' search for an economical method to remove salt from ocean water has provided a new technique by which drinkable water and electric power can both be produced in dual-purpose reactor-evaporators.

Unlike gas or water, electricity cannot be stored for use as needed. In the industry's early history, this characteristic of electricity sharply restricted its use and increased its cost; a power company fired up another boiler to take care of the peak demands, which usually occur during the morning and early evening hours. Now the extra boiler is unnecessary. As demand increases, a computer flicks a switch that brings in the needed power. Perhaps the extra power comes from a hydroelectric generator which, energized by running water that does not have to be heated, can be more economical for peaking power than steam- or nuclear-generated power. Or the extra power may come over long-distance, extra-high-voltage transmission lines from a plant in another time zone to the west where the day's peak demand has not been reached, or one to the east where the peak has passed. Similarly, long-distance transmission lines now under construction will transmit surplus power from the Columbia Basin south into California for summer air conditioning, and north from California to Washington and Oregon for winter heating.

The breakthroughs in the techniques of long-distance transmission of electricity permit power suppliers to meet demand without construction of costly standby plants to meet daily and seasonal peak loads. The resulting reduction in reserve capacity will save the industry some $3 billion by 1980.

Another means of reducing power costs is the construction of generating plants at the mouths of coal mines and transmission of the power over long distances to population centers. It is cheaper to transmit electricity from mine-mouth plants by wire than to ship coal from the mine to distant generators by rail. Because of improved technology in power transmission, and despite the more than doubling of material and labor costs in the past 20 years, power is transmitted at lower unit costs than it was in 1947. Long-distance transmission can permit substantial cost reductions in regions such as New England and New York, where high fuel costs, the absence of federal "yardstick" dams, and outdated plants run by old-fashioned managers have kept the cost of power substantially above the national average.

The recent breakthrough in achieving truly low-cost nuclear power in large generating stations gives promise of relief for the high-cost power regions, such as New England, and for lower-cost electricity throughout the nation. This new, nuclear source of energy, developed at public expense, could save Americans billions of dollars—if rates to consumers reflect the lower costs.[4]

Today the most profitable power companies frequently are not those with the highest rates. Rather, the companies that prosper most are those that have advantageous connections—to low-cost wholesale power supply, to large numbers of customers who need more electricity—and other less obvious connections that will be discussed in due course.

The vision, technology, and money that have brought the United States into the era of giant power have come from some remarkable American individuals and from both public and private institutions. The vision came from Thomas Edison's young secretary, Samuel Insull, who grasped as did no other man of his time the national and financial significance of electricity and the advantage of large generating plants and interconnected power systems over small, isolated units. The vision came during the early part of this century from President Theodore Roosevelt and Pennsylvania Governor Gifford Pinchot; they shared Insull's concept of giant power, but were appalled by the growing monopoly in the electric-power business, "the most threatening which has ever appeared," Roosevelt believed.[5] The vision and leadership in later years came from President Franklin D. Roosevelt, from Leland Olds, onetime chairman of the Federal Power Commission, and from Philip Sporn, the former head of American Electric Power.

Three eighths of the world's power is generated in the United States, which pioneered and continues to lead in the technology of electricity. Other countries have made important contributions. Norway, Sweden, and the Soviet Union have led in the development of transmission of power over long distances through use of high-voltage lines. Norway, Canada, and Luxembourg produce more electricity per capita than does the United States. Norway, with its abundance of fast-falling rivers and hydroelectric plants, produces more than double our 5,340 kilowatt-hours per capita. Power sells in Norway, through a combination of municipal, national, and private power systems, for a third of its cost in the U.S.[6]

The money that has ushered in the era of giant power comes principally from private investment. Electric power is a $70-billion industry; the investor-owned segment of the industry alone represents about 12% of all capital invested in business in this country. The federal government has invested $1.5 billion in development of nuclear power and altogether has invested some $10 billion in electric-power generation, transmission, and research; much of the money is being returned to the U.S. Treasury through revenue from the sale of electricity.[7]

Americans pay a $14-billion annual electricity bill. Half the power goes to industrial customers, but they pay only 28% of the light bill; residential and commercial customers pay more for the smaller amounts they use.[8] At present rates the light bill in 1980, when use will have trebled, will be $41 billion. If the rates are reduced to reflect the tremendous savings now being realized, the total electricity bill in 1980 will be only $30 billion.

Is the American public going to realize that prospective saving of tens of billions of dollars, amounting to $11 billion annually by 1980? At this point the answer is no—unless drastic reductions are made in the electric rates charged by the giant investor-owned utilities—the I.O.U.s—and, to a lesser extent, by the customer-owned power systems.

The average residential rate for customers served by municipal power systems is 1.57¢ per kilowatt-hour.

For rural electric customers, the residential rate averages 2.33¢ per kwh.

For customers of I.O.U.s, the average residential rate is 2.51¢ per kwh, approximately half again as much as the average rate of the city-owned systems.[9]

Because of the lower rates charged by local publicly owned power systems, their customers buy half again as much power as those served by I.O.U.s. Even so, the total electricity bill paid by the consumer of the local public systems is smaller.

In addition, many of the public power systems finance city improvements, thus permitting decreases in local taxes. Swimming pools, ball parks, schools, hospitals, street lighting—the full range of community services—are financed in whole or in part by utility revenues, rather than by taxes, in many cities or towns that own and operate their own power systems.

Jacksonville, Florida, is such a city. It is paying off the $30-million cost of a big coliseum, auditorium, city hall, and street and sewer improvements largely through the municipal electric system, which is Jacksonville's largest source of municipal income. In 1963, the electric department contributed $16 million—64% of the city's operating expenses. During the past 21 years, the electric system has put more than $140 million into the city's general funds. Yet Jacksonville electric rates are well below those of investor-owned utilities in Tampa and Miami.[10]

The municipal power system in Springfield, Illinois, each year contributes more than half a million dollars in services to the city. Power revenues alone—not taxes—created nearby Springfield Lake, scene of national boat races and source of municipal water for Springfield and other communities. Nevertheless, customers of the Springfield municipal system pay $4 less each month for 500 kwh than customers in another part of the same city pay for the same amount of power that they must buy from Central Illinois Light, an investor-owned utility.

In one state—Nebraska—all the power systems have been publicly or cooperatively owned for many years. The rates in Nebraska are the lowest in the Midwest.[11]

Directors of municipal power systems are divided on the issue of whether power revenues should be used to finance city services. Some argue that the revenue for these services should be raised through taxes, and that power rates should be reduced proportionately. The reduction would point up the economy of municipal ownership. This idea is less appealing to elected city officials, who prefer use of power revenues for city services to the unpopular alternative of increased taxes.

Part of the sharp discrepancy between rates of city-owned and investor-owned power systems is related to the taxes paid by the I.O.U.s and the payments in lieu of taxes made by the publicly owned systems. In both cases the costs of the taxes or the in-lieu payments are included in the consumers' electricity bills.

The investor-owned and city-owned power systems each

pay about 10.5% of their operating revenue to state and local governments, as taxes or in lieu of tax payments. Unlike the city-owned power systems, the I.O.U.s also pay federal taxes. That takes an additional 13% of their revenue, for a total tax bill amounting to 23.5% of revenue, compared with the municipals' 10.5%.[12]

After allowing for the 13% tax differential, however, customers of municipally owned power systems usually come out ahead of those served by the I.O.U.s. For example, electrical service costs $12.5 million a year less in Seattle than it would if the rates charged by the nearby investor-owned system, Puget Sound Power & Light, applied. Puget Sound pays $4 million more in taxes than the Seattle municipal plant does, leaving a net benefit of $8.5 million to a city for providing its own power.[13]

The state and local taxes of rural electric cooperatives come to only 3.2% of their revenue.[14] They do not pay federal income taxes, because they are nonprofit organizations. They also benefit from 2%-interest loans from the Rural Electrification Administration, although in recent years requests for these 2% loans have exceeded the funds made available by the Congress and the Bureau of the Budget.

The co-ops have some disadvantages that offset the low taxes and cheap interest. Indeed, the rural electric co-ops came into existence to meet the need that the I.O.U.s claimed they could not meet. The cost of furnishing electricity to rural areas with few customers is much greater than it is in urban areas, where a mile of line will produce 15 times as much revenue as it will in the country.

Rural electric cooperatives are prohibited by federal law from initially providing service in any community with a population of 1,500 or more. Furthermore, as part of the loan agreement, all R.E.A. borrowers must provide area-wide service, even to remote customers whom it is costly to serve. Another disadvantage—the migration from country to city, although partially offset by suburban expansion in communities served by cooperatives, has resulted in abandonment of services that cost the co-ops about half a billion dollars to install.

Because they serve sparsely settled areas, the co-ops have about half of the electric-power distribution lines in the nation. Yet they have only 7.5% of the customers and about 6% of the sales. All the co-ops together serve fewer customers than are together served by three of the largest I.O.U.s—Consolidated Edison in New York, Commonwealth Edison in Illinois, and Pacific Gas & Electric in California.

That kind of setup means that revenue is relatively low for the co-ops, which average only 3.5 customers per mile of line, one tenth as many as the I.O.U.s, which have 34. The investor-owned utilities collect $7,820 in revenue per mile of line, 15 times as much as the co-ops' $516.[15] Because of their few customers and consequent low revenue, and despite the 2% loans, the co-ops have to pay relatively more of their revenue out as interest (7.4%) than do the I.O.U.s (6.2%).[16]

The tax and 2%-loan benefits that help co-ops are also available to investor-owned utilities. R.E.A. 2% loans have, in fact, been obtained by 25 I.O.U.s, including some of the big ones: Arkansas Power & Light, Florida Power Corporation, Montana-Dakota Utilities, and Public Service Co. of Indiana. The I.O.U.s discovered, however, that it is less profitable to provide service on the required area-wide basis with 2% money than to serve more populous territory selectively with money that carries higher interest charges.*

The tax differential between I.O.U.s and co-ops could be greatly decreased, provided the private companies chose to share the profits of their operation with the customers, as the co-ops and municipals do. John C. Satterfield, when president

---

* For list of investor-owned electric utilities that have obtained Rural Electrification Administration loans, see Appendix A, p. 255.

of the American Bar Association in 1961, told how this could be done:

> Tax favoritism, tax advantage or tax discrimination in favor of cooperatives does not exist. Every individual proprietor, every partnership, every corporation in the United States may enter into patronage contracts under which patronage refunds (or delayed discounts) are deductible or excludable from taxable income of the business. When the attacks upon farmer cooperatives are analyzed, it is found that in almost every instance the actual reason motivating the attacker is the competition which is given to the business of such person by cooperatives.[17]

On the other hand, if cooperatives paid interest and were taxed on the same basis as investor-owned utilities, the electric rates charged by the co-ops would have to be increased substantially. President W. W. Lynch of Texas Power & Light, when president of the I.O.U. trade association, Edison Electric Institute, in 1963, noted approvingly the drastic effect that additional taxes and interest charges would have on co-op rates:

> An analysis of the operations of 23 G&T [generation and transmission] cooperatives shows that if those cooperatives paid taxes on a comparable basis with the investor-owned electric companies and paid interest on their long-term debt of only 3.449%, this group would have to increase their revenue, and therefore their rates, by 28.9% to meet their costs.[18]

One of the reasons for the difference in cost of electricity, depending on who supplies it, is that each supplier is simply acting in his own self-interest. The people who own and manage municipal power systems, the public-utility districts, and the rural electric cooperatives are also the consumers. As consumers, they want as much electricity as possible for the lowest possible price. Each customer has one vote in a cooperative or public-utility district. The directors or commissioners are elected by those consumers. Local electric consumers are the constituents of city officials who control municipal power systems. In all these instances, customer control provides incentive for reduction of price and increase in sales. Customer control thus substitutes for the competition that cannot apply, in the usual sense, among one utility's captive customers.

On the other hand, the investor-owned utilities are primarily interested in the greatest possible profit for the management and the stockholders. More than four million individuals own electric-utility common stock, which constitutes 37% of the companies' overall capital structure, or preferred stock, which accounts for 10% of the companies' capital.[19] Additional millions of individuals indirectly own stock in the I.O.U.s by holding shares of mutual funds that have purchased utility stock. Indirect ownership of utilities is more widespread, because life insurance companies and pension funds have invested heavily in utility bonds, which provide 53% of the I.O.U.s' capital. Insurance companies alone hold $23 billion of long-term debt of the electric utilities. One insurance company, Metropolitan Life, owns $2.4 billion in utility bonds. This one insurance company has invested more than twice as much in the electric-power industry as the federal government has invested in the Tennessee Valley Authority.[20]

The specific ownership of an individual investor-owned utility, in sharp contrast with the ownership of other power systems, is frequently difficult to determine. The I.O.U.s are required to report to government agencies the names of their 10 largest stockholders and the amount of stock held by each. These listed large "stockholders" in most cases do not actually own the stock. They are investment brokerage houses or other firms that hold the stock for various companies and individuals. One brokerage house, Merrill Lynch, Pierce, Fenner & Smith, Inc., in 1961 was listed among the 10 top stockholders of 53 of the 143 I.O.U.s with annual revenues of $10 million or more. Twenty-one other brokerage houses, insurance companies, and trust funds and one college—Harvard—were each among the 10 top stockholders of 10 or more of the 143 utilities.[21]

The difficulty in determining actual ownership of the stock held by the top "stockholders" was illustrated in 1964 by the frustrating experience of Holyoke, Massachusetts, city officials.

Holyoke has its own power system, which an investor-owned utility, Holyoke Water Power, sought to acquire. The city officials did not want to sell their power system, nor did many of the Holyoke customer-owners. Rates there were lower than in any other Massachusetts city or town.

Holyoke's city fathers decided to try to find out who was behind the I.O.U.'s plan to obtain their property. They saw from the company's reports that the 10 top "stockholders" apparently held more stock than all the company's actual stockholders in Massachusetts. The listed top "stockholders" were brokerage houses and insurance companies, most of them headquartered in New York. Aldermen Edward Sullivan and Patrick Lavelle, Attorney Maurice Ferriter, and Frank H. King, manager of the gas and electric department, climbed into King's car and wheeled toward Interstate 91 and New York, to find out who really owned Holyoke Water Power.

Two of the brokerage houses advised the delegation that their firms held the stock for investment companies, Standard Shares in one case and Central Securities in the other. An official of a third firm that the delegation visited, A. G. Becker & Company at 60 Broadway, said that the Holyoke Water Power stock in Becker's name belonged to 12 clients, including one in Switzerland, one in France, and a foreign bank. But the brokerage house would not identify the owners. "It is not our policy to reveal the names of these clients," said a spokesman for A. G. Becker & Company, "as they have requested that we hold the shares in our name for their own purpose."

Then the Holyoke delegation walked over to 70 Pine Street, headquarters of Merrill Lynch, Pierce, Fenner & Smith, Inc. It is the world's largest investment brokerage house. More important to the delegation, it is also one of the 10 top "stockholders" in Holyoke Water Power.

Merrill Lynch, Pierce, Fenner & Smith, Inc., was courteous to the delegation. But the firm would not tell the city officials who owned the Holyoke Water Power stock that was listed in the firm's name.

The delegation received a statement of policy from Merrill Lynch, Pierce, Fenner & Smith, Inc., written by William E. Conrad of the company's General Services Division:

> While we can appreciate your desire to know with whom you are dealing, firm policy prevents us from divulging the names and addresses of clients for whom we are holding securities. Our dealings with our customers are confidential in nature, and we pledge to keep this confidence at all times.
>
> The only way we may provide such information is upon receipt of a duly authorized and executed court order, spelling out the terms of the request. If such an action is possible on your part, we will be most happy to provide the information you seek.[22]

The delegation returned to Holyoke, wiser in the ways of Wall Street, but still in the dark about who was trying to acquire the city power system. The city officials dismissed the suggestion that they seek a court order, because of the expense involved. Instead, they tried some Yankee dickering. The company had sought to lease the municipal plant. The city officials suggested that, instead, the company sell its plant to the city. Holyoke Water Power—whoever it really is—did not accept the offer.

Although it is difficult to evaluate the influence of unknown stockholders on company policy, the identity of the actual owners of I.O.U. stock is of less consequence than the Holyoke experience suggests. I.O.U. stockholders divide into two categories: (1) the person or few persons who hold the proxy votes and decide policy and elections, and (2) the other 99.99%, who usually sign a proxy and mail it to management before the annual meetings and elections that ordinary stockholders seldom attend.[23]

Of the 200-plus major I.O.U.s, 53 are controlled by one of 15 utility holding companies.* One of these holding companies is Middle South Utilities. Headquartered in New York, it controls Arkansas Power & Light, Louisiana Power & Light, Mississippi Power & Light, and New Orleans Public Service. The former chief financial officer of Mississippi Power & Light, the late James T. Stietenroth, told a Congressional committee how decisions were made in his company:

> [The former president of Middle South] has a proxy when he comes down to the Mississippi Power & Light stockholders' meeting, which makes it almost absurd for us to go through the monkey motions of voting the shares. . . . At the annual stockholders' meeting, he comes in without a proxy but an authorization to vote the shares. He is the company.[24]

Stietenroth testified 12 years ago, but annual elections of investor-owned utilities, in contrast to the democratic elections of customer-owned utilities, are still nothing but ratifications of foregone conclusions. At the 1963 annual meetings and elections of 210 of the 222 major I.O.U.s, more than 90% of the votes were cast by proxy, or by one of the holding companies. In 189 instances, more than 99% of the votes were cast in similar manner. In 132 companies—almost 60% of the big ones—every single ballot cast was by proxy or by a holding company. In only 12 of the 222 major companies were less than 90% of the votes thus cast. And in those dozen

---

* For list of electric-utility holding companies and subsidiaries, see Appendix B, p. 257-259.

instances, a few individuals or companies together cast a majority of the votes.

Consequently, what appears to be overwhelming stockholder support for utility actions and management is often nothing more than a utility leader patting his own back with proxies. The president of Oklahoma Gas & Electric, Donald S. Kennedy, who is a former president of Edison Electric Institute, told a reporter in 1963 how "at our recent annual meeting stockholders commended the company management for the prompt disposal of the pending antitrust settlements" (with equipment manufacturers who had been convicted of price-fixing). "To us, that's a pretty important test of our policies." [25]

The proxy solicitation that Oklahoma Gas & Electric had sent out said nothing at all about forthcoming stockholder ratification of the antitrust settlement. A total of 17,879,425 votes were cast at the meeting, 98% of them—17,598,428— by proxy, and the proxies named Kennedy as one of the company officials authorized to vote the proxies.[26]

The stockholders of Oklahoma Gas & Electric probably still don't know that "they" commended the company's management.

Chapter 2.

I.O.U.s—INVESTOR-OWNED UTILITIES— ARE DIFFERENT

The investor-owned utilities, different in important respects from consumer-owned utilities, also differ fundamentally from other investor-owned businesses.

I.O.U.s have the right of eminent domain; that is, the right to take private property upon making reasonable compensation. Free-enterprise business does not.

I.O.U.s supply an indispensable service on a monopoly basis, with government protection; free-enterprise business does not.

Customers can choose which free-enterprise business they will patronize, but cannot select the company from which they purchase power.

A free-enterprise businessman makes money only if he can keep his costs low enough to make a profit at selling prices fixed by competition. I.O.U.s operate on a cost-plus, sole-source basis. Government virtually guarantees I.O.U.s all expenses, including taxes and salaries, plus profit.

Free-enterprise business sometimes fails, or fails to make much—if any—profit. There is an occasional *electrical* failure even in the era of giant power, such as the paralyzing blackout in the Northeast late in 1965 and another in the Southwest shortly thereafter. But I.O.U.s do not fail *financially,* because of the immense privileges bestowed on them by government.

Nor do the I.O.U.s fail to profit more than most free-enterprise businesses. In 1964, leading manufacturing corporations averaged 6.1% in after-tax profit out of each sales dollar. Only two of the 41 major industry groups—drugs and cement—took home more than a dime out of each dollar. The leading nonmanufacturing corporations averaged 6.3% in after-tax profit. Public utilities—electric, gas, telephone, and telegraph—took home more than twice as much, 14¢ out of each revenue dollar. For the 34 major I.O.U.s that dominate electric power the net profits averaged 16¢ on the dollar.

The net profit was 20¢ or more for six companies. Pacific Power & Light, a Maine corporation that serves parts of Oregon, Washington, Wyoming, California, Idaho, and Montana, netted 22.1%. The other five big winners were Houston Lighting & Power, Virginia Electric & Power, Ohio Edison, Public

Service of Indiana, and Texas Utilities, the latter a holding company in Dallas that controls three operating companies— Dallas Power & Light, Texas Electric Service, and Texas Power & Light. The transportation industry kept as profit only 6.2¢ out of every revenue dollar. And 1964 was the best year since 1957 for transportation. The transportation industry took home only 3.4¢ out of each dollar of revenue in 1961. That year the 34 giant power companies made 14.8% profit on each revenue dollar, and the percentage has gone up every year since.

It would not be fair to the power companies to compare only the profit–sales ratios. The large amount of capital investment required by the electric industry accounts for some of the extraordinarily high profit–revenue ratio. An average investment of $4.44 in plant facilities is required to produce a dollar of revenue. Thus profits should be related to the total amount of invested capital. In 1947, the I.O.U.s had an industry-wide return on invested capital of 5.6%. In 1961, the return on invested capital of the 34 predominant investor-owned utilities was 9.1%. The return kept climbing upward, 9.5% in 1962, 9.7% in 1963. In 1964, it reached 10%, approximately twice as high as the average for the 50 leading transportation companies.

Seven of the 34 power companies had a return on invested capital of more than 11% in 1964. Houston Lighting & Power topped the list, with 14.9%, followed by Illinois Power (13.5%), Florida Power & Light (12.3%), and Commonwealth Edison, which serves Chicago and the surrounding area (11.9%). The fifth-ranking company, with 11.7%, was Central & Southwest, a Delaware holding company which from a Chicago office controls four operating companies— Central Power & Light in Corpus Christi, Texas; Public Service Company of Oklahoma; Southwestern Electric Power in Shreveport, Louisiana; and West Texas Utilities. Ranking sixth and seventh were Detroit Edison (11.4%) and Texas Utilities (11.2%). American Telephone and Telegraph is often considered to be the best blue chip on the board of the New York Stock Exchange. Yet in 1965 all but one of the 34 biggest electric utilities had a higher return on invested capital than did A.T.&T.

The following year—1965—Houston Lighting & Power's net profit climbed to 16% of its invested capital. Four of the 35 electric utilities with individual assets of more than half a billion dollars netted more than 14%. (The other three were American Electric Power, 14.9%, Central & Southwest, 14.3%, and Texas Utilities, 14.3%.) Eleven of the giants netted more than 12%. Only six of the 35 netted less than 10% of their invested capital. The 35 averaged 11.4%.*

The consistency as well as the proportion of I.O.U. profits sets the investor-owned, government-protected utilities far above the free-enterprise businesses that battle for profit and survival. During the dizzying boom years of 1928 and 1929, the utilities edged the all-industry average in profit as a percentage of net worth—the net worth being the sum of the corporation's surplus and the book value of its stock.

During the depths of the Depression, resourceful or lucky free-enterprise businesses merely survived, without profit or without losing too much; utility earnings declined only slightly when the rest of the economy crashed. In 1932, the average income of all leading corporations amounted to two tenths of 1% of their net worth, but the I.O.U.s averaged 6% even then. From 1940 to 1957, the all-industry percentage of profit

* The ratio of profit to invested capital for utility holding companies published in *Fortune*'s annual directory of earnings was understated prior to 1965, because publicly held preferred stock of subsidiaries had been excluded before arriving at net profit. *Fortune*'s 1965 statistics, published in the magazine's July 15, 1966 issue, excluded common and preferred stock of subsidiaries for the first time. A table showing the net profit in 1965 of the 35 principal electric utilities, as a percentage of invested capital, appears in Appendix G, p. 287.

slightly exceeded that of the power companies. Every year since 1957, however, the investor-owned utilities have earned more than the all-industry average. In 1964, the net profit of investor-owned utilities amounted to 11.1% of their net worth, compared with 10.3% for the all-industry average.

By another measure of profit—return on common-stock equity—the profits of the large utility corporations today approach the spectacular. During 1963, 44 of the major power companies earned a return on common stock exceeding 15%.

In three cases, the return on common stock exceeded 20%. Indiana & Michigan Electric, a subsidiary of American Electric Power of New York, earned 20.83%. Texas Power & Light, a subsidiary of Texas Utilities, earned 20.73%. Ohio Power, another subsidiary of American Electric Power, made 20.27%.

In 1964 Indiana & Michigan Electric's return on equity rose to 22.27%, but was topped by Florida Public Utilities, with 23.33%.[1]

Eleven of the 44 companies with 15%-plus earnings are headquartered in Texas. Three are headquartered in each of the following states: Illinois, Indiana, Iowa, and Pennsylvania. Florida, Michigan, Missouri, Ohio, and Oklahoma are each home to two of the companies. The other high-return companies operate in Colorado, Delaware, Louisiana, Maryland, Mississippi, Montana, Nevada, New York, South Carolina, South Dakota, and West Virginia.*

Thus profits by the government-sheltered utilities are consistently greater than profits of risk enterprises—in direct conflict with announced policies of regulatory commissions and decisions of the courts, which have said that, because of their protected status, utilities should earn less than risk enterprises. The reasoning behind these regulatory and court principles

---

* A table showing the return on equity of investor-owned electric utilities appears in Appendix C, pp. 260-268.

was succinctly stated by a former head of the California Public Utilities Commission, Everett C. McKeage:

In considering any proposition brought forward by the public utility industry which seeks an advantage or benefit to that industry, regulatory bodies and the courts must keep in mind that they are trustees for the public and that the public utility performs a function of the state—a function that the state itself would perform were the same not performed by private effort—and that the public utility occupies a privileged position.

The public utility industry is not a private industry in the same sense that other industries not under regulation are considered private industries. A public utility is not entitled to earn profits that can be earned by private industry not subject to regulation. Being entitled to ask the state to call upon the public to contribute to its revenues by increasing its rates, a public utility places itself outside of the field of speculative profits or the right to claim such profits.[2]

The U.S. Supreme Court has said that after all it is the end result of utility rates that is important. "Rates which enable the company to operate successfully, to maintain its financial integrity, to attract capital, and to compensate its investors for the risks assumed certainly cannot be condemned as invalid," said the Court, even though they might appear meager. "The return to the utility equity owner," said Justice William Douglas for the Court, "should be commensurate with risks on investments in other enterprises having corresponding risks." [3]

It is not easy to apply the Court's guideline. There simply is no other enterprise with as little risk as electric utilities. Each year some 13,500 free-enterprise businesses fail.[4] No investor-owned electric utility has failed for a generation or more, because of the extraordinary privileges bestowed on I.O.U.s by government. The power companies' profits, accumulated from tens of millions of captive customers, regularly surpass those of the free-enterprise, risk-taking sector of the economy, despite the courts, despite regulatory commissions.

PART II

HOW IT GOT THERE:
How the Consumer Is Regulated

Chapter 3.

LOGJAMS, AND THE REGULATORY LAPSE

> The electric companies understand the need for regulation and its aims, and cooperate with regulatory agencies in every way.
> —Policy statement, EDISON ELECTRIC INSTITUTE, 1964
>
> The best regulation is little or no regulation.
> —EDWIN L. MASON, Chairman, Florida Public Service Commission, 1965 [1]

Regulation of public utilities is centuries old. During the 17th century, ferryboat operators in England enraged the public by charging exorbitant tolls and providing poor service. Consequently, Lord Hale, chief justice in the reign of King James I, laid down the basic rules of regulation:

> Each ferry ought to be under a public regulation, to wit, that it give attendance at due time, a boat in due order and take but reasonable toll. [2]

Utility regulation in the United States is based on Lord Hale's philosophy and dates from 1877. In that year the Supreme Court declared, in *Munn* v. *Illinois*,[3] that a business affected with a public interest must submit to public control.

Beginning in the latter part of the last century, state legislatures established regulatory agencies variously known as the public utility commission, public service commission, state corporation commission, state commerce commission, railroad and public service commission, or some similar title. In that era, railroads were the principal industry under commission jurisdiction. As electric companies, telephone companies, and other utilities became established, they were in most instances placed under some degree of commission regulation by the state legislatures.

The federal government began limited regulation of power companies during the early part of this century. The issue then was: To what extent, if at all, should government control the damming of rivers by power companies? In 1909 President Theodore Roosevelt vetoed a bill authorizing private construction of a dam on the James River in Missouri, arguing that "to give away, without condition, this, one of the greatest of our resources, would be an act of folly." [4] Prior to World War I, Congress considered legislation to provide a measure of public control over private dams. Power-industry spokesmen agreed that the only legislation necessary was a law "to provide some way by which the government can part with its title and invest it in somebody else who desires to develop the power." [5]

In 1920, Congress created the Federal Power Commission and empowered it to issue licenses for non-federal hydroelectric projects. Most licenses were to be granted for 50 years. Congress also included in the 1920 act the right of the United States, upon the expiration of a license, to recapture, maintain, and operate licensed projects, or issue a new license to another party, on the condition that the United States pay to the previous licensee its net investment in the project plus severance damages, if any.[6]

In 1935, Congress passed the Wheeler-Rayburn Act, which extended Federal Power Commission jurisdiction to interstate transmission of electric energy and its sale at wholesale in interstate commerce. The 1935 act gave the F.P.C. limited jurisdiction over securities, mergers, consolidations, acquisitions, and accounts of power companies. The act also gave another federal agency, the Securities and Exchange Commission, authority to simplify the complex public-utility holding company structure.[7] (One utility official, Samuel Insull, had been president of 11 companies, board chairman of 65, and a director of 85.[8])

Today, as always, the main responsibility for regulation of electric utilities rests with the state commissions. In 1963, Iowa became the 46th state to authorize a commission to regulate power companies. The four states with no commission having jurisdiction over investor-owned electric utilities are Minnesota, South Dakota, Texas, and Nebraska—the latter having no I.O.U.s that would come under commission jurisdiction because all of the power in the state is distributed by consumer-controlled systems.

Commissioners' terms of office are for six years in two thirds of the states, but run from three years in a few states to indefinite appointments in two. Commissioners are appointed by governors in 34 states, chosen by the legislature in South Carolina and Virginia, appointed by the President in the District of Columbia, and elected in the other 10: Alabama, Arizona, Florida, Georgia, Louisiana, Montana, New Mexico, North Dakota, Oklahoma, and Tennessee.

In 1964, the state regulatory commission staffs ranged in size from eight to 773. About half the commissions had fewer than 50 persons on the staff. The total annual budget of all the state commissions is about $50 million. The annual expenditure by each of 14 commissions was less than $200,000 in 1961, and in 30 states it was less than $400,000. The number of utility groups under state regulation ranges from two in Alaska to 19 in California, averaging 11 in each state, with from one to hundreds of different companies in each utility group.

Thus, for example, in 1963, the Michigan Public Service Commission had regulatory responsibility over 400 major bus and truck companies and 1,200 small ones, 87 telephone companies, 24 railroads, 16 electric companies, 14 oil transmission companies, 38 gas companies, 11 gas distribution companies, and 8 gas transmission companies—a total of 1,798 utilities and carriers.

The California commission regulates steam railroads, interurban railroads, street railroads, express corporations, freight forwarders, car loaders and unloaders, car loaning and renting corporations, common carrier and for-hire boats, pipeline, gas, electric, telephone, telegraph, water, toll bridge, passenger stage and heating corporations, wharfingers, warehousemen, air transportation, and a variety of highway transportation companies and contract carriers—more than 2,000 companies in all. The New York commission has regulatory responsibility for more than 3,000 companies, the Washington commission more than 4,000.[9]

Responsible for protection of the public interest in many and diverse fields, but lacking the staff and funds with which to exercise their responsibility, some commissions are able to do little more than accept and approve what is put before them by the hundreds of companies under their jurisdiction.

The chairman of the District of Columbia Public Service Commission, James A. Washington, agreed in 1965 to look into the rising profits of Potomac Electric Power, but acknowledged that the company itself would have to do much of the investigating because of the lack of commission funds.[10] In Maryland, the counsel to the Public Service Commission, Francis X. Gallagher, resigned after trying to regulate more than 200 utilities with a small budget and a staff dwarfed by batteries of experts retained by the utilities. He, too, said his commission did not have the necessary staff to check company books:

The pendulum of control is shifting to the utilities and the state regulatory agencies are powerless to reverse this trend without aid from legislative bodies. We ask the impossible when we expect a corporal's guard to analyze the rate schedule submitted by scores of utilities to determine their inherent fairness, to weigh the nuances of rate structure and to safeguard against one class of consumers carrying too heavy a burden. . . . We have to accept the figures given to us by the utilities.[11]

Nevada was worse off than Maryland. Its commission did not even have a full-time lawyer who could resign in protest. In 1964, the Nevada commission urged the legislature to provide it with "a full-time legal counsel." They didn't get one.

The Nevada commission, if it had had the staff to work up the figures, could have buttressed its case for a full-time counsel by pointing to the return on common stock earned in 1963 by the two power companies that supply power for 96% of Nevada's residential customers, 16.31% by Sierra Pacific Power, which serves Reno, and 14.94% by Nevada Power in Las Vegas.

The Alabama commission (whose new chairman is Eugene "Bull" Connor, former Birmingham commissioner of public safety) reported in 1962 that studies necessary for processing utility rate cases before the commission could not be done "until additional funds are available for the employment of the technical staff with proper training and experience to engage in this work." The last general electric rate case in Alabama dates back 36 years, to 1930.

South Carolina's commission has not had an electric-utility

rate case since 1933. The Delaware commission, whose members receive $4,500 a year and which has a staff of eight people, has not had an electric rate case since it was organized in 1949. Nor has Mississippi, since the commission was given jurisdiction over electric utilities in 1956. Thirteen or more years have elapsed since Georgia, Louisiana, New Mexico, Virginia, and West Virginia commissions undertook electric-utility rate cases. About eight years have elapsed since the last cases in Colorado, Kansas, Rhode Island, and Wisconsin.[12]

Thus most rate changes are initiated by the utilities and simply approved by the commissions, which are not equipped to inquire into the reasonableness of the rates. Although cost of producing electricity has been steadily decreasing, the net effect of rate changes until 1962 resulted in higher rates. In 1963, the rate changes amounted to a net rate reduction of only $30 million.[13] Rates should be going down on the average of almost a billion dollars a year to meet the goals for 1980 recently suggested in a study prepared by the Federal Power Commission in cooperation with all segments of the electric-power industry. Consumers are paying dearly for the regulation that protects and benefits the investor-owned utilities at the expense of their regulated customers.

Regulation of utilities is a complicated business, but the principles are easy to understand. Because competition cannot determine the price paid for electricity, the companies are allowed to earn a percentage of their investment. If the company has an investment or rate base of $300 million and the commission decides that 6% is a fair rate of return, the company is entitled to make $300 million $\times$ .06, or $18 million. Projected operating expenses (for this size company they might amount to about $42 million) are added to the $18 million to obtain the net operating income, which would be $60 million. Rates are then set to produce annual revenue of $60 million.

Here is another way of putting it:

rate base ($300 million)
   multiplied by
rate of return (6%)
   equals
net operating income ($60 million revenue minus $42 million
                       operating expenses, or $18 million)

All rate controversies involve one of those three items: the rate base, the rate of return, or the net operating income.

It is easy to see why each is important to the consumer and the company. If the rate of return of the company in the example above increased from 6% to 7%, the net operating income would increase to $21 million. If expenses stayed the same, that would mean an extra $3 million for the company.

Or suppose the rate of return stayed the same, but the rate base—the value put on the company's plant investment—was increased by $50 million to $350 million. Six percent of $350 million is $21 million, so that could also produce an extra $3 million in profit.

Third, even if the rate base and rate of return are stable, an increase or decrease in the operating expenses will change the net operating income. In the example, a reduction in operating expenses from $42 million to $39 million would be a third way to increase the company profit by $3 million.

One other important point—the return on common stock of the investor-owned utilities is usually much larger than the rate of return. The reason for this is that on the average the I.O.U.s obtain almost two thirds of their capital from debt (bonds) and preferred stock, on which the carrying charges are 4½% or less. In the example above, the company would pay $9 million to service at 4½% the $200 million of its capital that is in bonds or preferred stock. That would leave the other $9 million of its $18 million net operating revenue to apply to the $100 million worth of common stock, thus providing a 9% return on common stock. The return on common stock averages twice the rate of return for the companies that have the highest return on equity.

So much for the basic principles. Now, on to the practice.

Chapter 4.

THE RATE OF RETURN

Every homeowner knows that a small increase in the interest payment costs a lot over a period of years. A family buying a $20,000 house, with a 25-year mortgage at 5%, pays about $117 per month—$35,100 in all. If the interest rate is only 1% higher, 6%, the monthly cost increases almost $12, to $129. The total cost over the 25 years will be $38,700. The 1% increase hikes the cost of borrowing $20,000 by $3,600.

Increases in the power companies' rate of return similarly increase the size of the electricity bill. The only difference is one of degree—the power company makes more than the bank that holds the house mortgage.

The theoretical rate of return that most commissions allow investor-owned utilities has been about 6%. This has proved sufficient to attract capital, finance expansion, and provide a fair return for investors. Actually, however, most of the big companies now have a rate of return exceeding 7%. Of the 188 largest companies, 165 had a rate of return of 6% or more in 1963. For a majority of the companies—111—it was 7% or more. The rate of return was 8% or more for 55 companies, 9% or more for 20 companies, and above 10% for three: New Orleans Public Service (which is regulated by the city rather than by the Louisiana state commission), Blackstone Valley Gas & Electric in Rhode Island, and Montana Power.[1]

The few companies that had less than a 6% rate of return included one that serves rural customers on a nonprofit basis and some companies that sell wholesale power only, to parent utilities. Counting them in, the companies with a rate of return of less than 6% totalled 23, which makes them more than twice as rare as whooping cranes.[2]

The 55 companies in which the rate of return was 8% or more are located in 26 states. None of the 55 are headquartered in any of the eight states with lowest residential rates. Ten of the 55 are located in five states—Florida, Iowa, Massachusetts, Maine, and New York—that are among the nine with the highest residential rates.[3]

Nine of the 55 companies are headquartered in Texas; four are in Illinois. Three are located in each of the following states: Iowa, Kentucky, Louisiana, and Massachusetts. Ten states—Colorado, Florida, Indiana, Kansas, Michigan, Missouri, Nevada, New Mexico, Oklahoma, and Wisconsin—each had two companies with a rate of return of 8% or more. The other 10 companies operate in Maine, Minnesota, Montana, New York, North Carolina, Pennsylvania, Rhode Island, South Dakota, Vermont, and Wyoming.*

In 1964, the number of companies with a return of less than 6% stayed the same as it was in 1963. But the number of companies in the 10% super-exorbitant-rate-of-return class doubled from three to six. New Orleans Public Service and Montana Power were still there—Blackstone Valley Gas & Electric slipped down to 9%. The new 10-percenters were Texas Power & Light, Nantahala Power & Light (North Car-

---

* A table showing the rate of return and return on equity of major I.O.U.s appears in Appendix C, pp. 260-268.

olina), Edison Sault Electric (Michigan), and Citizens Utilities of Stamford, Connecticut, which operates in Arizona, Idaho, and Vermont.

The difference between what some individual companies actually make and what each would make with a 6% rate of return is measured in tens of millions of dollars. During the seven-year period from 1956 through 1962, eight companies each obtained over $100 million more than they would have with a 6% rate of return. The companies, and the overcharge:

Commonwealth Edison (Ill.)	$186,476,000
Pacific Gas & Electric (Calif.)	129,620,000
Virginia Electric & Power	118,416,000
Texas Electric Service	114,405,000
Houston Lighting & Power	111,891,000
Appalachian Power (W.Va. and Va.)	107,274,000
Public Service Electric & Gas (N.J.)	106,226,000
Ohio Edison	103,187,000 [4]

These companies overcharged their customers less than some other utilities did. The eight companies listed have more customers than other companies that have a higher rate of return; thus $10, $20, or $30 extra from each residential customer each year added up to the $100-million-plus overcharges. Some of the smaller companies did much better. As the mining engineer in Butte, Montana, figured out on his slide rule, Montana Power had overcharged each of its 134,000 residential customers an average of $85 to accumulate the $11.5 million that the company made annually over and above what a 6% rate of return would have allowed.

And how about the businessmen who paid a high commercial rate for electricity? Weren't they overcharged, too? Big industries can often buy power virtually at cost. Large industrial firms can and frequently do set up their own power-generation systems, if they cannot buy electricity cheaply. Thus they can provide a degree of competition—they have solid bargaining power. It is impossible, however, for most individuals or small commercial businesses to provide themselves with electricity in this era of giant power. The Butte engineer computed what the annual overcharge averaged for all the 134,000 residential customers and 19,000 commercial customers served by Montana Power. It was $75 a year, as much as the 1964 federal income-tax reduction for many families.

When a businessman who has to meet the competition charges too much, he loses his customers. When a cost-plus contractor charges too much, he probably will have to go before a renegotiation board that will go over his books and make him pay back the excess profit. When a utility charges too much, neither of these things happens. The customers have no place to go. There is no renegotiation and refund, because of a principle of utility regulation called the "water over the dam" rule.

Under the "water over the dam" rule, if a company's net operating revenue is less than was anticipated when the rates were set, the utility will not make quite as much profit as was anticipated. The customers are not required to make an additional payment to bring the revenue up to the sum foreseen. If, on the other hand, the revenue is more than was anticipated when the rates were established, the company pockets the extra income. Past underpayments or overcharges are "water over the dam."

The trouble with this rule, from the customer's viewpoint, is that usually only the companies benefit from it. Costs are decreasing consistently in the power business, but rate reductions have not reflected most of these cost savings. Neither the customers nor the commissions have the professional assistance and funds to challenge all the data presented by the utilities at rate proceedings. By the time a commission conducts an electric-utility rate case—if indeed it is one of the commissions that ever does—and if the commission has sufficient staff to make an independent study which shows that revenue is greater than anticipated, the issue is no longer pertinent.

A recent episode in Virginia shows how the "water over the dam" rule works, and provides insights into the entire regulatory process. In 1953, Virginia Electric & Power (VEPCO) sought a $4.8-million rate increase. Officials of Arlington County, a populous Washington, D.C., suburb in northern Virginia, considered protesting the proposed increase. Unlike most communities, Arlington County had a public-utilities commission. It was strictly advisory, with no jurisdiction over VEPCO rates, which are subject to regulation by the State Corporation Commission in Richmond. The Arlington commission consisted of seven unpaid members, an executive assistant who received $6,382.48 a year, and a clerk-typist.

The Arlington County officials were well aware of the cost of making an effective presentation to the state commission. VEPCO's engineers, lawyers, accountants, and financial experts would present a massive case for the rate increase. Arlington County had no expert witnesses; utility experts who oppose utilities would be hard to find, perhaps expensive to hire. There would be other costs, too—just the transcript of all the testimony at the hearing would cost the county hundreds of dollars. The utility's case would be financed by the customers and tucked into the light bill. The cost of the county's case would have to be financed by taxes, obviously a less popular and less convenient method.

On the other hand, the Arlington officials doubted that a VEPCO rate increase was really necessary. Through the years, the county public-utilities commission had been comparing the rates of the two electric utilities that served the county, VEPCO and PEPCO, the Potomac Electric Power, headquartered in Washington, D.C. Typical electricity costs of county residents on the west side of North Courthouse Road, served by VEPCO, already were 24% above those of Arlingtonians on the east side of North Courthouse Road, served by PEPCO. Service areas of the two utilities in the county were comparable, and VEPCO had more customers in Arlington County than PEPCO did. The county decided to protest the rate increase before the State Corporation Commission and hired a public-utility consultant, Laurence S. Knappen. Shortly after he was hired, the State Corporation Commission abruptly concluded the hearing.

Arlington County's special assistant attorney, Maximilian George Baron, obtained a continuance that at least permitted the county to cross-examine VEPCO witnesses. Attorney Baron had scant background in utility regulation and little time to prepare cross-examination. Nevertheless, with the assistance of Knappen, he was able to probe into several areas where costs of electrical service seemed to be going down, rather than up. One line of questioning dealt with the company's recently instituted practice of sending out electricity bills every other month, instead of monthly. Wouldn't the company save money, asked Baron, by sending only six instead of a dozen bills a year to its hundreds of thousands of customers? Shouldn't those savings be passed on to the customers in rates lower than those proposed by the company?

The company treasurer testified that there would be practically no savings by the new billing procedure. The State Corporation Commission rejected Arlington's argument and accepted the company's. In his opinion, Commissioner H. Lester Hooker wrote,

> [Arlington County] has also asserted that expenses should be reduced because of savings to be anticipated from bimonthly billings. . . . The savings from bimonthly billings are, as the treasurer of the company testified, of a very modest amount and almost all of the savings that are practical have been already realized.

The Commission also disregarded the recommendation of its staff, which said VEPCO's rates should be increased by only $3.2 million, instead of the requested $4.8 million. The Commission put the $4.8-million increase into effect, stating that this increase would permit the company to realize a 6% rate of return. Arlington County appealed to the Supreme Court of Appeals of Virginia, which upheld the Commission's decision. The rate increase went into effect March 1, 1954.

Six years later, VEPCO's Board Chairman, E. H. Will, journeyed to New York, where he was interviewed by *The Wall Street Journal*. He told the *Journal* how well things were going in the Old Dominion. The *Journal* reported:

[VEPCO's] ratio of operating expenses to operating revenues was 41.72% last year, according to Will, reflecting a gradual decrease from 49.07% five years ago. He said the company estimated a "further slight improvement" in this ratio in 1960. Contributing toward a lower ratio, Mr. Will states, was the company's method of billing its customers every other month, saving $2 million last year over the cost of monthly billing.

As it turned out, Board Chairman Will understated the saving in billing. Two years later—in 1962—VEPCO President A. H. McDowell, Jr., told stockholders, "we pioneered and have one of the most extensive bi-monthly meter reading and billing programs in the country, which results in annual savings of about $2.5 million."

The State Corporation Commission apparently did not check the company books, the report to stockholders, or *The Wall Street Journal*. In 1964, when a VEPCO customer asked the Commission about VEPCO's savings by bimonthly billings, he was told, "We do not have any specific information concerning the amount of money saved by the Virginia Electric & Power Company by the use of bimonthly billing."

Further, a commission official told the VEPCO customer:

Any reduction in expenses made by a regulated public service corporation benefits the rate payer. The rates are designed to produce sufficient revenue to allow the utility to meet its expenses and earn a reasonable return on its investment. Any reduction in these expenses will lessen the revenue required.

Less revenue was required, yes, but it was nevertheless collected and not refunded, because of the "water over the dam" principle. During the decade 1954–63, VEPCO's earnings per share rose from 73¢ to $1.58. The market value of the stock rose from $10.10 to $44.37. Yet during the 10-year period, VEPCO's residential customers became eligible for a *maximum annual* rate saving of only 60¢.

By 1962, VEPCO's rate of return, as calculated by the Federal Power Commission and the Arlington County Public Utilities Commission, had risen above 7%. The State Corporation Commission, using a different method, computed the rate of return at between 6% and 7%. The State Corporation Commission did not initiate any rate changes, even though by its own measurement the rate of return had exceeded the "allowed" 6%. Virginia's actual policy toward utilities in 1963 was, as Commissioner Hooker stated it, "If they don't go over 7[%], we don't bother them." [5]

Florida is another state whose commission, as a matter of policy, permits utilities' rate of return to exceed what the commission originally allowed. The Florida commission, said its executive director, Lewis W. Petteway, in 1963, "has been fairly consistent in its adherence to its longstanding policy that it will not disturb a utility's rates unless its return, for at least two quarters, exceeds the permissible rate by at least one half of one percentage point."

This policy, said Petteway, "has worked quite well for a number of years, and, I believe, has been helpful in avoiding numerous rate cases which are costly and burdensome to the utility, the state, and the consumer."

From 1961 to 1963, the rates of return of all major investor-owned utilities in Florida increased, in one case by more than one percentage point. Tampa Electric's rose from 7.64% to 8.92%; Gulf Power's from 7.36% to 7.73%, Florida Power Corporation's from 7.54% to 7.87%, Florida Power & Light's from 7.74% to 8.31%. Yet the Florida Public Service Commission did not schedule rate hearings until 1965—after the *Miami Herald* ran a series of articles about utility overcharges and the city of Miami hired an aggressive public-utilities consultant.[6]

Even in a state with a public-minded utility commission, such as California, the "water over the dam" principle that is written into utility law carries extra millions in overcharges out of utility customers' pocketbooks. Utilities drag on rate cases for months, even years, secure in the knowledge that an eventual rate reduction will not be retroactive.

A mere one-week postponement of a reduction can extract an extra million dollars from customers of one utility, electric or telephone. In 1964, San Francisco, Los Angeles, and San Diego urged the California commission to act quickly to decrease the telephone rates, pointing out that "telephone subscribers have been required to pay more than $150,000 per day in excess rates to the Pacific Telephone and Telegraph Company, no part of which excess can be refunded to the rate-paying public under existing law."

The commission nevertheless, upon reducing rates, directed the company to refund $80 million in overcharges collected by the company since initiation of the investigation. In 1965, the California Supreme Court held that the commission lacked the power to order refunds.

The law was on the utility's side—and so was the $80 million.

Chapter 5.

THE OPERATING EXPENSES

> Corporations collect [taxes] from the people who buy their products, and then turn the money over to the government. Neither the owners nor the employees of the corporation can have any of this money.
>
> —EDWIN VENNARD, Managing Director, Edison Electric Institute, 1964 [1]

Each year a few employers illegally keep money they have deducted from employee paychecks for federal taxes—for income, social security, railroad retirement, and unemployment taxes. Negotiation and federal tax liens reduce the uncollectable taxes to $50 or $60 million a year. Some of the employers have gone broke, losing their money and Uncle Sam's, too. The taxkeeping employers are subject to indictment, fines, and jail sentences.

Investor-owned utilities also keep money that they collected from customers for taxes. The I.O.U.s keep millions of these dollars. The government never gets them; the customers do not get them back. Yet officials of the power companies that keep these tax dollars are never indicted, fined, or jailed.

The reason for the contrasting policies is that in tax matters, as in other significant ways, the I.O.U.s are different from other businesses. "No other industry operates under such special and peculiar circumstances," a public-utility economics professor wrote recently. "Almost every aspect of the utility business is different from that of 'other businesses' and taxes are no exception." [2]

Taxes are not itemized on the electricity bill. Telephone utility bills usually list only one tax—the excise tax.* Itemized or not, federal, state, and local taxes are considered as operating expenses by public-utility commissions. Stockholders and utility officials pay none of the taxes; the customers pay them all, and all other operating expenses as well. Rates are set to cover all reasonable and likely expenses connected with furnishing utility service and to provide profit, as well. These expenses include maintenance, advertising, promotion, public relations, salaries, wages, pension plans, vehicles (including airplanes), depreciation, research, legal services, reserves for property damage, personal injuries and uncollectible accounts, the expense of the utilities' presentations before commissions in rate cases—everything related to provision of electric service, including taxes.

A utility is not likely to underestimate its expenses. To do so would decrease its revenue. Some expenses anticipated when rates were established do not have to be met. When rate cases are conducted infrequently or, as in some states, never, when a utility is not required to justify its various reserves, more money accumulates than is needed.

Despite increasing utility profits, the percentage of utility revenue required for federal taxes is decreasing because of many favorable changes in the law. The investor-owned utilities have received nine federal tax benefits since World War II.

The most recent was the reduction in corporation income tax approved in 1964. It provided for a 2% cut that year and another 2% cut in 1965. These reductions amounted to about $50 million for the I.O.U.s in 1964, and $100 million in 1965 and thereafter. These cost reductions could be easily identified and refunded to the customers.

---

* In some local jurisdictions a consumers' utility tax is levied, and itemized.

Some power-company officials regarded the 1964 tax reduction as too trifling to bother about. One company president, who is also a former president of Edison Electric Institute, the I.O.U. trade association, put it this way:

If the $1 million is passed on as a rate reduction, it is such a trivial reduction that a customer has trouble finding it and no one benefits to any worthwhile degree. I suggest that this is an instance of over-regulation. . . .[3]

In this case—Montana Power—following public criticism of the company's cavalier attitude, the state commission decided otherwise. It ordered the company to reduce its rates by $1¼ million to reflect the tax cut.

A *New York Times* survey in mid-1964 on utility handling of the 2% tax cut showed that "while a great number of utility companies had already passed on their tax savings to the consumer or had requested permission to do so, many others preferred to invest tax savings in new capital construction and equipment."

The Times reported that in New York State only two utility companies had cooperated with the state public service commission and requested rate reductions following the federal tax cut. The major utilities in New Jersey had taken the position that increased state taxes and investment in new construction made it impossible for them to reduce rates. No rate-reduction requests had been received from utilities by state commissions in Nevada, Missouri, and Rhode Island. In Utah two companies refused to recommend a rate reduction. No action had been taken in Michigan, Wyoming, or Louisiana.[4]

In 1962, Congress considered a tax credit for companies that made capital investments. President Kennedy's Secretary of the Treasury, C. Douglas Dillon, recommended that utilities be excluded from this tax cut, pointing out how they differ from other businesses:

The public utilities are regulated monopoly industries . . . in return for their authorization to operate as regulated service corporations, they are assured consumer rate charges which will cover their cost of operation, including federal income taxes, plus a just and reasonable rate of return on investment.[5]

Congress nevertheless authorized power companies to deduct $3 from their federal taxes for every $100 invested in new plant and equipment. The 3% tax credit benefited electric utilities by $58 million in 1962, $82 million in 1963, $97 million in 1964.

Most consumers did not benefit directly from this tax concession, however, because of an amendment that Congress approved two years later. When the 1964 tax bill came out of the House Ways and Means Committee, it included a provision—Section 203 (e)—which said that federal regulatory agencies could not require utilities under their jurisdiction to pass on to the customers the savings permitted by the 3% tax credit (unless it was spread over the life of the property) without the consent of the utility itself (which would hardly be likely). No hearings had been held on this section in the House committee. The rules under which the bill was considered provided no opportunity to amend the bill on the House floor. Section 203 (e) became law, by a two-vote margin in the Senate Finance Committee and a five-vote margin in the Senate.[6] *

Since World War II, the utilities have also benefited from repeal of the excess profits tax, repeal of the federal 3⅓ gross electric revenue tax, and from several revisions of Treasury rules on depreciation. The utilities' biggest tax break, however, derived from two sections of the tax law approved in 1954. Section 168 of the 1954 law permitted five-year amorti-

* In October 1966, Congress suspended for 16 months the 7% tax credit for non-utility corporations and 3% tax credit for utilities.

zation or "fast tax write-off" of all or part of the cost of emergency facilities related to national defense. Through 1964, 115 power companies accumulated more than $1 billion under this section.

Section 167 of the 1954 act permitted rapid depreciation of utility property. Through this one section, 121 electric utilities accumulated $711 million through 1964.

Ironically, this section also leads to distribution by some companies of *tax-free* dividends. Some I.O.U.s charge customers for taxes the companies never pay, then issue to stockholders dividends that are wholly or partially free of federal tax. It happens this way: Section 167 permits companies to keep two sets of books, one for the tax collectors, the other for the regulatory commissions. When income in the "regulation" book exceeds income in the "tax" book, the difference can be paid to shareholders as a tax-free return of capital.

In 1954, $21.6 million in tax-free dividend payments were made by power companies. Since 1958, they have distributed more than $90 million worth of tax-free dividends each year. In 1962, the payments totalled $101.7 million. In 1963, they totalled $123.9 million. The total in tax-free dividends distributed by 57 I.O.U.s in the decade ending with 1963 was $741.6 million, almost three quarters of a billion dollars. And they started the next decade off big, with $112 million worth of tax-free dividends issued in 1964.[7] *

Stockholders of five companies received almost half of this windfall. Detroit Edison distributed $86,488,401 in tax-free dividends; Pacific Power & Light, which operates in six Western states, $80,960,784; Niagara Mohawk in upstate New York, $80,617,324; Union Electric, which serves parts of Missouri, southern Illinois, and Iowa, $64,469,449, and Pacific Gas & Electric in California, $54,425,928. Consolidated Edi-

---

* Electric utilities that have issued tax-free dividends are listed in Appendix D (table 3), p. 279.

son of New York did not start issuing tax-free dividends until 1963, but in that one year passed out $18,705,147 worth, and Con Ed's tax-free dividend distribution more than tripled in 1964, to $64,497,018.[8]

In sum, the federal taxes paid by investor-owned utilities decreased from 14.7% of revenue in 1955 to 13% of revenue in 1963.[9] Thus on the average the $10 monthly electricity bill in 1955 included $1.47 for federal taxes; the $10 light bill in 1963 included only $1.30 for federal taxes. In other words, the monthly bill should have been reduced by 17¢ to $9.83 by 1963 and should have been further reduced in 1964 and 1965 to compensate for additional federal tax benefits that became effective in those years. (This example is simplified; rate adjustments must take into account other costs, as well. Therefore, rate reductions in many cases should have far exceeded 17¢, because of generally decreasing costs.)

Many utilities have taken the 17¢ out of the "tax reserve" and put it into construction or some other account. The effect of this investment of utilities' tax funds was pinpointed recently by Dr. Martin T. Farris, professor of economics at Arizona State University. Commenting on the different ways in which the 1964 tax reduction was being handled, Farris observed that the diversion of tax collections violated one of the basic principles of regulation:

Since taxes are *collected* from the customers by the utilities, the effect of the utility using the tax savings for investment is to *raise capital from the customer!* A customer should pay a fair price for the service. This price should adequately reflect all costs and include a fair return on a fair value. But a customer should *not* be required to *donate capital* to the utility. [his emphasis] [10]

Despite the violation of a basic principle of regulation, the customers are increasingly required to donate capital to I.O.U.s. The customers receive no stock, no dividends, no interest.

They do not get their money back. The companies use the excess revenue collected from customers to finance new construction, instead of going to the marketplace and selling stock to investors, or to provide extra sweets for stockholders.

During the past decade, utility financing has been significantly altered. In 1954, two thirds of the industry's $2.8 billion worth of new construction was financed by sale of securities; the remaining one third by what the trade calls "internal cash generation," that is, money set aside for depreciation and amortization and retained earnings. By 1963, the situation had reversed. One third of the industry's $3.3 billion in construction was financed by sale of securities; two thirds was financed by internal cash generation.[11] Part of this marked shift was made possible by the 1954 and 1962 tax laws, which permitted the companies to keep and invest funds collected from customers for taxes. Retained earnings, that is, profit which the company chose to invest rather than pay out as dividends to stockholders, provided only 15% of the internal cash generation.

Utility folklore pictures the power industry busy in the marketplace trying to raise new money for construction. "As the money for the expansion must be raised on the free market, the utilities must pay the market price of money or investors will put their money elsewhere," Managing Director Edwin Vennard of Edison Electric Institute wrote in *The Electric Power Business,* published in 1962. "The company must earn enough to pay the market price of money required for expansion." [12]

Actually, however, many companies are switching to a full pay-as-you-go basis. More than half of the 100 utilities surveyed in 1963 by a trade publication said they could probably avoid the sale of common stock for four or five years, thanks to internal cash generation. A banker, William F. Craig, writing in *Investment Dealers' Digest* in 1964, foresaw a situation "under which equity financing will be unnecessary for some [electric] companies for extended periods."

Some companies are generating not merely all the cash they need, he said, but up to "about 120% of the funds required" for new construction.

Without even hinting that the utilities could cut the rates that produce the excess revenue, Craig discussed the "problem of fund employment for companies generating cash in excess of requirements." Rural electric cooperatives pay a low 2% interest on money needed for new construction, if and when the Rural Electrification Administration has money to lend them. But the I.O.U.s with excess cash would not have to borrow at all or sell stock. They could make money on their surplus, too.

A serious problem for the I.O.U.s—too much money. What to do?

Chapter 6.

GIVE—TO THE CHARITY OF *THEIR* CHOICE

> *Facile largeri de alieno.* (It is easy to be generous with other people's property.)
> —Latin Proverb

William C. "Bill" MacInnes, president of Tampa Electric, smiled broadly in the picture accompanying his article in a 1964 issue of *Investment Dealers' Digest*. He had reason to be happy. Tampa Electric had everything going its way.

The company's rate of return had climbed steadily since Tampa Electric pushed through a rate increase in 1959. The rate of return had moved up from 7.64% in 1961 to 8.33%

in 1962, and 8.92% in 1963. This high rate of return brought in about $7 million more each year than a 6% rate of return would have, and permitted an 18.88% return on common stock in 1963.

Prospects for the future were even brighter. The old folks were flocking to sunny Tampa Bay; the company's service area would grow an estimated 73% within the decade. Expansion of the U.S. Strike Command permanent headquarters at Mac-Dill Air Force Base and of Tampa's deep-water port, the biggest between Mobile and Norfolk, was stimulating the economy. Additional new generating facilities would be needed to meet growing loads, but the company had no plans to sell additional stock. Internal cash generation would provide much of the needed money.[1]

There was another thing going for Tampa Electric. The company was known and honored for its philanthropies:

> Boy Scouts, Girl Scouts, American Legion,
> Boys Clubs, colleges, schools in the region,
> Civic, community causes eclectic
> Profited greatly from Tampa Electric.

The president shared his company's reputation. He received the Tampa Civitan Club's coveted "Outstanding Citizen of the Year" award in 1960, and in 1964 was named campaign chairman for the 1964 Greater Tampa United Fund.

And best of all, from the company's viewpoint, the customers financed the utility's philanthropies. The company, of course, got the credit.

In Florida and in an increasing number of other states, contributions to charitable organizations are considered part of investor-owned utilities' operating expenses. The customer gives to the charity of *their*, not *his*, choice.

Here again the I.O.U.s are different from most businesses. An individual gets a tax deduction of 20% or so on his charitable contributions, depending on his income. For many businesses the tax deduction will amount to 48¢ out of each dollar. A utility, however, wherever regulators permit the practice, loads donations in the light bill, to be paid by the customers who also pay all the utility's taxes and other expenses.

Florida and Tampa Electric are typical, rather than exceptional. Tampa Electric's donations of $86,928 in 1963 were well below the total in various states where donations are permitted as operating expenses. In 1963, Cleveland Electric Illuminating reported $514,479 in donations, Florida Power & Light $361,605, Dayton Power & Light $271,657. Iowa Electric Light & Power, Public Service Company of Colorado, and Virginia Electric & Power reported donations of more than $100,000.[2]

Power-company reports do not necessarily show whether donations have been charged to the customers. The reports may give the opposite impression. The donations may be listed as a nonoperating expense, supposedly to be charged to the stockholders. Nevertheless, the donations can be included as an operating expense by a state regulatory commission and charged to the customer.

It is necessary to distinguish between the accounting of donations, or any other expense, and the treatment accorded the accounts when rates are determined. Generally speaking, rates are determined on the basis of operating revenue, operating costs and rate base as listed in a utility's accounts, and the rate of return established by the state commission. Operating expenses are usually entered in accounts "above the line," to use the accountants' phrase, and are borne by the customers. Nonoperating expenses are usually entered "below the line" and are borne by stockholders.

To assure uniformity, the Federal Power Commission decides how electric-utility accounts should be kept. But a state commission usually decides what expenses will be included as operating expenses and passed on to the customers—no matter how the expenses are entered in the accounts.

For example, Virginia Electric & Power (VEPCO) made donations of $225,485 during 1964 and accounted for them "below the line" as a nonoperating expense. The State Corporation Commission verified that these donations had been properly accounted as a nonoperating expense. Yet the state commission permitted all the donations to be included as operating expenses and thus paid for by the customers.

Probably many VEPCO customers would have agreed with most of VEPCO's selections—hospitals, schools, neighborhood and road improvement groups, and a variety of other worthy causes. However, the customers would have undoubtedly preferred, had they been given the opportunity, to receive a tiny reduction in their electricity bills, make their own contributions in their own names, and get a tax deduction for it. And some of VEPCO's customers who were among the 558,-038 Virginians who voted for President Johnson might not have agreed with VEPCO's donation in their behalf, in 1964 as in 1963, to Young Americans for Freedom, whose chief goal was the election of Senator Barry Goldwater as President.

In 1956, utilities could require customers to pay for the companies' contributions in about one third of the states. By 1963, the practice was permitted in about half of the states: Arizona, Arkansas, Colorado, Delaware, Florida, Idaho, Illinois, Indiana, Massachusetts, Minnesota, Mississippi, Montana, Nebraska,* New Hampshire, New Mexico, North Dakota, Ohio, Oklahoma, Rhode Island, South Dakota, Utah, Vermont, Virginia, and Wyoming.

In addition, there were no court or commission rulings against the practice in seven more states: Alaska, Georgia, Hawaii, Iowa, North Carolina, South Carolina, and Tennessee.

---

* There are no electric utilities to profit from this lenient policy in Nebraska, but other utilities, such as telephone companies, can benefit there.

All utilities generally enjoy the same special privileges that electric utilities do in the matter of contributions. A state regulatory commission that permits one type of utility to include charitable donations in the rate structure will usually grant the same privilege to another type of utility.

The Federal Communications Commission has long required interstate telephone utilities under its accounting jurisdiction to list contributions as nonoperating expenses. In 1963, the telephone industry asked the F.C.C. to change the rules, so that contributions could be listed as operating expenses. The telephone industry argued that an increasing number of state commissions were permitting it to add company contributions to the phone bill. So why not change the bookkeeping procedure to conform with the rate-making practice? More than 125 colleges and charitable organizations wrote F.C.C. in support of the telephone industry's position.

Nevertheless, in a 4–3 vote, the F.C.C. held to its previous rule that contributions be listed as nonoperating expenses. The state commissions could and many, of course, would continue to require telephone users to pay for the charity of American Telephone and Telegraph, which is the nation's largest corporation.[3]

Although it has rate jurisdiction over relatively few electric utilities, the Federal Power Commission for years had a policy against allowance of contributions as operating expenses in rate-making. In 1964, the F.P.C., which since 1961 has generally worked in the interest of the consumer, lapsed and gave its blessing to utility-selected, customer-financed charity. The commission held in the United Gas Pipe Line case that "contributions of a reasonable amount to recognized and appropriate charitable institutions constitute a proper operating expense."

One member of the F.P.C., Commissioner David S. Black, opposed the policy switch. Charitable contributions, wrote Black, as commendable as they may be, are properly accounted for as income deductions, not operating expenses. They bear no relationship whatsoever to the necessary costs of providing utility service and, therefore, should not be borne by the utility customers. Charitable contributions, if made by the company, should be the sole responsibility of the stockholders. It is argued that a public utility has a community and civic responsibility and should, therefore, be encouraged to support deserving charities. I agree. But the financial burden of donations to charities should not be shifted to the consumer who has no voice in their selection.[4]

The Commission's reversal delighted Editor Francis X. Welch of *Public Utilities Fortnightly,* an I.O.U.-oriented publication. Welch wrote:

If the utility company management is put under the pressure of taking all such donations out of earned income, there could be some hesitancy in meeting this responsibility in a satisfactory degree. Certainly, organized charity of this type cannot be permitted to fail.[5]

It is difficult to follow his reasoning that the extraordinarily profitable utilities would or should hesitate to meet community responsibilities on the same basis available to other businesses and individuals. Electric utilities control so much of the nation's wealth that a proportionately tiny contribution from each soon pyramids into a very substantial sum. Actually, however, utilities give less proportionately than free-enterprise businesses, despite the widespread practice of passing the cost of utility gifts on to the customers.

In 1962, 33 utilities, of which 27 were electric or electric-gas combination companies, donated more than $11.3 million to charitable organizations, according to a study by the National Industrial Conference Board. If the donations of those companies were an accurate sample of the industry, the 220 major electric utilities donated about $75 million during the year. The utilities gave *more* than any of the 19 other industries surveyed. But they gave substantially less in proportion to income than any of the other 19 industries. The N.I.C.B. study showed that contributions for all industries averaged three fourths of 1% of net income. Non-utility industries gave away from one half of 1% to 3% of their net income. The utilities contributed only one fourth of 1% of their net income.[6]

The one state where a commission has recently reversed the trend toward customer financing of utility charity is California.

California's Public Utilities Commission used to require utilities to split the cost of contributions, 50–50, between stockholders and customers. This policy had bothered members of the commission. One of them, Ray E. Untereiner, an economist who had been employed by the National Association of Manufacturers, had expressed his doubts this way:

I do not question for a moment that utilities must participate in business organizations and contribute to civic undertakings and charities; and these things cost money. There is a real question in my mind, however, whether they should expect the ratepayers to contribute toward these costs. Since it is the utility that gets the public credit for a contribution to the Community Chest, for example, it would seem reasonable that it should be the utility that makes the sacrifice; that the stockholders, rather than the ratepayers, should pay the bill.[7]

In 1964, the California commission abandoned its 50–50 policy and in a decision subsequently affirmed by the state Supreme Court, declared "henceforth to exclude from operating expenses for rate-fixing purposes all amounts claimed for dues, donations and contributions."

The utility involved in the California case, Pacific Telephone and Telegraph, "desires its ratepayers to give," said the Commission, but "should not be permitted to be generous with ratepayers' money."

The California commission also disallowed the utility's

claimed deduction for lobbying and for increased executive salaries. The state Supreme Court, in upholding the commission on these points, noted that from 1956 to 1962, the number of executives employed by the utility increased from 201 to 334, and their pay increased from $3,125,967 to $7,217,687— while the company's employee force declined by more than 4,000.[8]

Such curbing of monopoly abuses by a strong state commission has not damaged the California utilities, according to one of their leading spokesmen. In 1965 President J. K. Horton of Southern California Edison told the New York Society of Security Analysts that "we have learned in California to function effectively under a system of regulation which we believe to be firm but fair." Horton continued:

It is true beyond question that ours is a strong commission and that it has a highly competent, well qualified staff. But this has not meant, in my judgment, and based on our continuing relationships with them, that its strength and competence have been misused or that arbitrary acts or unreasonable demands have been imposed on us. . . . We believe our record of earnings growth over the last several years, which has been achieved under regulation as it exists in California, speaks rather convincingly for itself on the subject of regulatory atmosphere.[9]

Unfortunately for consumers, state commissions that seek to exclude questionable donations or other expenses in rate-making are hampered by lack of details furnished voluntarily by the utilities. Before deciding how to treat a questionable item, the commission has to *find* it. That is why accounting detail is so important in utility regulation. *The whole regulatory system rests on the accounts.*

To facilitate discovery of questionable items, the Federal Power Commission in 1963 revised its accounting regulations to require electric (and gas) utilities to itemize their nonoperating expenditures, including contributions and political expenditures. The F.P.C. emphasized that the new accounting requirements would "not constitute a determination that the expenditures should be excluded from a utility's rate of service." [10] The accounting changes would simply permit state and federal commissions to identify questionable expenses readily. Rates could still be set high enough to cover the cost of a utility's charity and political activity, if the commission with jurisdiction approved.

The new regulations were to be effective with the 1963 annual reports, filed in the spring of 1964. Many companies disregarded the new regulation. Detroit Edison, for example, reported "Donations to Community Funds, Education Institutions, Civic and Religious Organizations . . . $645,830.04." The company knew to the penny what donations cost, but itemized none of them.

Perhaps some of the failures to itemize were due to lack of timely notice about the change in regulations. However, many power companies did not itemize nonoperating expenses in their 1964 annual reports, submitted 27 months after the new regulations had first been proposed and 15 months after they had been issued.

Philadelphia Electric, for example, reported as an operating expense $184,413 in unitemized contributions to "Chambers of Commerce and other civic and economic groups."

Detroit Edison had increased its annual charities to more than three fourths of a million dollars. It did not itemize the contributions. And it reported them as operating expenses.

Michigan is one of the states that does not permit utilities to pass on to customers the cost of charity. Nevertheless, itemization is helpful in such cases, because it enables ordinary stockholders, who bear the cost, to determine whom they are assisting. Detroit Edison did itemize its 1963 contributions, after receiving a second request from F.P.C. The company had given to a wide range of local civic, cultural, community, business, and educational organizations.

The second-largest contribution to an educational institution was $30,000 to Cornell University in Ithaca, New York, far outside Detroit Edison's service area. Cornell is a great institution. Possibly no one appreciates that fact more than Detroit Edison's board chairman, a former president of Edison Electric Institute, Walker Cisler (Cornell, M.E., 1922). However, stockholders of the company, had they known where their money was going, might have wished to emphasize aid to Michigan colleges.

Detroit Edison was more cooperative than some other companies that did not itemize all donations despite specific requests by the F.P.C. Houston Lighting and Power failed to describe $67,000 listed as "minor items." Montana Power revealed that $17,000 in contributions to Montana Chambers of Commerce and the Montana Taxpayer's Association were among the costs of producing its electricity, but declined to itemize $17,000 in other contributions and dues, which it had also put in the books as operating expenses.

When the F.P.C. originally proposed the 1963 accounting regulations requesting itemization, it suggested the reporting of expenditures "having any direct or indirect relationship to political matters, including the influencing of public opinion with respect to policy." The power industry had objected to that section. The Commission watered down the controversial requirement when the regulations requiring more detailed accounting were ordered late in 1963. Commissioner Black emphasized at the time, though, that efforts by utilities to influence fundamental attitudes or beliefs bear no reasonable relationship to necessary utility service and should be borne by the industry. Inadequate accounting regulations, he said, might cause such expenses to become "lost" in various operating expense accounts.

Audits by the Commission staff in 1964 buttressed Commissioner Black's point, and indicated that the new regulations fell short of the Commission's original objective, the proper reporting of political expenditures by utilities. The Commission reviewed reporting practices of 17 utilities (11 electric and 6 gas transmission), which had been selected at random. The review showed that the 17 companies "had included items totalling about $125,000 in operating expenses which the staff believed to be political in nature."

Audits of utility accounts by a regulatory commission are rare. The Federal Power Commission, with only 38 field auditors in 1965, could only plan to audit the books of electric and gas utilities "every seven to ten years." [11] All of the state regulatory commissions together had less than 500 accountants in 1963, only one in 10 a certified public accountant. And about 40% of the state-employed accountants worked for one of only three commissions—California's, New York's or Pennsylvania's.[12]

Just as policemen protect the public against crimes of violence, it is the accountant principally who protects the public against unscrupulous use of position and power by protected monopolies. Yet some state commissions have no accountant at all, others only one or two. Utilities account for some 20% of the business of this country, but you could lose all the state and federal regulatory commission accountants in the country among the cops called out to police one big parade.

Chapter 7.

THE RATE BASE

> Some commissioners don't understand our statements even though we attempt to make them in *Reader's Digest* terms. We feel we need 8% on the present value of our property. The opposition says we need 6% on the original cost. When commissioners don't understand what we are talking about and don't understand what the opposition witnesses are talking about, we get these compromise decisions.
> —GEORGE N. STEINHAUER, Utility official, 1962 [1]

A homeowner's property tax is based on two figures. One is the assessment; the other is the tax rate. The assessment may not be what he paid for the property, or what it is worth now. His house may have cost $20,000 and be worth $25,000 now, but if it is assessed at $10,000, he pays a percentage (the tax rate) of $10,000.

The tax rate may change from year to year. Unless the local government reassesses the property, though, each year the tax will be based on the $10,000 assessment.

A utility rate base and rate of return are comparable to the homeowner's assessment and tax rate. If the rate base (the plant investment) amounts to $300 million and the rate of return is 7%, the rates will be designed to bring in $21 million in net income.

Obviously, if the rate base increases, the revenue can be increased, without increasing the rate of return. A rate base of $400 million with the same 7% rate of return would permit rates designed to bring in $28 million in net income, an additional $7 million.

The rate base has another feature similar to the homeowner's tax assessment. If an assessment is too high, a taxpayer is overcharged year after year, whether or not the tax rate changes, until the assessment is lowered. Similarly, if a rate base is too high, the electric consumer's overcharge will go on and on, unless the rate base is scaled down. Thus the makeup of the rate base is all-important in determining the price of utility service.

The rate base includes the value of the plant and equipment used by and useful to the utility, less depreciation. The rate base also includes an allowance for working capital and in some states includes the value of construction work in progress and property held for future use.

When a regulatory commission decides what value to put on the property included in the rate base, it determines the size of the electricity bill, just as municipal assessors determine the size of the property tax bill when they evaluate real estate. Thirty state commissions, the District of Columbia commission, and the F.P.C. evaluate the rate base—with some variations—according to the original cost of the property, less depreciation. Thirteen state commissions use the "fair value" rate base, which is determined by considering the actual cost, the cost if the plant had to be reproduced new, plus various intangibles.

Rate bases tend to be comparatively higher in "fair value" states than in "depreciated original cost" states, because replacement cost is generally higher than original cost, and because of the intangible factors to which some commissions assign a cost. The 13 "fair value" states are Alabama, Arizona, Delaware, Illinois, Indiana, Kentucky, Maryland, Mississippi, Missouri, Montana, New Mexico, North Carolina, and Pennsylvania.[2]

There is no state regulation of investor-owned electric utilities in four of the seven other states, Texas, Minnesota, Ne-

braska, and South Dakota. As for the others, the Alaska and
Iowa commissions were just established. In Ohio, the rate
base is established on the basis of a plant's reproduction cost,
less depreciation. However, in Ohio, electric rates are negotiated between utilities and municipalities; the state commission is simply a board of appeals on electric rate matters.

The method of computing the rate base is academic in states
that never have had electric-utility rate cases, such as Delaware
and Mississippi. It is practically academic in states such as
South Carolina, where there has been no electric rate case in
recent years and where there is no statutory method of rate
base evaluation.

Even in some states that occasionally conduct rate cases, the
rate base is de-emphasized. In 1964, *Miami Herald* reporter
Juanita Greene attempted unsuccessfully to find out from the
Florida commission the rate base of Florida Power & Light.
"I'm sure there must have been a rate base worked up of some
kind," the director of the commission's finance department told
her, "but where it is, if it still exists, I don't know." That's as if
the county assessor could not show an ordinary taxpayer his
assessment.

Mrs. Greene concluded, after further investigation, that "the
near empty files of the Florida Public Service Commission
offered little last week except the suspicion that it is regulating
the utilities by ear. Or at best, by scratch pad." [3]

As a consequence of inadequate state commission staffs and
budget and lax regulation by some commissions, rate bases
tend to bulge with overpriced or unused equipment. Through
the years Federal Power Commission auditors have removed
$1.6 billion from utility plant accounts.[4]

Lately, in some states, sums equivalent to what customers
paid to cover utilities' tax bills—but which the companies
never needed because of the 1954 and 1962 tax reductions—
have crept into the rate base. The customers are required to

pay the utility a profit on what is really their own money. And because the "tax" money went into the rate base, the customers pay on it year after year. The utility eats the customers' cake and has it, too.

Some or all of the 1954 and 1962 tax accruals are permitted in the rate base by the commissions in Florida, Idaho, Kansas, Montana, New York, Michigan, North Dakota, Ohio, Oregon, and Virginia, and apparently also in Indiana and Massachusetts. State commissions in Arkansas, Delaware, Louisiana, Maryland, Mississippi, North Carolina, and South Carolina were still, in 1965, pondering what to do in this matter.

Utilities are especially anxious to increase the rate base. That is because net operating revenue has been rising faster than the rate base has proportionately increased. This has pushed the rates of return above the level theoretically allowed by state commissions.

To put it another way, if both the numerator (net operating revenue) and denominator (rate base) of the regulatory formula increase proportionately, the quotient (the rate of return) will remain the same:

$$\frac{\$21 \text{ million (net operating revenue)}}{300 \text{ million (rate base)}} \text{ equals } 7\% \text{ rate of return.}$$

However, if net operating revenue goes up $3.5 million, and $50 million is added to the rate base:

$$\frac{\$24.5 \text{ million (net operating revenue)}}{350 \text{ million (rate base)}}$$

also equals 7% rate of return.

Utility trade literature suggests a variety of methods to expand the rate base—"invest in well located land and bring in the utilities necessary for development . . . put overhead wiring underground . . . offer to bring in three-wire service . . . look into the purchase and lease of major load builders." Or "set up outside [of] regulation" subsidiary companies to provide broad credit for purchase of major appliances.[5] Some of these suggestions are for worthwhile activities that most rate-payers would endorse but others amount to a bald pitch for entry of the government-protected utilities into real estate and banking, as a device to forestall rate reductions.

* * *

> People of the same trade seldom meet together, even for merriment and diversion, but the conversation ends in a conspiracy against the public, or in some contrivance to raise prices.
>
> —Adam Smith, *Wealth of Nations,* 1776

It was a dull Saturday afternoon in May 1959 in the newsroom of the Knoxville (Tennessee) *News-Sentinel.* Reporter Julian Granger thumbed through news releases. One from the Tennessee Valley Authority told about contract awards for electrical transformers. It looked routine—except for a parenthetical comment:

(On this bidding Allis-Chalmers, General Electric and Pennsylvania Transformer quoted identical prices of $112,712.)

Granger's curiosity was aroused. How could three companies submitting separate, sealed bids arrive at identical prices, to the dollar?

He called Aubrey J. (Red) Wagner, general manager (now chairman) of T.V.A. The conversation confirmed his suspicion that he was onto something big and serious.

Granger knew that T.V.A. was concerned about high, sharply rising prices of American-made electrical equipment, as well as identical bids. On February 6, 1959, T.V.A. had purchased a 500,000-kilowatt turbogenerator from C. A. Parsons & Company, Ltd., of England. The purchase price—$12,905,800—was more than $6 million lower than the bids of the only other bidders—Westinghouse and General Electric.[6]

The "Buy America" act required that a bid from a qualified foreign firm had to be at least 6% less than that of a domestic firm to be considered. The law permitted more than a 6% differential in certain circumstances. T.V.A., in an effort to give American equipment firms full consideration, stated in its invitation for bids that it would accept the lowest bid from a U.S. manufacturer if it did not exceed the lowest foreign bid by more than 20%. But the differential between the British and American firms was so great that after allowing for a 20% differential—and a $1.5 million import duty—the American bids were still higher.

T.V.A. had been criticized for inviting, let alone accepting, foreign bids. T.V.A. bluntly explained why it invited foreign bids in a press release on February 27, 1959:

> For some time, T.V.A. has been disturbed by the rising prices of turbogenerators. There are only three American firms which manufacture large turbogenerators. Since 1951, the prices charged by these manufacturers for such equipment have increased by more than 50 per cent, while the average wholesale price of all commodities has increased only about 5 per cent.
>
> It was this history of price increases by the only United States suppliers which led T.V.A. to invite bids from qualified foreign manufacturers as well as domestic ones.[7]

During that same week, the city-owned power system in Los Angeles was also under attack for saving money by purchasing foreign-made equipment. The Los Angeles Department of Water and Power had accepted the bid of a Swiss firm, Brown Boveri Corporation, for two huge steam-turbine generators. General Electric tried to pressure the Los Angeles City Council into overruling its municipal power system. G.E. questioned the city's action in a full-page newspaper ad.

> What price national security? . . . Should a foreign firm be entrusted with producing power equipment that would be in critical need in this community in case of national emergency?[8]

At a City Council hearing the following week, officials of the municipal power system told of price differentials between American and foreign suppliers similar to those reported by T.V.A. The Board of Water and Power Commissioners, said its chairman, J. C. Moller, Jr., "has a responsibility not only to live up to the City Charter, but also to act in the best interests of the people of Los Angeles in maintaining low electric rates."

This we have done. The savings of more than $5 million are important to every user of electricity and will help hold the line on costs of service. If anyone can show me how we can legally award to an American bidder and how the difference of $5½ million can be made up in some other way, I—for one—would welcome such information.

The general manager and chief engineer of the municipal power system, William S. Peterson, told how bids of American suppliers had skyrocketed:

In May of last year, we opened bids for the two generator units for the Haynes steam plant, and we were shocked to find that they showed a 69% increase in cost per kilowatt of capacity over the generators then being installed at Scattergood steam plant. This was true despite the fact that the capacity per unit was larger and should have given relatively lower costs per kilowatt than a smaller sized turbogenerator. Bids at that time were received only from American manufacturers.

There were substantial cost savings to Los Angeles besides the $5½-million difference in bid price. Peterson estimated that the American-made machines would cost about $28 million more to operate. Additionally, General Electric in its bids on two previous units had included a price escalation clause of 20%, which the company had exercised. This permitted the company to charge 20% more than the price it had bid. In the bids now at issue, General Electric had included a price escalation clause of 30% for the first unit and 40% for the second unit. If exercised, said Peterson, the escalation clauses could add more than $5 million to the price differential, and the cost of buying the equipment from General Electric would be more than double Brown Boveri's bid.

The revelations of T.V.A. and the Los Angeles public power officials received scant public attention early in 1959. Most of the press wasn't digging, yet. However, Congressional investigators were.

During the spring of 1959, the Senate Antitrust and Monopoly Subcommittee, headed by Senator Estes Kefauver (D-Tenn.) began hearings on a bill by Senator Joseph O'Mahoney (D-Wyo.) dealing with "administered" prices. Kefauver and O'Mahoney, both vigorous advocates of competition, were disturbed by what appeared to be artificially high prices in industries dominated by few manufacturers. One of the witnesses, heard in May 1959, was Ralph Cordiner, chairman of the board of General Electric, whose price increases had shocked the Los Angeles Department of Water and Power. Cordiner testified that the customers determined the cost of his products:

In all instances, the price is completely subject to the force of competition in the marketplace and the value the customer believes he is receiving. The interplay of flexibility of prices, rising and falling in response to market change, is essential to the task of adjusting the allocation of resources to match the desires of people for goods and services.

Meanwhile, *News-Sentinel* reporter Granger had been working since February on the story he had sensed behind the T.V.A. press release concerning identical bids by General Electric, Allis-Chalmers, and Pennsylvania Transformer. His first story splashed across the Knoxville *News-Sentinel* eight days after the General Electric board chairman said that prices were set by competition in the marketplace. "Some American manufacturers, primarily in the electrical field," said Granger in his lead paragraph, "have regularly submitted identical bids on T.V.A. purchases of equipment and materials."

Kefauver and his subcommittee staff did their homework on electric supply, then went to Knoxville and opened hearings. Two big questions loomed: Was there a pattern of identical bidding? If so, were the identical bids a result of unlawful conspiracy?

With painstaking detail, Kefauver, his staff, and T.V.A. officials developed the pattern of identical bids. Eleven equipment manufacturers had each bid $1,404.15 on an electric transformer. Eight companies had submitted identical sealed, "secret" bids of $12,936 on an order of insulators. The hearings showed that sometimes the bid of one company would be slightly lower than the others. The next month, another company's bid would be slightly below the rest. And while the price of electrical equipment had gone up 50% since 1951, the prices of electrical appliances produced by the same companies, but sold in a keenly competitive market, had decreased. A pattern of identical bidding, rotation of low bidder, and a sharp rise in equipment needed to produce and transmit electric power emerged from the Knoxville hearings.[9]

Kefauver had put the executive branch on notice that if it did not get on with the job of investigating what appeared to be a giant price-fixing conspiracy, the legislative branch would. Under pressure from Kefauver and the Scripps-Howard papers, the Justice Department got in gear. Grand juries in Philadelphia (some of the alleged price-setting conspiracy had taken place in eastern Pennsylvania) began to investigate.

In February 1960, the Department of Justice returned its first indictments, charging a number of companies and individuals with violations of the Sherman Antitrust Act in connection with the sale and distribution of various heavy electrical products. The defendants were charged with conspiring to fix prices, terms and conditions of sale, allocation of business among themselves, and submission of noncompetitive, collusive, and rigged bids, "so as to eliminate and suppress competition."

Federal District Judge J. Cullen Ganey began hearing the cases in Philadelphia in March 1960. A number of companies pleaded "not guilty." Meanwhile, four grand juries kept grinding out indictments—20 in all. The enormity of the case became clear—$7 billion dollars worth of equipment was involved.

The trial developed the pattern of conspiracy. The price-fixers had met at various lodges and hotels around the country during the Fifties. Codes had been developed; price leaders switched positions according to a "phase of the moon" formula. The general managers and vice presidents responsible for carrying out the conspiracy dispatched intercompany memos about upcoming jobs and the price that each company was setting.

As the evidence unfolded, the conspirators heeded Judge Ganey's warning that he would not be lenient with companies that pleaded "not guilty" and were later proved guilty. Pleas were changed to "guilty."

At least one official of an investor-owned utility, McGregor Smith, chairman of Florida Power & Light, had been disturbed by the high prices of equipment and unseemly camaraderie between suppliers early in 1957. The price-fixing had been an open secret within the equipment industry for almost a decade (although General Electric Board Chairman Cordiner insisted he didn't know about it). At least some of the principals in the cartel were also aware that the conspiracy was illegal. As F. F. Loock, president of Allen-Bradley, put it bluntly:

No one attending the gatherings was so stupid he didn't know the meetings were in violation of the law. But it is the only way a business can be run. It is free enterprise.

The industry press apparently was also aware of what was going on. In 1958, one of the General Electric officials, George Burens, had resolved to stay clear of the cartel. However, according to *Fortune,* he was persuaded to meet with other industry people by none other than Fischer Black, who was then editor of *Electrical World.** Black invited the cartel set to his suite in New York's Astor Hotel, told them to order lunch, and then departed. Yet it had taken cost-conscious T.V.A. officials, assisted by an inquisitive Scripps-Howard reporter, a persistent Senator, and finally all three branches of the federal government to force the issue. Early in 1961, Judge Ganey found 29 companies, which supply almost all the equipment used by electric-power companies in the United States, guilty of price-fixing on products ranging from $2 insulators to multimillion-dollar turbine generators. Seven corporation executives went to prison; 23 received suspended sentences; fines of $2 million were levied on 29 companies.

The antitrust case proved that electric utilities had been overcharged hundreds of millions of dollars for equipment. The court permitted utilities to seek triple damages. The Federal Power Commission directed that settlements received by the utilities, plus interest, should be used to reduce the plant account—that is, taken out of the rate base, in the year of settlement.[10]

In other words, the utility customers, who had been paying for the overpriced equipment, would have the overload reduced, to the extent that the utilities vigorously went after the price-fixers. However, because the price-fix padding could not be removed from the rate base until settlement, the customers would pay the utilities a percentage of the padding year after year, until settlement. A utility makes money on any purchase allowed in the rate base, and if price-fixing, inflation, or any other cause increases the price, it can also increase the profit.

* Mr. Black is now executive vice president of Tampa Electric.

Thus big settlements would benefit the customer; small settlements would benefit both the utilities and their chief equipment suppliers, among whom, as *Electrical World* observed, a "close, family-like relationship" had existed.[11]

Recent annual reports of investor-owned utilities indicate that while some power companies have aggressively pushed their claims others appear to have been lenient with the price-fixers.

A former public-relations man for General Electric, William H. Dinsmore, recently noted his difficulty in finding any meaningful report on the price-fixing settlements in annual reports of I.O.U.s. Dinsmore wrote:

> Many utilities were less than crystal clear in reporting on damages collected as a result of the recent price-fixing rulings. . . . In reporting on its out-of-court settlement with an electrical manufacturer, one public utility said it had "obtained completely satisfactory price adjustments," while avoiding "costly" legal expenses, and had applied the resultant cost reductions to a "reduction of our property base accounts." No figures were given. Another utility said it had "effected satisfactory settlements," and credited the net amount recovered to the "applicable plant accounts." Again no mention of the sums involved, although stockholders might well be curious since utilities which had taken their cases to court had won damages amounting to tens of millions of dollars.[12]

By 1965, settlements totalling about $400 million had been made by utilities and equipment manufacturers. The settlements had cost General Electric $225 million, Westinghouse Electric $110 million, and Allis-Chalmers $45 million. One hundred twenty electric utilities had claims pending.[13]

Many electric consumers are still absorbing the cost of the great electric conspiracy whenever they pay their light bill. And they pay for it again when they pay their tax bill. The tax bite results from a 1964 ruling by the Internal Revenue Service that permits the antitrust violators to deduct the damage payments for tax purposes as a necessary business expense! That ruling will cost the U.S. Treasury about $150 million a year.[14]

Chapter 8.

STOCK OPTIONS—WHIPPED CREAM
ON THE DESSERT

> In actual practice, government regulation prevents
> spectacular stock benefits in the electric power business.
>
> —Edward Vennard, managing director, Edison
> Electric Institute, 1962 [1]

The hierarchy of the investor-owned utilities serving the Rocky Mountains was gathered in Jackson Hole, Wyoming, to discuss the state of the industry. Business was excellent, as usual; the price of utility stock was moving to new record highs and the Eisenhower administration in Washington, well into its second term, continued friendly. It had cut back the federal power program, skeletonized the staffs of the Federal Power Commission and the Securities and Exchange Commission and installed commissioners who did not bother the I.O.U.s.

The featured speaker at this meeting of the Rocky Mountain Electrical League was one of the region's own utility presidents, who was also serving that year as president of Edison Electric Institute, the industry's national trade association. The gloomy picture of the future that he painted contrasted sharply with reports on utilities issued by investment firms, which glowed like the gorgeous sunrise over the Tetons.

If present trends continue, said the president of E.E.I., "in 25 years private business in America is almost certain to be on the downgrade and our heritage lost." "We who are in business today have no right," he declared, "to allow a general deterioration of opportunity and of freedom." [2]

Opportunities were not deteriorating for this utility executive. His heritage was not about to be lost; it was going to be enhanced appreciably. On October 5, 1959, not long after his speech, he exercised options on 30,000 shares of stock in his company. The market price of the stock that day was $23.75. He, however, paid only $11.24 each for 9,000 shares and $11.48 each for the other 21,000. Thus in one day he made a windfall profit of $370,000. That was more than twice as much as the total annual salaries of the three commissioners and 18 staff members of the state commission that is supposed to regulate his and other utilities. It was more than the average American makes in a lifetime.

In 1966, this utility president—J. E. Corette of Montana Power, whose annual salary is $87,500 and whose accrued annual retirement benefits exceed $50,000—still held unexercised options on 35,000 shares, with a market value of about one million dollars. Seven hundred and fifty thousand shares —about 10%—of the company's stock had been set aside under restricted stock option plans for purchase by his company's insiders. By 1966, the company insiders had already acquired almost 500,000 of the shares, worth about $14 million. Some company officials paid only one third or one fourth of the price paid by ordinary stockholders.

Other utility officials have done almost as well during recent years by purchasing stock in their companies at below-market cost through exercise of options. Another former president of Edison Electric Institute, President W. W. Lynch of Texas Power & Light, has made $200,000 in option windfalls since 1957, plus his $71,000 annual salary. G. L. MacGregor, the

$92,150-a-year president of Texas Utilities, the holding company that owns Texas P. & L., has made $350,000; H. L. Nichols, chairman of the board of Southwestern Public Service, which serves portions of Kansas, New Mexico, Oklahoma, and Texas, $200,000; C. A. Tatum, Jr., president of Dallas Power & Light—another subsidiary of Texas Utilities—$100,-000. R. O. Linville, vice president and controller of Kansas City (Missouri) Power & Light, made more than $100,000 in option windfalls in one transaction in 1964.[3]

The restricted stock options from which they benefited are rights extended to a limited number of persons to purchase common stock at a price that is often much less than the market price. The option device works simply. A company sets aside so many shares for company officials. An option committee, formed from the board of directors, decides who gets options to buy the shares, and how many. Later, when an optionee actually buys the stock, he pays what it cost when the option was granted, rather than the current market price.

The initial windfall, when an official buys stock for a fraction of its market value, is only the first benefit; the tax treatment accorded option windfalls provides additional aid. If an executive buys 1,000 shares at the option price of $30 per share, for $30,000, and the market price is $100 per share, or $100,000, he pays no tax upon receiving the $70,000 windfall. When he sells the stock, the tax is computed at the long-term capital gains rate of 25% or less. If he gives the stock away—to his wife or his children, to a family foundation or a favorite charity—or, as in the case of one Texas utility official, to a prospective daughter-in-law, he pays no tax on it.

Furthermore, in many cases, the market value of the stock, not the lesser option price which he paid, can be deducted from his own personal income before taxes. His family is happy; his favorite charities are happy. He becomes known as a great philanthropist and is viewed with reverence and respect by the ordinary utility stockholders and customers who, for the most part, are blissfully unaware that in a sense it was their money he gave away, to his considerable tax advantage.

A case can be made for granting restricted stock options in risk enterprises whose success or failure depends largely on the ability of an executive to develop and sell a product profitably in a competitive market. If he does not succeed, the company does not succeed; the market value of the stock drops, and the options are worthless. The executive may lose his job, or go broke. If he does succeed, the market value of the stock will ordinarily rise, and he will benefit from exercise of the options and the consequent tax concessions.

An official of an investor-owned utility is in an altogether different category. Government has granted the I.O.U. an exclusive market for a product the public must have. Government has sanctioned a price for the product, a price that covers all expenses, plus profits which, because of inadequate regulation, become excessive. Government has permitted those expenses to include generous compensation, exclusive of options, in addition to liberal retirement benefits. The annual salary of chief executives of investor-owned utilities averaged $89,000 in 1963. That was four and a half times as much as that paid chief executives of the large city-owned electric systems.[4]

Option compensation differs from salaries of utility executives in that it completely escapes the rate-making process, because no one can forecast the future value of stock. Options directly affect ordinary stockholders because the option stock, sold at below-market price, dilutes their equity. The executive who buys his share for $15 gets as large a dividend as the stockholder who paid $40 for his. When stock is sold for less than market price, more capital has to be raised elsewhere. Some of it comes from the excess collections from customers for the utility's taxes; some from retained earnings, from which ordinary stockholders might obtain larger dividends except for the watering of their stock by options.

The more the I.O.U.s use retained earnings and tax accruals for construction, the less new stock they have to issue, and the more attractive the common stock already issued and the executives' options become. The average price of stock in the 125 industrial corporations charted by Moody's Industrial Service, Inc., rose by 50% from 1957 to 1963. During those six years, the average price of Moody's 24 electric utilities increased by 100%. Even so, the price of Moody's 24 selected utilities did not increase as much as that of the 70 electric utilities whose market performance Moody's regularly charts. The stock of 41 of the 70 companies more than doubled in value during the six years; for seven of the companies it tripled. Stock value of only three of the companies gained as little as the 50% all-industry average. The average market value of stock in aluminum, cement, copper, secondary steel, and the paint industries decreased after 1957; it remained about the same in the aerospace, steel, and machine-tool industries. The market value of stock in individual companies in a variety of industries plunged downward. But the trend of every one of the 70 electric utility stocks during the six-year period was upward.[5]

Since 1953, use of restricted stock option plans has grown steadily among power companies and utility holding companies. The lax attitude toward utility regulation that characterized the Eisenhower administration hastened the spread of utility options, but the stage had been set years before in a Democratic administration.

The only major investigation of the electric-power industry, conducted from 1928 to 1935 by the Federal Trade Commission at the instigation of Senator Thomas Walsh of Montana, revealed a variety of methods, including stock options, by which utility officials were making exorbitant profits.[6]

Senator Burton K. Wheeler of Montana and Representative (later Speaker) Sam Rayburn of Texas introduced legislation to curb the financial abuses. During the Congressional hearings, even utility officials agreed that restricted stock option plans were improper for utilities. Wendell L. Willkie, who was to become the Republican Presidential nominee in 1940, but was then president of Commonwealth & Southern, a New York utility holding company, testified in 1935 that the stock option was one of the "types of securities that we should not have gotten out . . . because it created a market for those things which, in my judgment, was bad. . . . If I had my way and we were to do it again," said Willkie, "we would never get out options." [7]

The Wheeler-Rayburn bill, which became the Public Utility Holding Company Act of 1935, contained what appeared to be a flat prohibition against utility option plans. Section 305 (a) of the act read:

It shall be unlawful for any officer or director of any public utility to receive for his own benefit, directly or indirectly, any money or thing of value in respect of the negotiation, hypothecation, or sale by such public utility, or to share in any of the proceeds thereof, or to participate in the making or paying of any dividends of such public utility from any funds properly included in capital account.

In other words, stock was to be used to raise capital—not to enrich utility insiders. A sleeper slipped into the act, though, at the suggestion of the National Association of Railroad and Utilities Commissioners. NARUC suggested during the Senate hearings that another section of the bill be amended to exclude from Federal Power Commission jurisdiction the security issues of those public utilities organized and operating in states where security issues were regulated by state commissions.[8] The Senate committee did not accept the amendment.

The House committee did, however. The Senate-House conference committee retained the House version, which became Section 204 (f) of the Federal Power Act.

The 1935 act gave the Securities and Exchange Commission regulatory responsibility for holding-company stock issues; however, the holding companies controlled only a minority of the utilities. Most states had some kind of legislation authorizing a state commission to regulate security issues. So the effect of Section 204 (f) was to exclude the security issues of most power companies from federal regulation.

A Democratic Congress finished setting the stage for the modern-day utility option plans in 1950. The revenue act approved that year provided that profit on stock acquired by options could qualify as a capital gain. This meant that the tax on it would not exceed 25%, and might be substantially less.[9]

In 1953, restricted stock options plans were initiated by Texas Utilities and Eastern Gas & Fuel Associates. Both were holding companies, with electric utilities among their subsidiaries. Texas Utilities controlled Dallas Power & Light, Texas Electric, and Texas Power & Light; Eastern Gas & Fuel controlled Boston Gas, a combination electric-gas utility. Both holding companies, however, were exempted from jurisdiction by the Securities and Exchange Commission because they were intrastate companies; S.E.C. jurisdiction extended only to major interstate holding companies.

Montana Power and Central Kansas Power initiated their option plans in 1954, Green Mountain Power (Vermont) and Nevada Power in 1955, Southwestern Public Service, which serves parts of Texas, New Mexico, Oklahoma, and Kansas, in 1956. Cleveland Electric Illuminating, Missouri Utilities, and United Gas Improvement, a combination electric-gas company in Philadelphia, joined the option club in 1957, Kansas

City Power & Light, New Mexico Electric Service, and Washington Water Power in 1958, Tampa Electric in 1960.[16]

Because of the amendment to the Wheeler-Rayburn Act that had been proposed by the National Association of Railroad and Utilities Commissioners, only one of the companies that adopted stock option plans up to that time had to obtain approval of the Federal Power Commission. That company was Montana Power, then headquartered in New Jersey and operating in Montana, whose commission at that time did not have jurisdiction over security issues. Federal approval of utility schemes was not difficult to obtain in 1956. The F.P.C., without a hearing, summarily approved Montana Power's stock option plan. The other utilities obtained the approval of state commissions, except for the Texas holding company which, being under no state or federal commission, needed only to vote stockholder proxies for the option plan.

As late as 1960, none of the 16 active utility holding companies subject to Securities and Exchange Commission regulation had stock option plans. Middle South Utilities of New York, which controls Arkansas Power & Light, Louisiana Power & Light, Mississippi Power & Light, and New Orleans Public Service, had proposed one, however, and the S.E.C. ordered one of its examiners to conduct a hearing on the proposal.

The case for Middle South's option plan was argued by two other holding companies, the Southern Company and Ohio Edison, by a legal firm representing Middle South, and by one of Middle South's directors, George F. Bennett, president of an investment company. They argued that an urgent corporate need for options existed to attract competent executives, hold the present ones, and improve performance. The $95,000-a-year president of Middle South, testified Bennett, would "do everything he is doing in a more extraordinary way . . . scan the operating expenses more carefully . . . sharpen his pencil a little sharper on construction programs . . . make his people who are negotiating with labor a little tougher," and be certain his company was earning a "full return," if only he could have some options.

The S.E.C. staff opposed the option plan, contending that it would adversely affect ordinary stockholders and utility customers and that the company was in no way suffering from its inability to issue options. The Commission overruled the staff and approved the plan on February 7, 1961.

All the holding company then had to do was to get final approval of its stockholders, an easy task, considering the manner of proxy voting in utility corporations. However, in this case, dissent was not improbable. A renowned educational institution—Harvard—was the largest stockholder of Middle South, although its holdings were relatively small. The dean of Harvard's law school, Erwin N. Griswold, had been a consistent critic of restricted stock options. Dean Griswold had told the House Ways and Means Committee, two years previously:

Stock options are inherently discriminatory. They can be limited to one employee or a few employees, and ordinarily are. They can be granted in very large amounts, without any of the mild safeguards against discrimination which are provided in the case of pension plans. Indeed, I think it can fairly be said that they are somewhat insidious in their operation and effect, for they operate mysteriously and quite haphazardly. Whether they are actually worth anything turns on the fluctuations in the value of the stock. Whether they are taxable or not depends upon many technical considerations. Although they are usually authorized by stockholder action, very little is known about the extent to which they are exercised or the extent of benefits which have actually been obtained, or are potentially available to the favored recipients. No matter how one looks at it, the benefit obtained from stock options prior to their exercise has no capital element in it. If it has any justification at all, it is as compensation, and compensation cannot fairly be taxed to some persons at the special capital gains rate when it is ordinary income to other people. . . . The stock option is a "heads I win, tails you lose" device.[11]

Dean Griswold felt that options were especially inappropriate for a public-service company. His advice on options apparently was not solicited by the managers of Harvard's investment portfolio. Harvard cast its votes for the Middle South option plan, which was approved May 19, 1961, by a vote of 14,013,597 shares to 296,496 shares, a comfortable 98% margin of victory.[12]

By that time, Ohio Edison, which controls Pennsylvania Power, had also obtained S.E.C. approval of its option plan. No hearing was held; policy had been set in the Middle South case. Utility option plans were okay with the S.E.C.[13]

During the next year, several new members were seated on the Securities and Exchange Commission.* When the Middle South and Ohio Edison option cases were decided, all of the S.E.C. commissioners had been Eisenhower appointees. By 1962, deaths and resignations had reduced the Eisenhower appointees to one; the others had been named by President Kennedy. But the change in S.E.C. commissioners did not change the option policy. In 1962, the S.E.C. approved without hearing the option plan of Central & Southwest, a Delaware holding company which from a Chicago office controls four southern and southwestern utilities—Public Service Company of Oklahoma, West Texas Utilities, Southwestern Electric Power of Shreveport, Louisiana, and Central Power & Light of Corpus Christi, Texas.[14]

Meanwhile, two more utilities whose securities were not subject to federal jurisdiction—Central Louisiana Power and Florida Public Utilities—initiated option plans. That brought up to 32 the number of electric-utility corporations which through

* S.E.C and F.P.C. commissioners are appointed for staggered five-year terms; a vacancy on both of the five-member commissions ordinarily occurs each June.

restricted stock options had begun, during the decade, the generation of additional executive compensation that escaped public notice and the rate-making process.

Although a change in national administration and commissioners had wrought few changes at the S.E.C., the atmosphere was different at the Federal Power Commission only five blocks away. By March 1962, less than 14 months after President Kennedy's inauguration, a combination of resignations and deaths at F.P.C. enabled the new President to name all five commissioners—men with a rich background in utility regulation, law, and accounting, led by Chairman Joseph C. Swidler.

When a utility stock option came before the new Commission in July 1962, from Black Hills Power & Light of South Dakota, it did not get routine, unquestioned approval. A majority of the Commission—Chairman Joseph C. Swidler, Commissioners Charles Ross and Howard Morgan—voted to deny the Black Hills Power & Light application on the grounds that the company had not justified its option plan, but they left the door open for the company to come back with evidence to prove, if it could, that the stock option plan would be compatible with the public interest, necessary, and appropriate. Commissioner Morgan argued that the F.P.C. could not approve the stock option plan even if it wanted to, because Congress had specifically proscribed the practice when it wrote Section 305 (a) * of the 1935 holding company act.

The company subsequently presented its case for options; the F.P.C. staff presented the case against them. In 1964, the Commission in a 3–2 opinion by Chairman Swidler with Commissioners Ross and David Black (who had replaced Morgan) concurring, denied the application for a stock option plan, citing five principal objections:

* Quoted on p. 77.

First, such plans disguise the extent of managerial compensation and thus make it easy for the top managers to receive excessive compensation. As the staff showed in this case, there is no practical method of accounting for stock options which will give a clear indication of their cost to the company. Over the years, the accounting for costs has been made the foundation of knowledgeable regulatory control. Since there is no disclosure of service costs under these plans in the accounts of the utility, the use of the stock option form of executive compensation distorts the real cost of electric utility service. On the other hand, increases in cash salary payments are immediately evident. Entered into the books of account, they are disclosed and understood by investors, consumers and regulatory officials alike.

Second, stock options usually prefer the top executives and ignore the important role of the lower and middle management group. On a companywide basis, they may create a morale problem for the many which offset their claimed incentive value to the few.

Third, such plans lead to executive compensation which is often irrational, erratic and unrelated to the performance of the executive. General market trends and the growth of the economy in the company's market area may play a larger role in determining the value of the options than the efforts of the optionholders themselves.

Fourth—such options tend to make management focus more on common stock prices than on the service obligations of the company.

Finally, the impact of such options is to dilute the equity of the company.

Black Hills Power & Light had argued that it needed options to keep its valued employees from deserting them and joining nearby utilities with option plans—Washington Water Power and Montana Power. On that point, the F.P.C. observed that "without stock options the company has lost no employees with a salary in excess of $7,000 per year except by death or retirement."

The Commission also noted that of the three options of 1,000 shares or more that had already been granted by Black Hills Power & Light, subject to commission approval:

> ... One of the recipients is 72 years old and one is 66. Of the remaining 13 recipients, 5 are between the ages of 55 and 65. It could hardly be contended that the options are needed to retain the services of these veterans. Options on only 1,850 shares of stock have been received by employees under the age of 50. What is clear from this evidence is that since most of the present options are to be granted to older employees, additional stock options will soon have to be proposed, and authorization requested, to attract and retain the services of younger men.[15]

The only other stock option plan that had come before the F.P.C.—the Montana Power plan which had been approved eight years before the Black Hills case—illustrated the growth characteristic of option plans, once approved. The original Montana Power option plan for 100,000 shares became 300,000 shares after a three-for-one stock split in 1959. By 1961, 750,000 shares were subject to option. Montana Power's second option plan, for the additional 450,000 shares, had not gone before the F.P.C., because of the Section 204 (f) loophole that had been written into the holding-company act back in 1935.

A law providing for state jurisdiction over utility security issues—one of the two prerequisites of use of the Section 204 (f) loophole—had been approved by the Montana legislature in 1951, only to be vetoed by Governor John W. Bonner. He explained his veto bluntly:

> The Montana Public Service Commission does not have the facilities or the personnel to pass upon the issuance of securities of any corporation. ... The existing federal agencies have the trained personnel and the experience necessary for the uniform examination, investigation and regulation of public utility corpora-

tions, and the interest of the people will be better safeguarded by retention of the present system.[16]

Ten years later, in 1961, a similar bill slipped through the Montana legislature. John W. Bonner was no longer governor. The bill was signed into law.[17] Montana Power suddenly moved its headquarters from New Jersey to Montana, thus satisfying the second provision of the Section 204 (f) loophole. One week after the new law became effective, the state commission approved the option plan; the 450,000 additional shares were available for company insiders.[18]

Montana Power's escape from F.P.C. jurisdiction over its stock options and acquisition of its second bundle of options had been neat and complete, accompanied by a company press release attributing the utility's decision to leave New Jersey to its dedication to serving Montana.

Thus in summary the F.P.C., the one commission with a policy against utility stock options, cannot touch any of the existing option plans. Furthermore, F.P.C. jurisdiction over security issues of I.O.U.s that don't have stock option plans—yet—is dwindling. In recent years, Duke Power moved from New Jersey to North Carolina and Puget Sound Power & Light moved from Massachusetts to the state of Washington. Along with Montana Power's move from New Jersey to Montana, that has left the securities of only 29 power companies, many of them small ones, under F.P.C. jurisdiction.[19] And 10 of those 29 companies have not accepted the F.P.C.'s contention that their securities are under federal jurisdiction.*

Without the kind of examination of option plans now required by the Federal Power Commission—if it only had some place to exercise its policy—companies initiate and continue these plans on absurd grounds. Cleveland Electric Illumi-

* Electric utilities whose securities are subject to F.P.C. jurisdiction are listed in Appendix E, p. 283.

nating, for example, actually contends that options do not provide compensation. The utility claims that "no charge had been made to income in respect to the difference between the issue price and the market price since no compensation to employees is involved by the granting of options." Of all the major I.O.U.s, apparently only C.E.I. takes this position. Since 1962, Cleveland Electric Illuminating's board chairman, Elmer L. Lindseth, another former president of Edison Electric Institute, has received approximately $225,000 in windfall profits from options. Since 1960, he has obtained through exercise of options 28,000 shares of stock with a 1966 market value of more than $1 million—this in addition to his annual $110,000 salary.

Central & Southwest is another case in point. The holding company contended in its solicitation of proxy votes for the option plan that it was needed to assist the company and its subsidiaries "in competing with other industries and, particularly, with other electric utilities for the services of personnel presently employed, by giving them an opportunity to acquire an interest in the corporation." Central & Southwest already had and still has—in addition to the stock option plan—an "employee thrift" plan which permits company employees to buy stock more cheaply than ordinary stockholders can purchase it in the marketplace. Under the "employee thrift" plan, the company pays one fourth of the market price of stock in the company, or half if the employee has over 20 years' service.

Central & Southwest contended that the option plan would benefit able and promising new employees. The major beneficiaries, however, appear to be 14 veterans, each initially receiving options on more than a thousand shares of stock, led by President John S. Osborne, whose $85,000 annual salary was supplemented by options on 3,178 shares. This was the same John C. Osborne who in 1964 circularized a brochure assuring his stockholders and members of Congress that the day when acquiring "control" of electric utility companies was considered an interesting speculation has long passed; today there is no ulterior motive to acquire shares of electric utility companies. . . . Yesterday's vision of a handful of capitalists ruthlessly exploiting the masses fades in today's reality of a nation of capitalists freely investing their savings, individually and collectively, directly or indirectly, in enterprises of their own choosing.

"It is the people as a whole, not individuals, not financial institutions and not government officials, who thus decide which enterprises shall flourish and which shall not," said Osborne, thus conferring upon utility stockholders an imagined power which they do not have, in that utilities flourish because government bestows on them special privileges not accorded free-enterprise corporations.[20]

The utility stockholder, alas, receives practically no information on stock option plans, except for sketchy information in the proxy soliciting his vote to inaugurate the plans. The annual reports of some holding-company subsidiaries do not mention the options at all; the stock in these companies is, of course, totally owned by the holding company. Annual reports to stockholders do not indicate the full scope of the option plans. In most such reports, option plans are mentioned in one paragraph set in small type among the footnotes in the back of the report. Proxy solicitations for annual meetings will mention the number of options granted and exercised that year, the number granted or exercised by the officers and directors as a group and two or three of the leading officials during the year. These solicitations do not, however, tell who received and exercised options and usually do not list the cumulative totals of option benefits by the top company officials.

One company, Southwestern Public Service, reports to the Federal Power Commission the names of optionees and the number of shares optioned, but it is the exception. At least one company, Montana Power, has declined an F.P.C. request to disclose the names of its optionees, beyond the officers and directors who, in most of the companies, are required to report their stock transactions to the Securities and Exchange Commission. These reports on "insider transactions" usually list the amount of stock held by officers and directors, and the amount and nature of recent transactions, that is, whether acquired by gift, by purchase, through exercise of options or stock splitting, whether sold or given away.

However, officers and directors of companies that have only recently been required to register with the S.E.C. do not have to list how much of their previously-held stock was obtained by exercise of options, or the price actually paid for the stock. Thus, for example, stockholders in Tampa Electric, a recent registrant, cannot assess the dilution of their stock by the company's president, William C. MacInnes, who obtained options to purchase 19,000 shares, or its vice president, Fischer S. Black, who received options on 16,000 shares—all for $17.81 each.

The reporting requirements on insider transactions are not onerous, but nevertheless some of the reports are tardy or inaccurate. These reporting requirements were instituted by S.E.C. in 1956, to begin for the year 1957. It took a long time for the word on the new requirement to get from S.E.C. to one southwestern utility official, who in late 1959 told the S.E.C. he had not been "aware of the requirement for filing the report."

A former president of Edison Electric Institute, President W. W. Lynch of Texas Power & Light, finally got back to his insider transaction reports in 1964, after S.E.C. had called his attention to an error in one of his previous reports. "It also develops," Lynch wrote S.E.C., "that Form 4 reports were not made in 1963 on a gift by me of 100 shares in June, the exercise by me of options on 40 shares in July, and 136 shares in December, and a further gift by me of 67 shares in January 1964." [21]

Utility officials are busy, as almost everyone else is. Occasional delay is understandable. However, whenever erroneous or tardy, reports required by Congress in order to guard against insider benefit from advance information add to the workload of the small Commission staff and reduce the amount of time available to it for providing investors, regulators, and Congress with what scant information can be collected on the basis of existing reporting requirements. Corporate reports are filed by thousands of companies, of which electric utilities are but one segment.

In the early 1950s, the staff in the S.E.C. section of ownership reports totalled 14. During the Fifties, it was reduced to seven. It has since been increased by two. Yet, principally because of the expansion in the number of large corporations, the nine-man staff has twice as many ownership reports to review as it had when the staff was almost twice as large.

*   *   *

Despite the seeming prohibition against utility options enacted by Congress more than 30 years ago, this abuse of capital stock is likely to expand, unless it is publicized to the extent that ordinary stockholders and electric consumers rouse and require legislators or regulators to stop them. This need for more public understanding and discussion applies to the entire field of electric-utility regulation. As things stand now, the work of the regulators is frequently done by the I.O.U.s themselves, which in many states put through the laws establishing the commissions and the ground rules under which they operate.

As early as 1898, Samuel Insull in his presidential address to the National Electric Light Association, predecessor of

Edison Electric Institute, urged the industry to seek state regulation. His proposal horrified other industry leaders at the
time, but was heartily endorsed a few years later as a device
to stop expansion of municipal electric systems, which from
1902 to 1907 increased twice as rapidly as I.O.U.s. Insull and
his colleagues played the leading role in formation of some
midwestern commissions.[22] The pattern was applied with variations in some other states and has continued. The Iowa commission was established in 1963 under legislation described
approvingly by a committee of the National Association of
Railroad and Utilities Commissioners as "actively sponsored
by the utilities themselves." [23]

Indeed, regulation is so much desired by utilities that one
company not subject to regulation advertises that it is. Texas
Power & Light advertises that it is a "regulated industry." [24]
Yet the company contends before the F.P.C. that it is not
subject to federal jurisdiction. There is no Texas regulatory
commission with authority over power companies. An archaic
Texas law providing for municipal regulation of utilities is
neither used nor useful. The Texas electric consumer has
recourse only in the courts.

All too rarely are the commissions called upon to take the
public's side and provide the firm but fair regulation that utilities respect. One of these occasions occurred in 1962 when
Captain Douglas N. Jones, former associate professor of economics at the U.S. Air Force Academy, challenged the notion
that utility commissions should represent equally the interest
of the public and of the private company. Said Captain Jones:

> This is nonsense. The commission must represent the public in
> order that the interests of the unorganized many are not compro-
> mised by the organized few. The idea—sometimes voiced—that
> the interests of the utility and the interests of the public are one
> and the same seems to me a *Reader's Digest* view of the universe
> and largely without foundation. They are not the same in important

respects, and the commission must be "on the side" of the consumer.[25]

Jones's forthright statement recalled the standard set by Franklin D. Roosevelt, who comprehended the necessity of consumer-minded regulators. In his first Presidential campaign in 1932, F.D.R. laid down his philosophy of utility regulation:

The Public Service Commission is not a mere judicial body to act solely as umpire between complaining consumer or the complaining investor on the one hand, and the great public utility system on the other hand. [When I became governor of New York] I declared that, as the agent of the legislature, the Public Service Commission had, and has, a definitely delegated authority and duty to act as the agent of the public themselves; that it is not a mere arbitrator as between the people and the public utilities, but was created for the purpose of seeing that the public utilities do two things: First, give adequate service; second, charge reasonable rates; that, in performing this function, it must act as agent of the public, upon its own initiative as well as upon petition, to investigate the acts of public utilities relative to service and rates, and to enforce adequate service and reasonable rates.

The regulating commission, my friends, must be a tribune of the people, putting its engineering, its accounting and its legal resources into the breach for the purpose of getting the facts and doing justice to both the consumers and investors in public utilities. This means, when that duty is properly exercised, positive and active protection of the people against private greed.[26]

President Roosevelt's words ring as true today as when he uttered them 35 years ago. His pronouncement should be posted in the office of every regulatory commissioner, in the State House, and in the White House.

PART III

HOW IT STAYS THERE:
The Generation, Transmission, and Distribution of Propaganda

Chapter 9.

THE ADVERTISEMENTS—
THE WORLD UPSIDE DOWN

In 1878, a famous American visiting England was persuaded by an 18-year-old Briton to address his London literary society. The American, Phineas T. Barnum, the world's foremost publicist, promoter, and circus man, titled his speech "The World Upside Down." Barnum was "screamingly funny," wrote the young Englishman, who was profoundly affected by Barnum's presentation. Four years later the Englishman, Samuel Insull, moved to America to become secretary to Thomas Edison. Insull renewed and maintained his acquaintance with Barnum, learning the old master's techniques of humbuggery and applying them to the fledgling electric-power industry.

Enterprising and energetic, Insull acquired and consolidated small power plants, superimposed intricate networks of holding companies over them, and became acknowledged leader of the industry. When his native country went to war in 1914, Insull immediately began to arouse sentiment for U.S. involvement. Named chairman of the State Council of Defense of Illinois when the U.S. entered the war, he organized a militant and effective propaganda agency. Under his organizing genius, speakers' bureaus, neighborhood committees, newspapers, ministers, and labor and fraternal organizations aroused fervent support for the war effort. Thirteen state defense councils formed a coalition, and Insull was named chairman. At war's end he was hailed by the President, foreign governments, a score of governors, and the nation's press for his effort.

When Insull's attention again turned to utilities after the war, he found the industry in low repute. Rates were rising, and state regulatory commissions that he had established were under attack for being too lenient with the industry. The critics ranged from the Hearst newspaper chain to the Progressive Senators—Borah of Idaho, La Follette of Wisconsin, Norris of Nebraska, and Wheeler of Montana. Insull was prepared to counterattack. His Illinois war propaganda council was still a going concern, but without a mission since the war's end. Insull converted the Illinois State Council of Defense, man for man, into the Committee on Public Utility Information. "In creating the Illinois Public Utility Information Committee, Insull was never more astute," wrote his biographer, Forrest McDonald:

> To combat opponents of utilities who had used opposition to war as their springboard, Insull borrowed the propaganda machinery he had used during the war and sought to equate patriotism with a favorable attitude toward utilities. . . . Insull may be called the link between P. T. Barnum and Madison Avenue.[1]

Utility propaganda committees proliferated; electric utilities around the nation set up identical agencies. Soon the National Electric Light Association, predecessor of Edison Electric Institute, set up a general committee to coordinate the state committees. By 1923, as McDonald wrote, "these agencies were

turning out a stream of utility publicity that almost matched
the volume of patriotic publicity during the war; one could
hardly go anywhere or read anything without encountering the
fundamentals of utility economics."

The activities of the National Electric Light Association
during the Twenties touched everyone. N.E.L.A. and its affiliates, wrote historian Arthur Schlesinger, Jr.,

distributed literature to newspapers, libraries, schools and fraternal
orders. They dispatched speakers to clubs, forums, even to
churches. They buttonholed legislators and public officials. College
professors, students, editors, lecturers, were secretly placed on the
utilities payroll. Research was subsidized, and university funds
replenished. Textbooks that told the truthful history of utilities
finance were censored, and more agreeable writings procured in
their place. A relentless campaign was conducted against the Bol-
shevik heresy of public ownership. Rarely in American history has
business organized so powerful a propaganda offensive; and the
final brilliance lay in the fact that the expenses were borne by the
people themselves when they paid their electric bills.[2]

The excess of this period brought on the Federal Trade
Commission investigation of electric utilities, beginning in
1928, that shook the whole utility empire. In 1932, Insull resigned his 85 directorships, 65 chairmanships, and 11 presi-
dencies and abruptly departed for Europe, prior to his indictment for embezzlement, using the mails to defraud, and
violation of the bankruptcy acts.

The tarnished National Electric Light Association promised
to reform. It heard from the chairman of Niagara Hudson in
1932 that "this association has gone back to first principles. . . .
Any taint of propaganda, of lobbying, of trying to color facts,
or to influence anyone except with facts is definitely, and I
hope permanently, ended in this association."[3]

The permanency of reform was untested because, instead,
the association disbanded the following year, explaining that

it had been stamped, rightly or wrongly, with the reputation of a great propaganda organization and that it was best to end the association and start afresh. The same day the power company officials organized a new trade association, Edison Electric Institute.[4]

In 1941, another organization, E.C.A.P. (Electric Companies Advertising Program) was formed to handle the industry's national advertising. In 1945, the industry created the National Association of Electric Companies, a lobby. In 1949, P.I.P. (Public Information Program) was formed to handle public relations. The old National Electric Light Association was gone and, it was hoped, forgotten; in its stead the industry had four organizations.

The National Association of Electric Companies was headed by Purcell L. Smith, who had been president of the Middle West Corporation, the successor to Insull's 32-state Middle West Utilities, and chairman of Middle West Service Company, an adjunct of Middle West Corporation. Middle West Service Company was also to furnish eventually the managing director of Edison Electric Institute, Edwin Vennard, a former president of the utility service company. N. W. Ayer & Son was engaged to handle the industry's national advertising through the Electric Companies Advertising Program. A leading public-relations firm, Bozell & Jacobs, was assigned the industry's image-building task through the Public Information Program.

These four organizations are the cadre of the utility propaganda network that projects an upside-down image of the investor-owned utilities. As the spread between the cost and the price of power widens, the industry advertises that electricity is the biggest bargain in the family budget. While publicly proclaiming the desirability of utility regulation, the industry quietly works for repeal of the basic regulatory laws. While collecting more money than they need for taxes, and keeping the difference, they advertise themselves as the biggest taxpayer in the state, or "Your Tax-Paying (Not Tax-Eating) Electric Company." [5]

The industry fought construction of Hoover Dam in the Twenties, Grand Coulee Dam in the Thirties, Hungry Horse Dam in the Forties, Hell's Canyon Dam in the Fifties, and the Hanford (Washington) nuclear-steam plant in the Sixties, to cite only principal battles, in each case arguing that the additional power was not needed and suggesting lesser alternatives or none. And in each case—except Hell's Canyon, which the power lobby defeated—there was an immediate market for the power produced at the plants they fought.[6] Despite this history of their own making, the industry persistently advocates complete monopoly, advertising that it "can supply all the electrical power all of the people of America will ever need." [7]

Secure from competition and assured large profits, the industry alleges unfair competition, portraying itself in national advertisements as a fullback tackled by the referee, a track star leaping a high hurdle while his opponent clears a low one, or a baseball player, foot on the bag, tagged out by the umpire. Controlled by relatively few men, the industry contends that the industry's ownership—which implies control—resides among the millions of ordinary stockholders, and suggests that democratic customer ownership of power systems is undemocratic or socialistic. Sheltered by government, with market, price, and profit assured, America's largest monopoly maintains in advertisements, in reports to stockholders, in the trade press, and in company education programs that it is the essence of free enterprise.[8]

This transformation of a protected monopoly into what is represented to be a free-enterprise business had been, perhaps, the outstanding inversion of the real world of utilities. "One of the great triumphs of the propaganda trade," the Memphis

Commercial Appeal observed, has been "the plastic surgery which has made it possible for the dealer in electricity . . . an impostor in the role of a free enterprise businessman . . . to pass as a member of the tribe of salesmen of shoes, real estate and cottonseed." [9]

In advertising, as in other respects, the investor-owned utilities differ from shoe clerks, realtors, the Popsicle man, and any other free-enterprise businessman. The I.O.U.s do not have to advertise to attract the customer to the store; they already supply the power he must have. The companies do not have to beat the competition, because nobody else retails electricity in their territory. There is some competition for a supplemental market—heating—with gas and oil companies. However, 77 of the I.O.U.s, including some of the biggest ones, sell gas as well as electricity on a monopoly basis. These combination companies are not likely to promote one of their products at the expense of another.*

It would be foolish for an I.O.U. not to advertise, because the entire cost of the ads can usually be passed on to the customers. The manager of a shoe store might spend so much on advertising that his profits would be reduced despite increased sales. But he cannot turn to a government commission, as the I.O.U.s can, to obtain a price adjustment that all customers are required to pay.

After World War II, the national advertising campaign of the I.O.U.s continued to reflect Insull's precept that patriotism should be equated with a favorable attitude toward the industry. Through use of pictures and text, the I.O.U.s identified themselves with the Statue of Liberty, the Star-Spangled Banner, Independence Day, Abraham Lincoln, Ben Franklin, Patrick Henry, and George Washington, as well as with the Bible and childhood.[10]

---

* The 77 electric-natural gas combination companies are listed in Appendix F, p. 285.

The ads in the immediate postwar period did not directly attack the municipal, federal, and cooperative systems. The direct attack on other power systems started, if a definite time can be set, shortly after the surprise victory in November 1948 of President Harry S. Truman, a staunch supporter of the federal power program.

The groundwork was laid carefully. In January 1949, the industry undertook to find out how to arouse the public more through advertising. The Electric Companies Advertising Program ran a series of test ads, employing various appeals, in *Time* and *The Saturday Evening Post*. The tests showed that emotional ads had higher readership than unemotional, factual presentations, and that the public did not equate federal power with socialism.

"To link our fight to the T.V.A. question would run us into a lot of opposition," concluded the 1950 E.C.A.P. report on the test ads. However, "to link our fight to socialism is something else again. . . . We're on favorable ground there." Ads dealing with socialism, E.C.A.P. reported, drew the most readers.[11]

That same year Bozell & Jacobs, the industry's public-relations firm, sent utilities a "long-sought slogan to express the spirit of the electric industry's battle against socialization: 'GOVERNMENT IN ANY BUSINESS IS SOCIALISM.'" Bozell & Jacobs suggested the slogan be used for "stickers, imprints, posters and general advertising and to rally other business and professional interests for a joint undertaking."[12]

The power-company lobby, the National Association of Electric Companies, joined in. A 1950 N.A.E.C. pamphlet declared that many power companies foresaw the possibility of a "modified Marxist state" in this country, with nationalization of electric power followed by take-over of other key industries.[13]

The fourth arm of the power industry, Edison Electric Institute, increased the voltage behind its attack on those "socialists" who believed in competition in the power business. E.E.I.'s President Elmer L. Lindseth, who was also president of Cleveland Electric Illuminating, told the 1950 convention of the trade association that "this cold war against freedom of enterprise here in America is being waged without let-up. It is our prime obligation to hold the line against further socialization of the electric light and power business. . . ." Professor James E. McCarthy of Notre Dame told the convention the faith of many Americans "has been undermined by the sniping and sapping of misguided men who are inspired by alien ideologies." W. C. Mullendore, president of Southern California Edison, charged before the convention that "every trick and device, every abuse of power, every misrepresentation and deceit known to a large body of experts in all these lines, have been used by representatives of government to advance the cause of their first love—the socialization of the power industry." [14]

As the industry prepared to shift the tone of its advertising and public relations, an ad ready-made for national use appeared in Frederick, Maryland. Written in 1949 by Charles D. Lyon, then advertising manager and now president of Potomac Edison, and entitled "The Story of Ten Little Free Workers," it was a take-off on the old "Ten little, nine little, eight little Indians" song. The ad told how "the socialists got" the investor-owned utilities. Then, in quick succession, the socialists got the doctor, the railroader, the miner, the steelworker, the farmer, the lawyer, the grocer, the salesclerk, and finally the newspaper reporter. The Electric Companies Advertising Program adopted the ad for its own use. *Electrical World,* a trade publication, designated it "ad of the year" in 1950. Before the ad was a year old, 31 I.O.U.s and 20 other companies or organizations had asked permission to use it.[15]

By 1950, the I.O.U.s had firmly established themselves as

abundantly American, through their national advertising program. Now they were tooled up to establish the idea that non-I.O.U.s were un-American. Space was purchased in *Time, Life, Look, Newsweek, The Saturday Evening Post, U.S. News & World Report,* in the now defunct *Collier's* and *American,* in six leading farm magazines, and in three newspaper trade publications. From 1950 through 1952, more than half of the industry's national advertisements dealt with socialism. "A Socialistic U.S.A.?" asked one headline, beneath a map dotted by government dams and proposed government dams. Through use of pictures, federal and customer-owned power systems were identified with socialism, investor-owned power with the Bible and the Constitution.[16]

The public image of the I.O.U.s improved dramatically as the advertising became more critical of what the ads termed "socialist" power systems. In 1949, 24% of the public believed that I.O.U.s "would probably give you the lowest rates." Two years later the percentage had increased to 34%. During the same period, the percentage of persons believing the federal government would probably give them the lowest rates decreased from 37% to 29%. The percentage of persons who believed that city- or town-owned systems "would probably give you the lowest rates" also decreased, from 17% to 15%.[17]

This question on rate attitudes, asked for the industry by Opinion Research Corporation, ignored the fact that the federal government of course does not sell power to residential customers. And actually, rates of city-owned systems were then, as now, substantially less than those of investor-owned utilities. In other words, the I.O.U.s had convinced a substantial segment of the population that no is yes, that high is low, that of course the world is upside-down! By the end of 1952, *The Saturday Evening Post* credited the Electric Companies Advertising Program with having shifted "the great weight of public opinion in favor of the electric companies" and applauded the industry for it.

During the 1950s, the socialism theme was stressed in speeches before Edison Electric Institute, in mass mailings arranged by power companies, and in reports to stockholders. A former president of Edison Electric Institute, Louis V. Sutton of Carolina Power & Light, warned that the number of groups "devoted to socializing" the I.O.U.s was increasing.[18] Companies paid two organizations * to distribute a *Reader's Digest* condensation of John T. Flynn's *The Road Ahead,* which flashed the inverted image of utilities before its readers, then raised the specter of socialism:

> Privately owned power companies are weighted down by every form of government shackles. Private power systems must run at a profit or die. . . . The Socialist planners believe they have the private power systems on the run. . . . The drive is to socialize the power industry.[19]

"The eventual complete socialization of America's electric power industry" was being sought through federal development of nuclear power, charged Cleveland Electric Illuminating's president (now board chairman), Elmer L. Lindseth, in his annual report to stockholders. The financing of T.V.A. through the sale of bonds, rather than appropriations repaid from revenue, also endangered our free economy, he said. "The remedy to creeping socialism," said Lindseth, a former president of Edison Electric Institute, "lies in a fully informed citizenry, alert to the facts and their implications." Not a line in this annual report told the citizen-stockholders of the existence and implications of the restricted stock option plan adopted that year by Lindseth's company.[20]

Some of the ads, speakers, and industry publications carried

---

* The Committee for Constitutional Government and America's Future, which are discussed on pages 210-220.

a more ominous tone than the threat of socialism. *Electric Light and Power,* reporting on an electric consumers conference in Washington attended by the President of the United States, the Secretary of the Interior, and several Senators, including one who was to become Vice President, said "It's a good bet that plenty of the several hundred who attended the conference didn't know that they're getting into a Commie-front organization." (After Clyde Ellis, general manager of the National Rural Electric Cooperative Association, raised the prospect of a libel suit, the magazine corrected "an extremely wrong statement.") [21] *Public Utilities Fortnightly* carried an article in which, summarized the editors, "a parallel is drawn between the growth of the R.E.A. and establishment of communism in the U.S.S.R." [22] The managing director of Edison Electric Institute, Edwin Vennard, told the E.E.I. convention that the principal protagonists of trends within the United States "are of course the Communists, who are guided from Moscow." [23]

Late in 1957, utility stocks started climbing like a jet fighter.[24] The reduced costs, the massive tax advantages granted the industry in 1954, and the national de-emphasis of utility regulation had boosted utility prospects and profits to a new plateau. The free-enterprise sector of the U.S. economy was undergoing a recession, but the essential, cost-plus, monopoly utility industry was booming. After-tax profits of all corporations decreased 18% from 1957 to 1958. For the I.O.U.s, they *increased* 7.5%. Construction expenditures by American industry *decreased* 17.4% from 1957 to 1958. For the I.O.U.s, they *increased* 2.3%. The all-industry average of salaries and wages *declined* slightly from 1957 to 1958. Among the I.O.U.s, salaries and wages *rose* 4.5%.[25]

Yet in 1958, Edison Electric Institute received the grimmest report yet on the forces of evil that were supposedly crowding in upon the industry and the nation. The trade association asked Admiral Ben Moreell to address its convention. A retired naval officer, Admiral Moreell was board chairman of Jones & Laughlin Steel Corporation from 1947 to 1958, when he became chairman of Americans for Constitutional Action, a political organization formed that year to elect "constitutional conservatives."

Admiral Moreell had been a favorite of the power industry since 1955 when, as chairman of the Hoover Commission Task Force on Water Resources and Power, he had called for abolition of the federal power program and declared his satisfaction with utility regulation. His recommendations on abolition of the federal power program had drawn dissents from other task-force members, including two members of President Eisenhower's Cabinet—Attorney General Herbert Brownell and Secretary of Health, Education and Welfare Arthur S. Flemming.

Another task-force member, former Postmaster General James A. Farley, had termed the recommendations "dangerously close to inviting an abdication by the federal government of the responsibility to insure the proper development of the country's great natural resources." [26] Admiral Moreell told the utility leaders in 1958, the second year of the second term of the friendly Eisenhower-Nixon administration, that the United States was on a "suicidal" course to slavery. The nation was threatened, he said, by total state socialism. [27]

Other industries and groups picked up and used the I.O.U,s' advertising themes. *Human Events,* a mainstay publication of the right wing, suggested in a *Wall Street Journal* ad that to achieve economy in government "R.E.A. ownership can be transferred to local cooperatives," as if to say that the members of the rural electric cooperatives did not already own them. [28]

Republic Steel advertised in *Harper's* its dismay over government financing of electric power. [29] McGraw-Hill, the book and magazine publishers, took a full-page ad in *The Wall Street Journal* to state "The Electric Power Companies' Case for Public Confidence." In an enormous misstatement, Mc-Graw-Hill said matter-of-factly that the I.O.U.s "have received no public subsidies," then put the case for complete monopoly by the I.O.U.s:

By relying on these companies to meet its electric power require-ments, the public will fully protect its economic interest in ample and efficient service at fair prices.[30]

Guaranty Trust Company of New York chimed in with a full-page ad in *Electrical World*, the McGraw-Hill trade pub-lication whose masthead states its belief only in investor-owned utility systems. "The favored groups are not private power companies but consumers of 'public' power," concluded the advertisement by Guaranty Trust,[31] whose board chairman was also board chairman of Duke Power. (In addition, the bank's trustees included four officials of Consolidated Edison of New York, and one of its directors was an official of Public Service Electric & Gas of New Jersey.) [32]

As the power industry's attack descended to lower and lower levels, members of Congress and groups under attack by the ads began to question the propriety of the arrangements through which the multimillion-dollar cost of the campaign was financed. The I.O.U.s were firing away from a privileged sanctuary. Unwilling or unknowing customers and taxpayers financed their battle.

In 1957, Senator Estes Kefauver (D-Tenn.) put before the Internal Revenue Service a series of I.O.U. national ads which he termed "false and misleading." He did not suggest that the companies be prohibited from advertising in any manner. He did suggest that the stockholders should be required to pay for the propaganda. "Taxpayers and ratepayers are, indeed, paying for their own brainwashing," said Kefauver, "without having the democratic right to determine whether they wish to do so or not." [33]

The Internal Revenue Service ruled that the ads were not "ordinary and reasonable expenses," but rather were designed for "lobbying purposes, for the promotion or defeat of legislation or the development or exploitation of propaganda." Therefore, ruled Internal Revenue, the costs of the ads could not be deducted by the I.O.U.s as a business expense in filing their federal tax returns.

This was hardly an insufferable sanction. The utilities could pass on to their customers the slight tax increase resulting from the ruling. The industry, however, was aghast, and immediately denounced and misinterpreted the ruling. "Never before was there a more outstanding example of 'the power to tax is the power to destroy,' " declaimed the president of Edison Electric Institute, Montana Power's President J. E. Corette.[34]

Friends of the power companies joined in the denunciation. The president of the Advertising Federation of America, C. James Proud, termed the Internal Revenue ruling a "sinister gimmick." [35] The Butte *Montana Standard* portrayed a hapless power industry held by thugs, with the Commissioner of Internal Revenue giving the industry the brass knuckles. "If carried to its ultimate," said the *Standard,* "it could mean the end of free enterprise."

The Saturday Evening Post read into the ruling a federal "right to censor advertising." [36] *The Saturday Evening Post* was understandably interested in the advertising. It had received millions of dollars from the power industry for the more than 160 E.C.A.P. ads it had published. However, censorship, which *The Post* decried, was not at issue in any way.

An enormous misrepresentation was being spread throughout the land by the power-company ads and by the industry and press distortion of the Internal Revenue Service ruling. This propaganda campaign, if it led to the I.O.U.s' objective of complete monopoly, would spell disaster for the hundreds of city-owned and cooperative power systems. The trade association of the municipal power systems decided to ask the advertising industry to suggest some ground rules of ethical advertising by the I.O.U.s. Alex Radin, general manager of the American Public Power Association, put the request to President C. James Proud of the Advertising Federation of America. Proud responded that "I can understand your concern over the campaign of E.C.A.P. [Electric Companies Advertising Program], but it is our intent and purpose to protect the principle [that advertising be deductible as a business expense] rather than the specific campaign."

Radin then turned to the American Association of Advertising Agencies. It ducked, too. "It has been our opinion," wrote A.A.A.A.'s Senior Vice President Richard L. Scheidker, "that the advertising which you criticize is outside the scope of our committee and the A.A.A.A. Interchange of Opinion on Objectionable Advertising . . . and that it is more in the area of the Federal Trade Commission."

Radin wrote to the Federal Trade Commission. F.T.C. Chairman Earl W. Kintner threw the hot potato to Capitol Hill:

[E.C.A.P.] advertising . . . is of a nature separate and distinct from the type which is the subject of corrective action by the Federal Trade Commission. Were the Commission to look into the matter, any corrective action would have to involve proceedings of a judicial type, culminating in appeals to the federal courts. However, the courts have held, in a long line of cases, that political questions are matters for the legislature rather than the judiciary to decide. Additionally, the Congress has set its policy as to investigations by the Commission on its behalf. Under applicable law, investigations by the Commission in this area are conducted only upon joint resolution of both houses of Congress with funds supplied by the Congress therefor.[37]

In 1960, the Federal Power Commission ruled that the cost of the political ads should be entered in accounts as a non-operating expense.[38] Although the tax treatment of the propaganda ads had meant little to the utilities because of their priviliged tax status, the accounting treatment could be a different matter. If the ads were not allowed as an operating expense, their cost would have to be borne by the stockholders, a shocking development to utility officials who had grown accustomed to having the customer pay for the propaganda.

The power companies promptly appealed the F.P.C. decision. The courts sustained the F.P.C. The companies, said Circuit Court Judge Walter Pope in 1962, "are simply being required to keep their books in such manner as to indicate that presumptively those [political advertising] activities are to be paid for out of their own pockets rather than passed on to the consumer." [39] In 1963 the Supreme Court refused to grant review of the Circuit Court opinion, thus upholding the F.P.C.

Meanwhile, power-company ads reached a new low in innuendo. By use of pictures, government and consumer power systems were associated with Khrushchev, Castro, the Berlin Wall, barbed wire, and Red soldiers. One of the ads, termed "particularly ugly" by the late President John F. Kennedy, showed an elderly couple turned back into East Berlin by Communist guards at the Berlin Wall. "There's a quiet threat within," read the ad. "For 30 years the threat has grown . . . in the field of electricity. . . . When government owns business . . . it can tell you where to work and live, even what to do or say." [40]

During this period, the rural electric cooperatives instituted a program that was to have as much effect on the I.O.U.s' national advertisements as any action by the courts or the Federal Power Commission. The co-ops, through their trade organization, the National Rural Electric Cooperative Association, started to run national ads, too. N.R.E.C.A. started its ads after surveys showed that the majority of Americans, urban and rural, either did not know who owned rural electrics, or thought that stockholders or the government, instead of the customers themselves, owned and controlled them.[41]

N.R.E.C.A.'s advertising program, managed by Frank Strunk, was positive and high-toned. The ads did not reflect on the investor-owned utilities. However, N.R.E.C.A. let it be known that if the I.O.U.s did not stop their misleading ads concerning rural electrification, future N.R.E.C.A. ads would hit the big power companies hard.

Copy was prepared in 1964 for an N.R.E.C.A. ad headlined, "How Can the Power Company Charge $25,000 for a Line to My Place?" The ad copy told of an actual case where an I.O.U. wanted an advance of more than $25,000, subject to possible refund, plus at least $300 per month, to serve a rancher six miles from a utility line.

This was a bold plan on N.R.E.C.A.'s part—the big utilities could outspend and outadvertise them many times over. But N.R.E.C.A.'s decision to fight if necessary in the advertising columns, along with the Federal Power Commission and court decisions and President Kennedy's denunciation of the ugly insinuations in I.O.U. advertising, caused the utilities to reappraise and revise their national advertisements. The I.O.U.s, although doubling their national advertising budget in 1964, stopped using the socialism and Communism themes in their national advertising. N.R.E.C.A.'s ad about the $25,000 line was not published.

Industry officials, however, have not stopped using the theme in other ways. Possibly they have been so conditioned, like Pavlov's dog, that the cry of "socialism" is a reflexive response to critical discussion of the industry. In 1964, when the stock option windfalls of President A. R. Watson of Southwestern Public Service were publicized, he viewed the revelation as another step "to bring socialism to the electric power industry." [42] The board chairman of Washington Water Power, Kinsey Robinson, raised funds for the 1964 campaign war chest of the Business-Industry Political Action Committee (BIPAC) by charging that "we in business in this country are being badly hurt in Congress by dedicated socialists and do-gooders." He called upon other industries "for support in the battle of investor-owned utilities for survival." And this occurred a few months before he made a windfall profit of $78,000 from options on 6,000 shares of Washington Water Power stock. [43] Managing Director Edwin Vennard of Edison Electric Institute and Clarence Manion of Manion Forum,* a right-wing organization which considers public power to be "pure socialism," developed the same theme in a joint radio program in 1964. Manion led off:

The privately-owned, tax-paying electric power business is the bull's-eye on the big target of private property and private enterprise that Karl Marx said must be destroyed by the forces of socialism and communism. . . . People who wish to fight against the advance of socialism must know more about the present plight of those who are on the socialist gunners' bull's-eye—namely, investor-owned electric power companies.

Vennard, after stating that "it is an honor to speak on the Manion Forum," immediately reduced the choices before elec-

---

* Manion Forum, founded in 1954 by Clarence E. Manion, a member of the national council of the John Birch Society, broadcasts a weekly program over some 267 radio stations and 39 television stations in 43 states and the District of Columbia, issues a monthly newsletter and pamphlets, and promotes establishment of Conservative Clubs. Manion Forum summarized its activities in a March 27, 1961, promotional letter in these words:

"For 6½ years our distinguished speakers have (1) condemned wasteful 'foreign aid'; (2) labor boss dictatorship; (3) 'reciprical trade' agreements crippling our industries and throwing millions out of work; (4) they have repeatedly pointed up the evils of income tax; (5) they have fought 'public power' as pure socialism; (6) they have opposed federal aid to education; (7) they have fought for preservation of state sovereignty against the inroads of centralized power in Washington; (8) above all, they have condemned any appeasement of the gangsters in the Kremlin."

trical consumers to two—the free market or Communism, the former ludicrously impractical for an electric utility, and the latter as repugnant to people who own the power systems that serve them as it is to the owners of I.O.U.s. Said Vennard:

> I should like to spend the next few minutes talking with you about the electric power industry, and how it is related to the central issue facing the world today: That is, whether man will depend upon government for his welfare or whether he will depend upon himself. The choice is that simple, and people have been faced with it for centuries. The founders of this nation recognized it, and made their choice. . . . Either a person is free or he is not.[44]

The colloquy between Vennard and Manion became the April 26, 1964, Manion Forum newsletter, headlined "IN-VESTOR-OWNED POWER COMPANIES PRIME TAR-GET OF SOCIALIST PLANNERS." The title was reminiscent of the *Reader's Digest* reprint that power companies had paid the Committee for Constitutional Government and America's Future to mail out 15 years earlier.

There was no significant sentiment in or out of government to socialize the power industry when the I.O.U.s intensified their campaign of innuendo 17 years ago, and there is no significant sentiment for such a take-over today. The issue is as phony as Phineas T. Barnum's "Feejee Mermaid," contrived of monkey and fish—but even more profitable to power-company barkers than the "mermaid" hoax was to Barnum. Allegedly shot at by socialists for years and years, the I.O.U.s have miraculously suffered no casualties while capturing 103 of the municipal power systems and three rural electric cooperatives since 1949. During the same period, the federal government's investment in its power program was reduced from 1% of the budget to 0.6%, and the profits of the protected utilities rose above those of risk enterprises.

Advertisements on the socialism theme sponsored by individual utilities still crop up around the country. Despite the court ruling that political ads should be paid for by the stockholders, the cost is still borne by the consumer, unless commissions are eternally vigilant and well-staffed. Just before the 1964 general election, the ad that had helped start the industry's "socialism" campaign 15 years before suddenly appeared in hundreds of newspapers. That was the old "Story of Ten Little Free Workers" ad telling how "the farms have been collectivized" and nobody could criticize the federal government which was giving everyone free legal advice and had nationalized the power companies, the grocery stores, railroads, steel, coal, and medicine. By 1964, the ad had been copyrighted by Reddy Kilowatt, Inc.—a corporation built around a "Reddy Kilowatt" cartoon symbol of investor-owned utilities—and tagged with a line telling the reader to ask his Congressman to keep government out of business. The ad had also been turned into movies and stage presentations and been used by hundreds of utility and non-utility corporations.[45]

After the 1964 election, a member of Congress asked the Federal Power Commission to determine how two companies that had run the ad had accounted for its cost. The F.P.C. found in both instances that the cost was listed as an operating expense, $5,875 for Carolina Power & Light, which had put the ad in 109 papers in North and South Carolina and Tennessee, $4,893 for Montana-Dakota Utilities, which had placed the ad in 89 newspapers in North and South Dakota, Montana, and Wyoming.

This shifting of the cost to the customer was similar to what a California utility had done in 1963 with a "Story of Ten Little Free Workers" pamphlet. An F.P.C. employee in California found it stuffed in with his light bill from Southern California Edison. He asked the company for a copy of the voucher showing payment for the pamphlet. No, the company said, it would take a request from Washington to make such information available. The request from Washington came—from both the F.P.C. and California's Senator Clair Engle. The company's response showed that the $9,345 cost of the pamphlet was charged to operating expenses.

F.P.C. explained to Carolina Power & Light, Montana-Dakota Utilities, and Southern California Edison the already well-publicized regulations and court decision that such costs should go into the books as nonoperating expenses. Thus, it was hoped, these and other political expenses would be spotted by the state regulatory commissions and charged to the stockholders—provided that the commissions have the time, money, and staff to look at the utility books.

Four Florida I.O.U.s, in a joint advertisement, put a Communist connotation on the Federal Power Commission's requirement that they account for political ads as a nonoperating expense. "A 'Berlin Wall' [is] being built in America... constructed of subtle and gradual curtailments of traditional American freedoms," and F.P.C. "laid the first brick" by its accounting regulations, said the 1963 ad signed by Florida Power Corporation, Florida Power & Light, Gulf Power, and Tampa Electric. Gulf Power told the F.P.C. the ad was part of its "institutional or good will advertising," and should be paid for by the company's customers. Florida Power & Light had a quite different answer:

> The ad was neither reviewed or approved by the chief executive officers of this company. In fact, our name was included by mistake and consequently this company will not participate in the cost of the ad.[46]

That was a new twist. The customers of other power companies would pay for the smear ad that bore Florida Power & Light's signature.

In 1964, it appeared that even though the utility and advertising associations did not seem to care about the ethics of the

I.O.U. ads, someone in the advertising fraternity did. An advertising executive, Charles B. Jones of the Leo Burnett Company, criticized "the inept, puerile tactics" of utility advertising, which he termed "a cancer" in the industry:

> Advertising based on untruths, or outrageous exaggerations of the truth, is not uncommon, even despite today's many policing bodies. It seems to me that the utility industry is guilty of the creation and distribution of its fair share of such advertising, and I sense that the trend holds small promise for immediate improvement.[47]

Jones buttressed his case with a quotation from Father Henry J. Wirtenberger's *Morality in Business:*

> Sin is committed by unjustly injuring the good name of another in his absence or by revealing hidden faults or expressing sinister interpretations of his good deeds.

From Father Wirtenberger's text, Jones could have proceeded to say that power-company officials should not suggest that other power suppliers are socialists or Communists.

He might have discussed the morality of keeping taxes collected from customers.

He could have simply said that it's a sin to tell a lie.

He did not, though. His main suggestion was that utilities should not misquote prices, and the electric companies that push electric heating should not circulate newspaper clippings that tell about explosions of gas furnaces. They should use a more positive approach.

Good points, both of them, but they certainly do not go to the heart of the issue.

Nobody wants to criticize the Madison Avenue McCarthyism of the nation's largest and most powerful industry.

Nobody wants to bell the fat cat.

Chapter 10.

THE CONGRESS—
DON'T "BETRAY THE SOURCE"

The first rule of successful pressure politics—never
admit that it is only you who is talking.

—The House Select Committee on Lobbying Activities of the 81st Congress, General Interim
Report [1]

Members of the service club blink back tears as the movie
approaches its emotional climax. The camera sweeps toward
and holds on a statue of Abraham Lincoln. A voice intones:

You cannot build character and courage by taking away a man's
initiative and independence. You cannot help man permanently
by doing for him what he could and should do for himself.

The movie ends; the still darkened room is hushed. Then
slowly, one by one, the lights come on. The program chairman
rises, and speaks quietly but clearly:

I believe that you will agree that this is a challenge which affects
each of us. . . .

Simultaneously, his associate begins distributing stationery,
paper and envelopes of different colors and sizes and individually stamped. He passes out pens, a brochure and cards
carrying a brief message:

We the undersigned are becoming extremely concerned with increasing government encroachment into areas which by our American heritage have become free enterprise endeavors. . . . We are
particularly concerned with the unfair competition that exists from
the R.E.A. program against investor-owned power companies.

The associate also distributes a sheet of paper on which similar phrases are handwritten:

... We have been discussing the growth and apparent changing attitude of R.E.A. and are shocked by the way things are going on.

The program chairman continues:

... Take just one minute to help protect a way of life for all future generations, simply by reading this card. If you agree, sign your name as a sponsor of the message that will be sent by telegram to our Congressman tonight. ... On the sheet are the names and addresses of several of our legislative representatives. There is also a sample of a letter that has been written before about this very same problem. Please use it only as a guide. ... You may mail your letter yourself, or we will be happy to mail it for you.[2]

The half-hour Technicolor film, "The Power Within," which the audience had just seen was an elaborately conceived political-action production of the investor-owned utilities. The film was previewed by several hundred I.O.U. executives at the 1963 convention of Edison Electric Institute.[3] They were enthusiastic about its potential for arousing a mass of letters to Congressmen that reflected the industry's viewpoint. Officials of 30 companies estimated that more than 330,000 "grass roots" letters to Congressmen could be generated by members through use of the film in their service areas.[4]

Electrical World's coverage of the movie preview included a picture of three men who helped put the film and its supplements together. One was Robert Person, president of Colorado Public Service, which served as technical adviser on the film. Another was Wayne Bishop, president of Varicom International of Boulder, Colorado, which produced the film. The third was Edison Electric Institute's managing director, Edwin Vennard, author of one of the six tracts which, along with the film and a 119-page manual on how to use it, made up a Project Action kit, selling for $675 each, with discounts for quantity purchase. The electric utilities' Public Information Program—P.I.P.—handled arrangements for selling the Project Action package to individual companies.

The printed material included two scary brochures about customer-owned power systems, "The Creeping Shadow" and "Deviation of R.E.A.," a pamphlet titled "From Rural Electrification to Empire Building," and Vennard's "The Facts About the T.V.A. Power Business." The fifth item was a digest of the second Hoover Commission's recommendations on water resources and power. (In the digestion process, the dissents of Commission members Representative Chet Holifield (D-Cal.), former Postmaster General James Farley, Attorney General Herbert Brownell, Jr., and Secretary of Health, Education and Welfare Arthur S. Flemming had been completely eliminated.) Finally, there was a brochure entitled "The Power of the People," with suggestions on how best to obtain political action.

The film was billed by its producer as a device that "opens minds which have long been closed to the problems of the investor-owned utility industry . . . [and] prepares a path for further education or action, as your company desires." The thick manual accompanying the film set down with painstaking detail the techniques for getting the film before 75 types of organizations, for "opening the minds" of the audience, then obtaining "every ounce of motivation of receptivity possible" and getting results immediately, when the program chairman "will have control of action."

The manual stressed that the film was prepared as "a complete, self-contained mind opener, educator and motivator." Nothing was left to chance. After the minds had been opened, educated, and motivated, the person responsible for the film's showing was ready with pen, paper, and postage. Here, too, the planning was meticulous. The manual told why attention to detail was necessary:

Sample letters should be on various colored and sized stationery and handwritten. This will give members of your audience an authentic guide, yet, because it looks as though it is an actual letter someone has written, avoids the chance of copying and standardized letters coming from your audience to any one Congressman.

This will allow the action obtained to appear spontaneous to the recipient and not as though it were a planned concerted effort by any one interested group.

Program chairmen were also cautioned that letters to Congressmen should be individually stamped—not, for heaven's sake, taken back to the office and run through the postage meter. The office meter, cautioned the manual, "will betray the source of the letters to the recipient."

In contrast with the deceptive goals for its use, the film opens with a straightforward portrayal of the most touching scene in any family—a reunion, the return to the family farm of a young man who now lives in the city. Rugged Ed Jenkins, hands calloused from hard and honest work, glows with pride as his two young grandchildren tumble out of the car and head for Grandma's cookie jar. While his attractive daughter-in-law and Grandma begin to fix dinner, Ed settles down to hear how his salesman son, for whose education and success he worked so hard, is getting along. Young Bill Jenkins is glum, though.

"What's eating you?" Ed Jenkins asks his son.

Bill unloads his troubles. There's not enough money to go around. Things are different since Dad was young. It's those income taxes, state taxes, sales tax, property tax, luxury tax, school tax, and Social Security taxes. Why, says Bill, income taxes take "upwards of twenty percent of my income." (He does not add that with four dependents and assuming only a standard deduction, a 20% tax take means that his annual income is about $22,000.)

Then there is the competition, Bill says. He is in the printing business and finds it hard to cut into the accounts of established business or to get any contracts out of the new federal center, the military bases, and the federal research institute. "Government doesn't seem to let out any business; at least not enough to dip your toe into," he complains.

"That stinks worse 'n my hog pen," exclaims Grandpa Jenkins. And with that he goes to the phone and calls his old friend Alec, the local Congressman, who is conveniently nearby. Father and son climb into the car and go to see him.

The existence of government printing presses is no news to the "Congressman." "Confound it, Ed," says the "Congressman," "you're just pointing out one little facet of this thing . . . one tiny drop in an enormous bucket of swill."

Furthermore, says the "Congressman," Ed Jenkins himself is encouraging government-owned business, and "probably the most significant" of all the examples is membership in a "taxpayer-subsidized" rural electric cooperative, which provides "unfair" competition for investor-owned utilities.

Young Bill Jenkins ventures that a little government competition is a good thing, because utilities are a monopoly. "But a regulated, legal monopoly, Bill," replies the "Congressman," "regulated as to the prices that may be charged, regulated on the amount of profit that may be earned, regulated as to the dividends that may be paid to us as investors. This is the true and proper role of government—regulation, not competition."

Not only are the investor-owned utilities well regulated, they are locally owned, according to this remarkable "Congressman." "The owners of private utilities aren't they, but we. You and I and practically everyone here in Barnes County, and in counties all across the land. Take Margaret Lewis, the widow, for example. She actually owns some utility stock."

The "Congressman" reads to the farmer and his son from the Hoover Commission report—the line that federal competition in the power field is "the negation of our fundamental economic system." He tells them that just as I.O.U.s were "swallowed up by T.V.A., there now is a backdoor federal take-over of the investor-owned utilities." Back in 1932, he says, "the government owned only seven percent of the nation's power. Now that's jumped to twenty-four percent, and it's still expanding." By the time the "Congressman" says the private power companies are "owned and run by free enterprise," Ed Jenkins appears convinced that he has been working for the socialists and ready to disconnect the power line from his own rural electric cooperative.

"There's a word," says Jenkins, "for where all this is heading."

This film is a mixture of the misleading and the fraudulent. The federal government does not own and never has owned 24% of the nation's power. Furthermore, its percentage is decreasing. Federal power production decreased from its record high of 15% during the 1950s to 13% in 1962. The conversations in the movie dealt with the federal power program, and unknowing viewers were left with the impression that its relative role is twice as great as it actually is. To arrive at a figure approaching 24%, the film's producers had to include the generation of power by city-owned systems, public-utility districts, state-owned systems, and the rural electric cooperatives.

Both investor-owned utilities and rural electric cooperatives are privately owned. Both are eligible for and have received 2% loans from the Rural Electrification Administration for serving rural areas. To follow the tortuous reasoning used in the film, one would have to say that all electric power is government power, because of the substantial privileges that government confers on all power suppliers. Public Service Company of Colorado, the technical adviser for the movie, should be especially aware of this, having recently received a $47.3 million grant from the Atomic Energy Commission.

One can visualize what Wendell Willkie's rumbling reaction would have been to the statement in the film that power companies were "swallowed up by T.V.A." It was Willkie who, as the president of Commonwealth & Southern and the outstanding utility leader during the 1930s, negotiated the sale of utility properties to T.V.A. His record on that transaction helped propel him into the Republican Presidential nomination in 1940. He was criticized, not for letting the properties be swallowed, but for getting more from the government for the property ($78,600,000) than it was worth. Willkie stoutly defended the good deal he made:

They forget when they criticize me on the power issue that I was a trustee for a number of stockholders. What did they expect me to do? Give the company away? If I were a public official, then I would have the government's interest as my interest and I would work on behalf of the government's interests. The only test that could be logically and fairly applied was whether or not I was an effective representative of the people whom I was hired to represent.

Look what I did for them! I got $25,000,000 more than the government offered me for the Commonwealth and Southern properties in the T.V.A. area.[5]

Another point—the "Congressman" in the film pulled a sly trick on persons whose audio reception is poorer than their video. In explaining to Ed Jenkins how R.E.A. loans work, the "Congressman" drew an analogy with a monthly house payment of $50. Then the camera held on the paper where he was working out his example. He put the decimal *before* the fifty dollars, instead of after it, so it read $.50. Thus those in the audience who watched better than they listened received the impression that R.E.A. loans were comparable to paying a monthly house rent of only 50¢. That artifice was probably one of the "extremely subtle" subliminal motivation techniques mentioned in the film manual. "With the film there are many more uses of motivation, some extremely subtle," the manual read. "They have been carefully created and placed to avoid no one in the quest for supporters. . . . They transfer empathy and emotion into words and deeds."

Both of the quotations attributed to Lincoln at the film's emotional conclusion are notoriously fraudulent. They are number 9 and number 10 of "Lincoln's 10 Points," * which according to the Library of Congress apparently sprang from the imagination of the Reverend William J. H. Boetcker. He copyrighted and printed them in 1916. It was the Committee for Constitutional Government, however, that sold and circulated the spurious quotations and thus earned the dubious honor of having first associated Mr. Lincoln with the maxims. Lincoln scholars and magazine articles have dissociated Lincoln from the maxims.[6] The Republican National Committee has warned that the "10 maxims are not Lincoln's. . . . Do not use them as Lincoln's words."

The "Lincoln" quotes had been used before by an I.O.U. executive. President Gerald L. Andrus of New Orleans Public Service, one of the utility contributors to the Committee for Constitutional Government, closed his 1962 Junior Achievement banquet address in New Orleans with the 10 maxims. Andrus, since promoted to chairman of the holding company,

---

* The text of "Lincoln's 10 Points" most frequently used, according to the Library of Congress:

1. You cannot bring about prosperity by discouraging thrift.
2. You cannot strengthen the weak by weakening the strong.
3. You cannot help small men by tearing big men down.
4. You cannot help the poor by destroying the rich.
5. You cannot lift the wage earner up by pulling the wage payer down.
6. You cannot keep out of trouble by spending more than your income.
7. You cannot further the brotherhood of man by inciting class hatred.
8. You cannot establish sound security on borrowed money.
9. You cannot build character and courage by taking away a man's initiative and independence.
10. You cannot help men permanently by doing for them what they could and should do for themselves.

Middle South Utilities, said the maxims were "attributed to Abraham Lincoln." [7] And they were in vogue among the power company elite as recently as September 1966, when the *Edison Electric Institute Bulletin* carried the text of a speech by F. J. Funari, vice president of West Penn Power. Funari, objecting to a proposed computerized nationwide service for matching men and jobs as "remarkably similar to a recent Soviet plan" recalled that "As Lincoln reminded us, 'You cannot help men permanently by doing for them what they could and should do for themselves.' "

Within three months of the film's preview at the Edison Electric Institute convention, it had been shown by 51 companies in 38 states and at least one foreign country. Public Service Company of Colorado obtained 15 copies of the film and set as its goal 250,000 viewers by January 1, 1964. The information department of Public Service of Colorado announced meetings with the Junior Chamber of Commerce, Colorado Farm Bureau, Manufacturers Association, and others, in an attempt to get one or more of those groups to make Project Action one of their specific programs.

Community Public Service of Fort Worth reported that it had succeeded in obtaining "community leaders who are not associated with the company to introduce the film at clubs and civic organization meetings." The director of communications for Public Service Company of New Mexico arranged for the film to be shown at a Lions Club luncheon and to some visiting Shriners. He wrote Project Action headquarters that the film tied in with the Chamber of Commerce "Action Course in Practical Politics." The New Mexico utility executive reported that a precinct chairman had told him "we finally have a vehicle for presenting these facts to the average person."

The First National Bank of Englewood, Colorado, and the Englewood Chamber of Commerce promoted the film through an ad and tie-in news story in the Englewood *Herald*. ". . . Do

you know you are taxed to support competition against you?"
read the ad. "Do you know what to do about it? Hear and
see 'The Power Within' . . ." [8]

Five natural gas and telephone companies used the film. The
executive secretary of the National Tax Association showed
the film to the Iowa Independent Oil Jobbers Association.

Early in 1964, Sears, Roebuck borrowed a copy of the film
from Texas Gas Transmission Corporation and showed it to
store employees in Owensboro, Kentucky. However, Sears began to receive protests from persons served by rural electric
cooperatives. Shortly thereafter a Sears executive said, "You
can rest assured that the showing of this type of film is not a
national policy of Sears." Disgruntled electric customers could
not switch utilities, but the mail-order business is different;
Sears wasn't going to risk loss of customers to Montgomery
Ward.[9]

The amount of time, money, and planning spent by I.O.U.s
on "Project Action" is indicated by the 14-step plan of utiliza-
tion adopted by Public Service Company of Colorado, which
appeared in the September 1963 *Project Action* newsletter:

1. A meeting of the company's executive committee was called
and the program was explained in detail.

2. A special meeting of division managers was called and the
program was explained in detail.

3. A 1-day training session has been scheduled for division
personnel who will have the responsibility for presenting the program in the respective divisions. Two people will be called from
each division.

4. To assure support of the company's union personnel, Project
Action will be previewed by officials of the operating unions within
the company.

5. Regarding the central office in Denver, a meeting has been
scheduled for key department head personnel. Following their preview of the program, requests will be made for their services as

conference leaders. This will assure department heads' under-standing of the program and gain support in encouraging their personnel to participate.

6. Selected employees will then have a 1-day training seminar.

7. For the same reasons as outlined in 5, Project Action will be the subject of regularly scheduled supervisory development seminars.

8. During the month of October those who have been trained to use the program will present it to all the employees of the company during a series of 1-hour meetings.

9. Contacts would then be made immediately with all company personnel who are members of various civic groups in an effort to schedule Project Action on the programs of these various groups.

10. The company's information department will make a series of mailings, using the program's "Power Within" brochures, to various organizations in the Denver metropolitan area and begin scheduling meetings among the contacted groups. This same procedure would be undertaken in each of the company's divisions.

11. Company management will review the brochure, "The Creeping Shadow," and determine the feasibility of mailing it along with a letter from the company president to all stockholders.

12. Consideration will be given to showing the program to local stockholders during special meetings in Colorado.

13. Special consideration will be given to the desirability of contacting public, parochial and private school officials in order to determine if Project Action might be utilized in the high schools.

14. Lists of names of persons who have seen and are sympathetic to Project Action will be compiled from each of the meetings for future follow-up.

Public Service Company of Colorado reported that the film had been successful in motivating 63.4% of the viewers to participate in Congressional contacts. Requests for the films built up, chain-letter fashion.

"Each showing of the film," said an official of Colorado Public Service, "results in requests for additional showings."

The Project Action package was presented at seven regional meetings of the Electric Companies Public Information Program during the summer of 1963 and scheduled for presentation at eight regional meetings of the Public Utilities Advertising Association during the following fall and winter. Then, in January 1964, the complete text of the Project Action movie, manual, and tracts appeared in the *Congressional Record*. After that, questions to utility officials about Project Action evoked shrugs. The *Project Action* newsletter reportedly ceased publication. Project Action, if it continued to exist, had shifted to underground transmission.

How much did Project Action cost? Who paid for it— the customers or the stockholders?

The companies were supposed to report political expenditures as a nonoperating expense. There was a particular place in the books for such expenditures to be reported, Account 426 of the Uniform System of Accounts for public utilities, developed by the National Association of Railroad and Utilities Commissioners and the Federal Power Commission. There the cost could be spotted and disallowed in rate-making, if the state regulatory commissions chose to do so.

However, a commission first has to find an expense before disallowing it. The 1963 reports of the electric utilities to the Federal Power Commission did not mention Project Action or "The Power Within."

A commission seeking to probe the cost of that big project would probably be forced to hire a battery of psychologists and search the subliminal.

*   *   *

During May 1965, the U.S. Senate Commerce Committee conducted hearings on S. 218, a bill that would have eliminated Federal Power Commission jurisdiction over most wholesale power rates. S. 218 also would have completely exempted from F.P.C. jurisdiction any company whose facilities are within one state and not directly and permanently connected with those of a utility in another state. The effect of the bill would have been to free more than 50 of the nation's 180 major electric utilities from federal regulation immediately and to permit most other power companies to escape federal regulation by creation of new companies at state lines.

The 30-year-old laws that S. 218 sought to negate underlie the basic electric-utility regulatory responsibility of the F.P.C. These included the commission's authority to audit utility books, to prevent interlocking directorates to a degree, to see that local power distributors can secure needed interconnections on reasonable terms, and to establish uniform accounting systems. Regulation of retail electric rates was not at issue; the states have always had exclusive jurisdiction over them, whether the electricity originates from intrastate or interstate sources. However, a number of the states have no jurisdiction over wholesale power rates.[10]

Thus S. 218 posed a principal issue: Shall basic utility procedures continue under regulation by the F.P.C., or shall they not be regulated at all, except for such regulation as some state commissions might be able to achieve with their limited budgets, staff, and jurisdiction—in an industry so immense and interconnected that the Big Blackout of 1965 was not only interstate, but international? (Twelve investor-owned utilities in three states affected by the blackout in the Northeast would have been freed from F.P.C. jurisdiction over interconnections by S. 218.)

The right of state commissions to allow or disallow operating expenses was not at issue. The bill simply would have removed the requirement that books be kept according to uniform national standards, worked out years before in cooperation with state commissions so that, theoretically, they could find and evaluate questionable expenditures. The bill would have exempted the securities of at least 10 more companies from F.P.C. regulation, leaving the securities of no more than 19 electric utilities under F.P.C. jurisdiction.

One would suppose, from reading power-industry policy statements or from viewing the industry's Project Action movie, that the investor-owner utilities would oppose this bill to remove the regulation they endorse. "The electric companies understand the need for regulation and its aims and cooperate with regulatory agencies in every way," Edison Electric Institute had said in its 1964 policy statement.[11] Regulation of electric utilities "is the true and proper role of government," Bill Jenkins had been told by the "Congressman" in the Project Action movie.

And certainly one might suppose that the state regulatory commissions would favor regulation. Five months before the hearings began, at the Honolulu convention of the National Association of Railroad and Utilities Commissioners, NARUC President Nat B. Knight, Jr., chairman of the Louisiana Public Service Commission, had reminded fellow regulators of a special obligation:

> We in regulation have a special responsibility and an uncommon opportunity to contribute by the effective discharge of our duties, to stimulation of the public awareness and evaluation of the worthiness and importance of state government, and of regulation in general, federal as well as state.[12]

Five weeks before the Senate Commerce Committee hearing opened, representatives of the National Association of Electric Companies and the National Association of Railroad and Utilities Commissioners met in Miami's DuPont Plaza Hotel. The utility lobby was represented by Robert C. Dolan, assistant to the president. NARUC's representative was Edward D. Storm, a member of the Maryland Public Service Commission. Also attending, among others, were Edwin L.

Mason, chairman of the Florida Public Service Commission, the Florida Commission's executive secretary-general counsel, Lewis W. Petteway; President Robert Fite and Vice President Benjamin Fuqua of Florida Power & Light; and Harry Poth, from Reid & Priest, a New York law firm that represents utilities.

Together the regulators and the regulated mapped their strategy for testimony on S. 218. Dolan, the utility lobbyist, was named coordinator of the joint efforts of the "state commissions and all other interested parties." It was agreed that he would furnish state commission representatives with research reports and other helpful information, and that the state commissioners who testified on the bill would submit advance statements to Storm "for proper coordination."

The strategy evolving at the DuPont Plaza fitted perfectly into the investor-owned-utilities manner of handling legislative matters. Just as the industry's Project Action motivated others to wire and write Congress in behalf of the industry, now the state commissions would testify for the industry, which would coordinate the presentation. The "umpires" of the regulatory commissions were playing on the I.O.U. ball team, with the lobbyist for the principal utility group under their jurisdiction coordinating the effort.

One other detail had to be worked out—the batting order for the forthcoming hearing. It was agreed that the lead-off man would be Ed Mason, chairman of the Florida commission, appearing also for the Southeastern Conference of Utility Commissioners. A member of the Indiana commission, speaking also for the Great Lakes Conference of Utility Commissioners, would be on deck. In the hole would be a representative of the National Association of Railroad and Utilities Commissioners, to be followed by a spokesman for the Western Conference of Utility Commissioners and the chairman of the New York commission.[13]

The Miami strategists also discussed other possible witnesses. They knew that Edison Electric Institute was due to name its new president before the hearing convened. In the natural order of things, the vice president of the Institute would ascend to the presidency. Perhaps he, too, would testify.

At the hearing in Room 5110 of the New Senate Office Building, Chairman Swidler of the F.P.C. testified at length against the bill. Mayors opposed it. So did the A.F.L.-C.I.O. and the trade associations of the municipal and rural electric cooperative power systems. One of the bill's opponents, Mrs. Esther Peterson, Special Assistant to the President for Consumer Affairs, told the committee the question before it was "effective regulation versus no regulation."

The utility and state regulatory commission spokesmen followed the batting order that had been previously arranged in Miami, except for the substitution of two pinch hitters. The president of the Western Conference of Utility Commissioners and the chairman of the New York commission had been detained at the last minute, so associates read their statements. The utility witnesses and the state regulatory commissioners were all *for* the bill.

The new president of Edison Electric Institute was among the utility officials who testified for the bill. It was the same Edison Electric Institute that had issued its policy statement in support of regulation. The new president, Robert Person, was the same man who, as president of Public Service Company of Colorado, helped create and saturate his service area with the movie that told of the virtue of utility regulation. Person was all for the bill to disembowel the F.P.C. Nevertheless, he testified, "Edison Electric Institute does not oppose effective electric utility regulation." In other words, Edison Electric Institute was not opposed to effective regulation; it was just opposed to laws that permit regulation to approach effectiveness.

There was a slip-up, though. Commissioner Mason of Florida, under questioning, leveled with the committee and candidly stated why the I.O.U.s love "regulation."

If he had his druthers, Senator Gale McGee (D-Wyo.) had asked him, would he prefer not federal, not even state, but county regulation? Responded Mason:

We feel very strongly about that, yes sir. We feel if the county could and would regulate, this is the best regulation. The best regulation is closest to the people. The best regulation is very little regulation. This has been proven throughout the history of our country.

The chairman of the Florida Public Service Commission went all the way. "The best regulation," said Mason, "is little or no regulation."

His frank response brought laughter from some parts of the hearing room. Not from the I.O.U. officials, however, who clustered, frowning, for hushed conversations in the corridor outside the hearing room.

When the I.O.U.-state-commission team moved to the House Interstate and Foreign Commerce Committee for hearings on a similar bill, Mason was not on the roster.

No matter how good a rookie looks on the grapefruit circuit, no hits and a costly error against the Senators put him back in the minors.

Chapter 11.

THE PRESS—
FREEDOM *FROM* INFORMATION

The editor of the *Tampa* (Florida) *Tribune,* V. M. Newton, Jr., was delivering a ringing address on the "right to know" before the Arizona Press Association:

Only an informed public opinion can preserve the processes of free government. . . . As an editor of the free American press who has spent ten active years in the great fight for freedom of information I point a finger at Congress with the warning that the very future of American freedom is in their hands today. And I call upon each and every newsman in our land, as well as on the American people, to keep constant pressure on the individual Congressman to remind him that American government is the servant—not the ruler—of the American people.[1]

Editor Newton provided national leadership in his profession's fight against governmental secrecy, which culminated in the "right to know" law signed by President Johnson in July 1966. Meanwhile, however, back on Tampa Bay, Tampa Electric arranged an unneeded rate increase, piled a stock option plan on top of its employee stock purchase plan, and pushed its return on equity up to a super-exorbitant 18.88% in 1963. The editor of the *Tampa Tribune* was by no means the only newsman who overlooked the big local story of customer-gouging by Tampa Electric. "For several years now," the company bragged in its 1963 annual report, "the company has received no derogatory comments through the various press media."

The company attributed its immunity from criticism to participation by the company in community affairs (much of it financed by the customers) and expanded activity of its Speakers Bureau.

The Speakers Bureau had grown out of the company's campaign to put over the rate increase in 1959. Four years later, the coordinator of the Speakers Bureau, George D. Gentry, told other utility officials how his company had created the rate increase lobby and transformed it into a device for improving the company's image. The first step had been saturation of the community with company speakers.

"There turned out to be two basic ways" [to get company speakers before audiences], said Gentry, "one, by unsolicited invitation—of which there were a few—and two, by solicited invitation, sort of a sophisticated 'crashing the party' type of approach."

Where invitations had not been readily forthcoming, said Gentry:

contacts were made with business and civic leaders upon whom we could count for help—always "going through" employees where possible. From lists available through Chambers of Commerce, Presidents' Roundtables, county councils, etc., we found it a fairly simple matter to construct our own master list. . . . All the shots were called and virtually all the bird-dogging done from the office of our vice president of finance—by him—with our advertising and publicity manager, Virgil Price, serving as senior colonel on this militant staff. Carefully detailed records were kept of all maneuvers on both sides, locales pin-pointed on a system map—and with strategy and execution closely paralleling the recent "Big Lift." [2]

Then, said Gentry, after "face-to-face communications had been established throughout all our systems . . . the ground-work had been laid, the mechanics were in operation . . . the Speakers Bureau per se was formed." The Speakers Bureau circulated films as well as speakers, leading off with distribution of the film "Communism on the Map," a film conceived and produced by a member of the John Birch Society that shows all the world except Spain, Switzerland, and the United States as either red or pink—and with a big question mark on the U.S. If Editor Newton or other Tampa newsmen were to take their eyes off Washington long enough to cover local utilities, this film would help return the interest of the press to the District of Columbia, Afghanistan, and other places outside Tampa Electric's service area.

The big, hard news about utilities seldom gets attention from the press. In the spring of 1965 the Federal Power Commission, for the first time, published the rates of return of major electric utilities.* This study showed how regulation of the rates of the largest industry has broken down. Certainly the news value of the story was both national and regional.[3]

The Commission distributed a press release that told, in the headline, that for the first time it had compiled and published a uniform rate of return for major electric utilities.

The Commission did not comment on the rates of return. It simply called the attention of the press to a valuable and significant study. Result: No coverage.

Perhaps some reporters who saw the release did not realize the importance of the rate-of-return study. Perhaps they did not have time to do a little legwork. Perhaps, in some cases, there was enough handy copy around the office, sent over by the utilities.

Not until the rate-of-return study was placed in the *Congressional Record,* a week later, and a release was sent to the press galleries from a Congressional office, did the rate-of-return study receive some slight attention from the press.[4]

Disinterested newsmen could inform the public on utility matters better than interested utility officials or public officials can. Utilities, however, are a neglected beat.

* The rates of return of electric utilities appear in Appendix C, p. 260.

Serious questions about press coverage of all financial affairs were raised by the Securities and Exchange Commission in 1963. Reporting these findings in the August 1963 issue of *Harper's,* Peter Bart wrote:

> The S.E.C. chronicled in grim detail some hard facts which many editors would rather forget. Among them were these:
>
> Financial reporters and editors in many cases have held stock in companies about which they have written, or have accepted gifts, junkets and other favors from these companies.
>
> Financial sections often fail to distill truthful and important news from the dishonest and trivial; as a result, the financial press has been used over and over again by stock touts and manipulators to mislead the investing public.
>
> A close-knit camaraderie has developed between the financial press and financial public relations men—a camaraderie that works to the disadvantage of the ordinary newspaper reader.[5]

Bart, who has worked on metropolitan papers in New York and Chicago, noted that *The Wall Street Journal* and *The New York Times* have assigned bright young men to financial reporting, and that these two papers do not permit their reporters to accept the favors offered in lavish amounts by press agents. He learned, however, that even in the metropolitan press, some editors doubled as advertising salesmen and that castaways were assigned to the business and financial pages. Prepackaged puffery becomes "news" on big and little papers. Bart wrote:

> As newsmen have grown to rely more and more on this pre-digested copy, financial reporters have become lazy. Instead of using his legs and his brains, a man can concoct a story by simply calling a friendly flack and telling him about his problem. The item is readily supplied. But it is puffery, not news.

The public's right to know about utility affairs is being gradually eroded. Prior to 1954, the Securities and Exchange

Commission requested utility holding companies under its jurisdiction to report their "contributions, dues or other payments to social, educational, professional, trade or similar organization" and "payments or contributions to newspaper press associations, newspapers, magazines or other publications ... for purposes other than advertising." The utility industry had vigorously objected to reporting this information, arguing that it was of questionable value for enforcement purposes and that the costs of preparation were unduly burdensome. The S.E.C. agreed and, having received no request for a hearing, held none and deleted the reporting requirements on March 29, 1954.[6]

The itemization of utility contributions, no longer required by the S.E.C., could not be obtained at the Federal Power Commission. These unitemized contributions often amounted to hundreds of thousands of dollars annually from individual companies.

In 1963, as noted earlier,* the F.P.C. proposed regulations that would require electric and gas companies to include in their annual reports their contributions to charitable organizations and expenditures to influence public opinion.

Here was a clear-cut freedom-of-information issue. Did the public have the right to know what a utility, a quasi-public agent of the state, spent for purposes not related to its operations? Customers were required to pay many of these nonoperating expenses. Were they entitled to know what they were buying?

Nothing in the regulations would have diminished in any way the utilities' rights to say or spend or advertise as they pleased. Nor did the proposed regulations forbid utilities to make their customers pay these nonoperating expenditures.

The F.P.C. invited comments on its proposed regulations.

* Page 56.

A number of newspaper editors submitted their views. Every one of them *opposed* the proposed disclosure requirements.[7]

"Gag rule on advertising," said one. The regulations emanated from "socialists in the civil service," said another. Other editors held that the disclosure requirements would constitute "denial of an American right," be "another step toward the ultimate socialization of the utility industry," and "effectively gag private utility companies." Broadcasters and advertising associations joined newspaper editors in demanding freedom *from* information about power-company expenditures.

The F.P.C. was told by the Boise (Idaho) Advertising Club that its members unanimously opposed the regulations, that the club members "invariably oppose laws, rules or regulations which tend to restrict and in some cases virtually usurp the right of individuals and companies to use mass communications media for free expression in advertising." Either the club had been misinformed concerning the regulations or had misinterpreted them.

The F.P.C. modified its proposed regulations, which originally would have required companies to itemize contributions of $100 or more. The F.P.C. regulations put into effect in 1963 required itemization only of those contributions exceeding $1,000. As it turned out, the modification didn't mean much. Many companies simply disregarded the regulation requiring itemization of contributions. The F.P.C. has neither the time nor the staff to follow through on enforcement in every instance.

During recent years, the investor-owned utilities have quietly obtained revision of other regulations. These changes deny the public information which, when available in the past, provided valuable glimpses into utility operations.

Prior to 1948, electric utilities were asked to report to the Federal Power Commission the names and fees of persons retained for legal, financial, engineering, sales, and similar services. F.P.C. regulations were revised in 1948 to exclude reporting of payments under $10,000 per year for the Class A utilities (those with annual operating revenue of $2.5 million or more) and under $5,000 for Class B utilities (those with annual operating revenue between $1 million and $2.5 million). The reporting requirement was again amended in 1957 to excuse any Class A utility from reporting payments below $25,000.

Information on most utility retainers thus comes to light only during those rare and fleeting moments when a Congressional committee or a regulatory commission seeks and obtains it.

A hearing by the Senate Judiciary Subcommittee on Antitrust and Monopoly in 1954 revealed that Arkansas Power & Light paid more than a quarter of a million dollars to 46 legal firms or individual lawyers in 1950 and 1951. Former Arkansas Governor Sid McMath testified about the nature of some of the negative, nonlegal services sought by the company, in return for the fee:

> One lawyer friend of mine was called by Mr. Moses (C. Hamilton Moses, board chairman of Arkansas Power & Light), himself, and told that he had heard this lawyer was supporting me. Mr. Moses told him if he continued to support me, his A.P.&L. retainer would be immediately withdrawn.[8]

Mississippi Power & Light retained at least 21 law firms, who received from $15 to $1,158 a month, for which they rendered little, if any, legal service, according to testimony by the company's former chief financial officer before the subcommittee.

The subcommittee found "a whole range of political and public relations activities, including retaining of local lawyers in communities throughout the power company service areas and at the state capital, distribution of contracts and supplies, with the understanding that helpful political activity is expected."

One of the power companies' national advertisements in 1964 indicated that perhaps the companies were willing to divulge some of the information they usually are reluctant to impart, such as their retainers. Electric companies, said the ad, "answer any question you may have quickly, without making a federal case of it." [9]

Having some questions about the electric-utility industry, the authors accepted the advertised offer. The offer had been made by "more than 300 companies," according to the ad. However, the ad agency said, only 103 companies actually sponsored it.[10] So letters were written to each of the 103, referring to the ad and asking each of them 12 identical questions. One of them was: "What attorneys and legal firms were retained by your company during 1963, and what was the compensation for each?"

Fewer than half of the companies responded to the letter.

Of those answering, five said the question about retainers constituted an "invasion of privacy."

Six said the boss was out of town and more time was needed to prepare a response, which never arrived.

One official referred us to "my good friend Senator———" for a discussion of the company.

Three referred us to their parent company.

One said we wouldn't be interested.

Three said they were subject only to state jurisdiction.

One said attorney fees were a "minute percentage of the company's expenses."

One said it chose to defer a response.

Ten listed only the total payments for attorneys or fees in excess of $25,000 each.

Four said they retained no attorneys, and 16 companies listed all the attorneys and legal firms retained, and their compensation. Thus 20 companies, less than 20% of those offering to "answer any question you have quickly," responded to the question.

Although the press seldom explores utility ownership, options, advertising, nonoperating expenses, rates of return, and retainers, other aspects of power-company affairs receive wide publicity. This coverage, purchased unknowingly by some electric consumers as part of the light bill, is prepackaged in "canned editorial" factories. The editorials are distributed to editors who publish, often as their very own, prefabricated paeans of praise for the I.O.U.s.

During 1964, more than one million editorials praising the power companies were distributed to newspapers by one of these editorial transmission systems—the Industrial News Review of Portland, Oregon.

Each week Industrial News Review sends a packet of 12 or 13 editorials and a page of short "fillers" to about 11,000 newspaper editors. A survey of use of these editorials in one state—Colorado—showed that about a third of the editors used the editorials, frequently as their own and without change. Some editors used as many as 200 of the editorials during a year.

Many newspapers using I.N.R. material have a small circulation. The national impact of these editorials should not be overestimated. However, in many homes the small local paper, with its regular diet of pro-utility editorials, is the only newspaper read regularly.

Industrial News Review refuses to divulge information about its clients and fees. (A member of the family that has operated I.N.R. for more than 50 years did, however, admit to *The Washington Post* in 1965 that I.N.R. received an undisclosed fee from the American Medical Association.) Of course, I.N.R. does not have to say who the clients are. A remarkable pattern unfolds before anyone who analyzes the editorials.

After one has noted the pattern, he can determine, before opening the weekly packet from I.N.R., what organizations or industries are going to be lauded in 10 of the 12 or 13 editorials.

Every other week during 1964, one editorial praised each of the following: American Medical Association, American Meat Institute, the New York Stock Exchange, Pan American Airways, REA Express and chain food stores. The companies or organizations were frequently mentioned by name. In some instances the timetable varied slightly.

Every week one of the editorials extolled each of the following: the oil industry, the drug industry, the Chamber of Commerce or taxpayer associations, and the railroad industry. In the last case, the editorials sometimes did not mention railroads, but criticized the barge and trucking industries that compete with the railroads.

And every week, without exception, two of the editorials sang glory, glory to the I.O.U.s.[11]

One of the editorials, distributed in the June 29, 1964, packet, should be set to music:

No line of activity keeps the public better informed about its growth, operations and plans than does the investor-owned electric power industry in the United States.

Second verse:

This is largely due to the fact that a power company lives in a gigantic goldfish bowl, the size of the territory it serves.

Chorus:

Its every act is subject to public observation and local, state or federal regulation. . . .

In 1964, Industrial News Review sent out one laudatory editorial about the insurance business, one on the telephone industry, and two on banking. However, these samples apparently did not sell the service to prospective clients. On the other hand, two editorials in the spring of 1964 on the virtue and propriety of $200-million annual subsidies for American steamships apparently evoked a favorable response. Beginning June 1, editorials lauding the Committee of American Steamship Lines were distributed every other week. Similarly, distribution of editorials complimenting the timber industry and tree farming began June 8. Industrial News Review also furnished, on a somewhat irregular basis, editorials lauding investor-owned gas utilities and right-to-work legislation.

Miscellaneous editorials dealt with holidays, seasons, good government, International Printing Week, YMCA Week, Boy Scout Week, Future Farmers Week, Girl Scout Week, National Library Week, National Transportation Week, Chemical Progress Week, National Flag Week, Farm Safety Week, National 4-H Week, National Newspaper Week, National Bible Week, National Farm-City Week, and Red Cross Month.

Industrial News Review editorials distributed in 1964 said that power companies make only a "modest" profit, are "unfairly taxed" and are "constantly engaged in a battle for existence." Rural electric cooperatives were characterized as "socialistic monopolies," the Bonneville-California transmission line as "socialization, at taxpayer expense." In fact, 52 of the editorials distributed in 1964—enough for one a week— dealt with "socialism" in the electric-power industry.

I.N.R. grieved with the president of Edison Electric Institute, Walter Bouldin of Alabama Power, because power companies are "hobbled" by the "socialized power movement"; I.N.R. seconded the notion of *Reader's Digest* that investor-owned utilities could do the whole electrification job, without cost to the taxpayers. Always abreast of the power lobby's line, I.N.R. said that the Federal Power Commission should not have jurisdiction over wholesale power rates.

Public officials who sought to assure competition for the

I.O.U.s were promoting "further socialization of the industry," according to I.N.R. Even the sturdy New Englanders were said to be menaced by "socialism," in the form of the Passamaquoddy project, a proposed federal hydroelectric plant in Maine.

The editorials droned on in a similar pattern throughout 1965. The day before the Big Blackout of November 9, Industrial News Review assured readers that service standards of I.O.U.s are "of the highest"—and that their rate structure "allows only for the cost of providing service, plus a modest profit—usually about 6%."

The hand is Industrial News Review's; the voice is the I.O.U.s'. But to the eye of the unsuspecting reader, these editorials often appear to reflect the words and wisdom of the local editor.

Use of these identical editorials throughout the country leads I.N.R. and its clients to represent them as reflections of "the viewpoints of a majority of the American people." That phrase was applied by the American Medical Association to its collection of anti-Medicare editorials presented to Congressmen during the spring of 1965.[12] At least 44 of the editorials in the A.M.A. presentation came from Industrial News Review.

Seven of the editorials in the A.M.A. collection came from "Washington Exclusive," a product of another canned editorial service, the U.S. Press Association, which "for $175 will send your message to 1,199 weeklies and 150 daily newspapers." [13] The National Association of Electric Companies and the I.O.U.s' Public Information Program are among clients that have been listed by the U.S. Press Association.

Industrial News Review itself observed the "virtually unanimous" conclusions of "hundreds of editorials which recently appeared in papers across the country" in favor of one of its clients' causes. I.N.R. also noted "opposition to the [Knowles] dam [in Montana] has been increasing at a swift pace and papers within and without the state have taken up the fight" —this after having distributed editorials against the proposed Knowles Dam.

In a similar instance, newspapers in Pennsylvania, Ohio, and Georgia attacked the Internal Revenue Service ruling that the expense of power-company political ads should not be tax-deductible. The newspapers, all using the I.N.R. editorial as their own, declared in unison that the ruling "has stirred up a hornet's nest of editorial comment. . . . And the overwhelming mass of the editorial comment says, in effect, that the ruling is indefensible, amounts to an attack on freedom of speech, and violates the most basic Constitutional principles."

The Industrial News Review's leading role in transmission of power-company propaganda dates from the days of Samuel Insull, who expanded it into a national utility propaganda service during the Twenties.[14] I.N.R. received $84,000 a year from power companies during that period, according to testimony before the Federal Trade Commission by a member of the Hofer family, which operates the service. Apparently nothing short of a similar investigation by a federal commission or Congressional committee, however, will elicit the amount of current I.O.U. contributions to I.N.R. and other utility propaganda outlets.

Union Electric (Missouri) reported a $1,100 contribution to Industrial News Review in 1962. Pacific Power & Light and Portland General Electric each gave I.N.R. $1,300 during at least one year in the Fifties. However, some other companies hide these expenditures.

When the Federal Power Commission asked Texas Power & Light to itemize several hundreds of thousands of dollars casually listed as "other miscellaneous operating expenses" in its annual reports since 1961, there, tucked away, were $600 annual contributions to Industrial News Review.

Mississippi Power & Light was asked by F.P.C. to itemize its operating expenses for 1963. The breakdown showed that a $300 contribution to Industrial News Review, as well as "honorariums to former retainers," "honorariums to ministers," "expenses of college professors," and a lot of supplies at the company lodge were part of the price of getting the lights to burn in Mississippi.[15]

After Industrial News Review has noted overwhelming support for its principal client's position, the power companies' public-relations firm, Bozell & Jacobs, takes over.

It can combine the editorials written by utility-financed editorial services with opinion surveys conducted by utility pollsters and thus concoct their very own "public opinion."

A memorandum jointly distributed by Bozell & Jacobs and Central Surveys, Inc., of Shenandoah, Iowa, a polling organization frequently used by power companies, declared:

A new survey among county, daily and weekly newspaper editors, conducted by the Industrial News Review, confirms and enlarges on a similar study reported by the *American Press* magazine . . . 1,169 (out of 1,362) believe that T.V.A. and similar regional federal projects indicate a trend toward socialism. . . .[16]

And what is *American Press?* It was termed a "highly respected . . . outstanding . . . trade publication" by a president of Edison Electric Institute, after the magazine's description of the Internal Revenue Service ruling that utility propaganda is not an ordinary and reasonable tax-deductible expense as "another vicious invasion of our dwindling freedoms."

A different view of *American Press* was expressed by Ben H. Bagdikian, author and former newspaper reporter, who observed in the December 1964 *Harper's* that the reader of *American Press* "is almost never told that he is seeing something other than the considered product of his local editor." Perhaps the best comment on the reliability of *American Press* was the headline in its October 1964 issue:

PUBLISHERS PREDICT GOLDWATER VICTORY [17]

Use of prepackaged editorials is probably governed more by convenience than by conviction in the case of many newspapers, especially the small ones. One man may be owner, ad salesman, mailer, and makeup man, as well as editor. He has little time to write editorials, or to edit those furnished him.

As the newspaper's deadline approaches, the size of an editorial becomes more important than its message. So the editor reaches for a galley of editorials, of varying length, which he had set into type earlier. The copy may have been supplied by one of the canned-editorial services. Or it could have come from the local power company, whose public-relations staff has saved the editor the bother of rummaging through the exchange papers to find editorials to reprint.

A typical week's mailing to editors from Carolina Power & Light in 1963 included 13 such "reprint" editorials. Seven attacked the Rural Electrification Administration. Two lauded investor-owned companies. One applauded right-to-work legislation. One commended a professor for saying that profits are not too high. Another criticized a professor who had spoken ill of power companies. At least one of the editorials originated from Industrial News Review.

A Southern publisher whose paper has won numerous awards for excellence described the relationship in his state between the press and the power companies in these words, written in 1963:

The companies advertise fairly heavily and their representatives attend all the press association conventions, get cozy with most publishers, foot the bills at cocktail parties and flood the poor country editor's desk with ready-made editorials, editorial reprints from other newspapers that are for private power and against public power, etc.

The average weekly editor, being more of a printer, anyhow, accepts this indiscriminately and usually regurgitates it on the page in one form or another. The power company officials are pleasant to work with, pay promptly and their public relations practices are much smoother and more expert than the co-op's. Whenever we have a gold medallion [all-electric] home completed the power company people always help in getting tie-in advertising [from equipment dealers, builders and other companies associated with the new all-electric homes] and writing feature copy.

The power companies' own advertising amounts to a substantial regular portion of many newspapers' income. The copy frequently is in "mat" form, already prepared, requiring almost no production cost by the paper.

In 1961, for example, Montana Power paid 49 weeklies and 11 dailies more than $45,000 for publishing the company's series of cartoons by Reg Manning. That is to say, during 1961 each paper received on the average, depending on its circulation and rates, more than $750 for publishing the cartoons.

Just as many a lawyer retained by a utility ponders the attitude of the company toward his political activity, an editor must consider how the bills on his desk or his children's college fund might be affected if he becomes too inquisitive or critical about the operations of a major advertiser. One weekly in Montana Power territory, the *Western News* published in Hamilton, Montana, which has sharply criticized the utility, was written off as an advertising medium by the company 35 years ago; the company did not like the barbs thrown by the late Miles Romney, Sr. From 1930 to 1937, the paper functioned without a Romney at the editor's desk. The paper did not oppose the company during this period, and the utility ads resumed. In 1937, the present publisher, Miles Romney, Jr., a free-swinging editor like his father, took over. Two weeks later the company stopped advertising in the *Western News*. The utility has not placed one of the regular "institutional" ads, such as the cartoon series, with the paper since.

One of the company cartoons depicted the harassed taxpayer receiving a huge bill for "government financed projects." Similarly, Montana Power tried to hand the $50,000 bill (including $5,876.50 for cartoonist Manning) for this series to its customers, by charging off all the costs of this ad series as an operating expense.

The Federal Power Commission told the company that the cost of these political ads should be put in the books as a non-operating expense, where presumably it would be borne by the stockholders, in line with the court ruling in the Electric Companies Advertising Program case. The company protested strongly to the F.P.C.:

We are astounded that the Commission staff regards advertisements opposing communism and supporting the American system and containing basic concepts of economics as being "political controversy.". . . This series . . . won a Freedoms Foundation award . . . 38 of the advertisements dealt with such subjects as the advantages of Democracy over communism, free enterprise, business economics, the profit system and the freedoms enjoyed by American people.[18]

While many editors will not permit the viewpoint of a principal advertiser to influence their editorial decisions, utility officials in the past considered that a newspaper's editorial attitude was conditioned by utility advertising. The Federal Trade Commission investigation revealed some of the utility officials' attitudes on this point. As one utility official put it in a letter to a colleague:

Gee, what the country press is worth to people who are honest and use it honestly is beyond calculation. I have spent as much as $300 in three years entertaining editors, etc. Some of them do enjoy a little drink. All of them are "God's fools," grateful for the smallest and most insignificant service or courtesy.

"We are trying," wrote another utility public-relations man, "to promulgate the idea rapidly among the newspapers that public utilities offer a very fertile field for developing regular, prompt paying customers of their advertising columns. When that idea penetrates the United States, unless human nature has changed, we will have less trouble with the newspapers than we had in the past." [19]

Human nature apparently had not changed. And most major magazines give the industry even "less trouble" than the newspapers.

True, one major magazine executive scolded the power industry. But why did he scold it? For not advertising enough.

"I don't think that the $2 million or $2.5 million of the E.C.A.P. (Electric Companies Advertising Program) is nearly enough," *Time* executive Andrew Heiskell told the 1961 Edison Electric Institute convention. The I.O.U.s apparently agreed and budgeted $4 million for E.C.A.P. in 1964.

The Saturday Evening Post frankly admitted that utility advertisements "have been used in the battle along with the editorial comment to help turn the tide of public opinion" to the side of the power companies. *Life* portrayed the federal power program as a pork-barrel monstrosity.

The magazine that does the most for the investor-owned utilities is *Reader's Digest,* the one magazine with saturation coverage of the nation, a magazine that receives about a quarter of a million dollars annually from I.O.U. advertising.

A. L. Cole, the general manager of *Reader's Digest,* told the Edison Electric Institute convention in 1961 that several *Digest* editors were going to write articles favorable to the investor-owned utilities. As a result, he hoped, people will not "have to secure their electric service from any government."

In other words, *Reader's Digest* would help the companies campaign for complete monopoly.

"We are on your side," said Cole. "We have shown this repeatedly by articles published in *Reader's Digest* over a period of many years." [20]

Indeed it has, and to an audience twice the size of that reached by the next largest magazine. With a paid circulation of 25 million, the *Digest* goes into 15% or more of the homes in most parts of the nation, and into 25% or more of the households in about half of all counties in the U.S. More than 10 million copies of each issue are also sold overseas.

Digest readers were told in December 1963 that the Rural Electrification Administration is "a many-headed monster that is eating into the entire electric power industry—and into the taxpayer's pocketbook." The month before, *Digest* subscribers had read that rural electric cooperatives are engaged in "highly unfair competition with private, i.e. publicly regulated utilities." In May 1963, they were informed that "one of the shocking facts that taxpayers have not been told . . . [is that] the Treasury now has to pay up to 4⅞ per cent to borrow from the public the money which the Rural Electrification Administration lends out at a cut-rate two per cent to co-ops [which are] . . . in competition with taxpaying companies."

In July 1962, a member of the *Digest* staff attacked rural electrification and other cooperatives in an article entitled, "Should Those Co-ops Get Tax Privileges?" [21] The article, said Vice President (then Senator) Hubert Humphrey, contained "so many basic false assumptions and misconceptions about farmer co-operatives that I feel obligated to comment on it," which he did, point by point, in a Senate speech.[22] (It would be pointless to ask the *Digest* to correct the errors, as it does not print corrections or letters to the editor.)

Some 60 million Americans read the *Digest*. Others read *Digest* articles about how the poor power companies are harassed and abused through the *Reader's Digest* reprint department and use of the power companies' lists of stockholders, customers, and community leaders.

The reprint service provides for mass distribution of *Digest* articles that readers have found "of exceptional interest or usefulness." *Reader's Digest* perceives prior to publication which articles the readers will find exceptionally interesting and useful and publishes a box listing bulk reprint prices for them. Regularly, the articles selected include those castigating rural electric cooperatives, as well as attacks on medicare, urban renewal, area redevelopment, and the National Aeronautics and Space Agency.[23]

Metropolitan Edison (Pennsylvania) included a reprint of the December 1963 *Reader's Digest* attack on that "many-headed monster," the Rural Electrification Administration, with bills sent to the utility's 260,000 customers.[24] Duke Power mailed the reprint to thousands of customers, stockholders, and farm leaders in the Carolinas. President Walter Bouldin of Alabama Power, also then president of Edison Electric Institute, had his personal card clipped on reprints of the article circulated by his company.

Some companies featured the *Reader's Digest* reprint in their advertising. "For reprints of this authoritative article," said Southwestern Electric Power (Louisiana) in its ad, "write any of the investor-owned electric power companies listed below."

A month after the article appeared in *Reader's Digest,* its reprint editor told the York (Pennsylvania) *Gazette and Daily* that more than a million reprints had been sold. The reprint editor declined to tell the *Gazette and Daily* reporter whether arrangements for sale had been made with power companies prior to publication. Industrial News Review, ever mindful of its principal client, gave the lead position in its December 13,

1963, packet of free editorials to one in vigorous support of the *Digest's* attack on R.E.A.

By some variation of Parkinson's Law, the more the power companies spend on information, public relations, and advertising, the less the public knows about their operations. However, there is a wealth of information in the public record for any newsman who truly covers the beat, as Reporter Rice Odell of the *Washington Daily News* has proved.

There is nothing wrong with press coverage of utility affairs that could not be cured or at least improved by inquisitive and thorough reporters backed up by publishers who are willing to jeopardize an advertising account and be snubbed at the club. The press has informed Americans extremely well on matters such as medicine, space, and politics. The utility rate-of-return formula can be more easily understood and explained than the new math, and is more important to the family budget. But unless a few more reporters and editors occasionally leave the herd of newsmen covering the New Hampshire primary, or the civil rights demonstration, or in the press gallery, unless they read the literature of regulation and dig into the issues in the manner of the *St. Louis Post-Dispatch,* some Scripps-Howard papers, and a few others, Americans will continue to discuss electric power by exchanging slogans rather than by evaluating meaningful facts.

Chapter 12.

THE SCHOOLS—GUESS WHO TEACHER IS

> Against the sort of odds that exist today . . . the elec-
> tric light and power companies not only have the
> right, but a moral obligation, to "educate the pub-
> lic . . ."
>> —From an *Indianapolis Star* editorial distributed
>> to 11,000 editors December 7, 1964, by Indus-
>> trial News Review, on behalf of its principal
>> clients.

Most elementary and high-school teachers are not trained
to teach economics. The majority of them never took a course
in the subject. There is an acute shortage of texts and sup-
plementary material for the teaching of economics in elementary and high schools, and few teachers are trained to
evaluate them.

A letter received by the President of the New York Stock
Exchange illustrates the point. The letter came from a high-
school band director. He was teaching economics, for the first
time and without training. He asked the Exchange for "any
material you might have" that would help him and his students. The President of the Exchange observed philosophically
that many school officials "would rather have a band leader
teach economics than have an economist lead their band." [1]

In college, students may take an excellent general course in
economics without learning much about public utilities. The
popular and succinct college text by Paul A. Samuelson,
Economics, An Introductory Analysis, now in its sixth edition,
states that a utility rate base is "complex," that "any simple
yardstick comparison between private and public [utility] op-

erations [is] difficult if not impossible." The text alludes to the effect on the pricing system of "the great regional power projects such as the TVA and the Bonneville Dam," the latter apparently a reference to the Bonneville Power Administration, the federal agency that markets power from about 20 federally constructed dams, including Bonneville Dam. Samuelson writes about "marginal utility," "equal marginal utility," "psychological utility," and "total utility," but says practically nothing about the public utilities.[2]

College students who go beyond the basic economics course will probably find some discussion of public utilities in general survey courses called Government and Business or something similar. Perhaps they will engage in a discussion of utility rates and services. But the field of regulation is broad. A general survey course does not equip the student with an understanding of the fundamental differences between competitive, free-enterprise corporations, including competitive utilities such as transportation companies, and the monopoly public utilities, to which individuals pay thousands of dollars during their lifetimes without once having the opportunity to shop for a better bargain.

Academic attention to regulation in general, not just public-utility regulation, is decreasing. Samuel Krislov of Michigan State University and Lloyd D. Musolf of the University of California, editors of *The Politics of Regulation,* published in 1964, found it "ironic that as political scientists acknowledge increasingly the significance of the regulatory process and administrative procedures, teaching of, and emphasis upon, them decline in our universities." [3]

The major foundations have not moved into the vacuum with their scholarly and well-endowed resources. Studies in regulation do not fit into guidelines established by the Rockefeller Foundation. The venerable Brookings Institution of Washington, D.C., issued two studies of electric power during the 47-year period 1917–1964. Both were pamphlets, one written in 1942, the other in 1929. (In 1966, however, a study of the role of competition in the electric-utility industry was completed by a federal executive fellow at Brookings, Richard Hellman.) [4]

Research for term papers and theses leads some students in the general survey courses into detailed examination of particular aspects of the regulatory process. Students find, however, that it is much easier to locate resource material on, say, farm subsidies than on important aspects of utility operations. Thus each year a new class of collegians moves from campus to the world of work prepared to debate the merits of 75% of parity for farmers, but for the most part blissfully unaware that the local power company regularly receives well over 100% of parity, plus fringe benefits that no labor union has yet achieved.

The universities are producing many fiscal economists, labor economists, and other specialized experts. Few universities, however, produce authorities on the public utilities that account for about one fifth of American business. Rare is the campus that even offers a course in public utilities.

A few lonesome public-utility scholars have chronicled the withering away of their profession. Robert W. Meyer of the University of Illinois concluded that "academic attention to public utility economics in the form of scholarly articles clearly has dwindled almost to the vanishing point." [5] A survey by Professor John D. Garwood of Fort Hays Kansas State College indicated that not more than 75 or 80 of some 1,800 colleges and universities offered a course in public-utility economics. Among the many larger institutions that did not offer such a course, Garwood found, were the universities of Connecticut, Delaware, Florida, Kansas, Michigan, Missouri, South Carolina, and Virginia, plus Duke, Northwestern, Penn State, Wake Forest, Tufts, Kansas State, Brown, and Creighton.[6]

Since Garwood's survey was published, some of the leading utility authorities at major universities have retired, and the public-utility courses they taught have been dropped from the curriculum. Columbia University in New York offers courses ranging from Urdu to 12th-century French lute music, but it dropped the course in public-utility economics when the distinguished Professor James C. Bonbright retired and now touches only a relatively small part of the entire field of utility pricing in a course on welfare economics of price structure. When Professor Robert Montgomery retired after more than 40 years at the University of Texas, the public-utility course he had taught was dropped, to the great relief, one would deduce, of Texas Power & Light and Southwestern Bell Telephone. Both had tangled with the trenchant Montgomery through the years.

Another authority in the field, Professor Horace M. Gray of the University of Illinois, was scheduled to retire in 1966. Gray's vigorous advocacy of more competition in business has not endeared him to utility monopolists. The public-utility economics course at Illinois probably will not be offered after Professor Gray's retirement.[7]

At some institutions the public-utility course is taught by a utility official, by the editor of a trade publication that reflects the viewpoint of only investor-owned utilities, or by a teacher who dwells upon transportation rather than the monopoly utilities—the electric, telephone, gas, and water companies. Younger teachers with interest, training, and practical experience in the field are simply not available. Some of the bright possibilities have been hired by the utilities themselves, at salaries more attractive than those available at a university.

Obviously, few scholars are studying and few students are learning how regulated monopolies function. The question then arises: Who teaches the regulators?

No university or college offers the specific curriculum

needed to train members of regulatory commissions. Few courses are designed for regulatory accountants, attorneys, and engineers. This lack of preparation for accountants is especially significant, because good accounting is a prerequisite of fair regulation.

Regulatory accounting used to be a lively field for scholars. Federal Power Commissioner Lawrence J. O'Connor, Jr.— the first certified public accountant ever to serve on a federal regulatory commission—recalled recently how during the 1920s and 1930s, "regulatory accountants were most conspicuous for their activity in prescribing uniform systems of accounts; the related techniques and problems were discussed at length in professional periodicals and financial journals." But today, said O'Connor:

> Little reference is made to regulatory accounting in more recent accounting texts. . . . Few college or university courses, for example, give any coverage to the accounting concepts employed in regulation and the few that do are economics-oriented, being taught for the most part by economists for economists.[8]

As William J. Powell, technical assistant to F.P.C.'s chief accountant, put it, "not many students of accounting or even their teachers, much less the public generally, are aware of the necessity for regulatory accounting and how it affects the national welfare."[9]

What this adds up to is that practically the only persons who understand utility accounts are utility accountants. Even experienced investment analysts have trouble figuring out these accounts. That puts investors at a disadvantage. A committee of the Investment Bankers Association took a long, hard look at the state of utility accounts in 1965; the bankers did not like what they saw. Said the committee, headed by American Securities Corporation's Executive Vice President William N. Bannard:

Differences in accounting practices have placed the average investor at a great disadvantage. Indeed, even the institutional investor finds it difficult to follow and to determine comparable utility earnings.

The bankers reported "there is no consistency in accounting practices with respect to the treatment of the investment credit or deferred taxes due to accelerated depreciation." They termed current utility accounting practices "completely inadequate," showing "a greater lack of comparability than at any time since 1933."

"There must be proper communication," said the investment bankers, "to maintain investor confidence." [10]

One would suppose that the federal government, with its thousands of publications, would have at least one bulletin telling consumers about the $14-billion-a-year electricity bill. But it does not. *Consumers All,* the 1965 Department of Agriculture Yearbook, tells how to kill bugs, select rugs, remove stains, and relieve pains; it has sections about the house mortgage, insurance, medical bills, financing a car, and one on whether the wife should work. The section on saving energy is not about electric energy; it has to do with shelves within reach, and room enough for knees beneath a table. Nothing about the electricity bill, however, in the book for consumers issued by the Department whose agencies include the Rural Electrification Administration.[11]

Open one of the "Do You Know Your Economic ABC's?" pamphlets issued by the Department of Commerce and you will find discussion in everyday terms of profits, gross national product, depreciation, balance of payments, and the like. You'll read that "the consumer is king" because the dollars he spends in the marketplace decide which businesses profit.

But what about the businesses that King Consumer has to patronize, no matter what the price, because they are utility monopolies? The Department of Commerce pamphlet reads like a bedtime story by Reddy Kilowatt: "Our government can and does regulate . . . public utility prices so that a community cannot be overcharged for its use of gas, electricity, and water," soothingly assures Uncle Sam.[12]

There is an argument going on within the academic community and some companies about what economists call the "metrocorporation." That is a corporation that envisions itself as obligated by limitless social functions. Stockholders of some metrocorporations complain that the management should be in the business of making money for them, and let the stockholders handle their own philanthropy and good works with the profit, if they want to. "It is intolerable that public functions be performed by self-designated private officials," wrote the University of Chicago's leading conservative economist, Milton Friedman.[13] But where are the scholars who speak up for the captive customer of the utility, the unknowing and perhaps unwilling contributor to a variety of organizations, some charitable and some not, fostered by utilities that add the cost of their donations to the electricity bill?

Power-company donations flow as steadily as electricity into many well-motivated organizations that would logically make such inquiries. Any organization whose name indicates it has to do with economics is a magnet for utility contributions— the Bureau of Economic Understanding, the Council for Economic Growth and Security, the Economic and Business Foundation, the Economists National Committee on Monetary Policy, and the Joint Council on Economic Education with its state and regional affiliates in Arkansas, Illinois, Kentucky, Minnesota, New Jersey, and Pennsylvania. Utility influence has been especially heavy in the Texas Bureau of Economic Understanding, which has supplemented teacher salaries.[14]

Of course those who administer these programs will not necessarily be influenced by the donations. Yet a well-meaning professor who has finally raised a little money to do some research or adult education is not likely to start off by examining critically the industry that helped his project get started. If he were to do that, the budget might be smaller next year. The manner in which corporate gifts can be used to keep recipient educational organizations "in line" was put discreetly by Merryle Stanley Rukeyser in a recent issue of *The Freeman,* published by the Foundation for Economic Education, which has long been supported by utilities. Corporate gifts, said Rukeyser:

should be on an annual, or income, basis, rather than in the form of an unrestricted capital endowment. The promise of a recurrent gift gives the donor . . . an opportunity to be selective. . . . This procedure reserves the privilege of cutting off gifts to those educational institutions which fail to achieve scientific objectives and scholarly approaches to the dynamic problems of contemporary civilization.[15]

Unfortunately, the academic world has never recovered from the purge of public-utility textbooks and curricula engineered by the investor-owned utilities in the Twenties. During that period, I.O.U. officials spent a considerable amount of time seeing to it that, as one of them described it, "some of these inimical textbooks [are] discarded" through "quiet and diplomatic measures." [16] With many of the candid textbooks discarded or outdated, with little scholarly research in the field, with the wise teachers of public utilities retired and not replaced, the field is virtually wide open for education about utilities by the utilities themselves. And "educating" they are, at a tempo increasing since the late Fifties, perpetuating the wondrous myths that electric utilities are taxpaying, locally owned, bargain-offering free enterprises beset by competition and bedeviled by socialists.

At the 1957 convention of the Edison Electric Institute, its president hammered home the theme that companies must expand what the industry variously calls its "communications" or "education" program. "It is an undertaking," said E.E.I. President Donald S. Kennedy, the president of Oklahoma Gas & Electric, "which must be well-conceived and well-executed, and one in which it is hoped that the entire investor-owned part of the industry would share. . . . Many capable minds in our industry have been applying their best thoughts to means and methods by which this communications problem can best be solved, and the results show gratifying progress." [17]

His successor as E.E.I. president, J. E. Corette of Montana Power, followed up in 1958. "I am suggesting," said Corette, "that we embark immediately upon an expanded educational program which will make a lasting impression upon the American public." [18]

At the 1959 convention of Edison Electric Institute, retiring President Corette elaborated on this theme and equated love of country with love of I.O.U.s in the manner of the old Insull public-utility information committees:

Government ownership of utilities has always been the first goal of the socialists and communists. Because of this, the future of the American system of government is dependent on the electric business continuing in the hands of investor-owned taxpaying companies. This places upon everyone in our industry a double burden both as an employee and as a good citizen. Our problem is not only to save our industry, but to save the American system of government, with its great benefits to the people.

. . . My year as president of E.E.I. has caused me to spend more hours than ever before on the development of a program of what must be done if we are to stop the trends of the past 25 years, which lead to ultimate socialism, to ultimate loss of our freedoms, our wonderful productivity and our standard of living. . . .

With other good citizens we must actively carry on a major economic education program so that all the American people will realize and will protect with their last ounce of devotion the American system of government and business, the productivity, the high wages, and all the benefits that result from it.

And what were the perils so great that an industry not subject to democratic control had to take upon itself the education of the public? In his judgment, said the Edison Electric Institute president:

... nothing in recent years is more serious than the effort of the Internal Revenue Service for tax purposes, and the Federal Power Commission for rate purposes, to eliminate certain advertising expenses from the classification of ordinary and necessary business expenses. ... This is an outstanding example of what comes from centralized government.[19]

In other words, the industry might have to pay for some of its own propaganda, instead of including the cost in the light bill. And so a gigantic "education" program had to be launched by the utilities.

The American people have a proud record of giving their full measure of devotion to their country. American patriotism preceded utility advertising and education programs, and runs deeper than identification of national security with the goals of utility managers. The equation of the national interest with the personal advantage of an industry, a corporation, or an individual cheapens all America. The use of the facilities and personnel of a public-service corporation to mislead the public is tragic. Yet, day after day and night after night, around the country, utility spokesmen attack customer-controlled power systems and teach what they consider to be the principles of free enterprise to audiences which have not learned the fundamentally different principles of public utilities and which are left with the impression that utilities resemble risk enterprises.

Central & Southwest, the Delaware holding company, told

in its 1963 annual report to stockholders how its operating companies, "through individual interviews, have told a large number of their customers of the unfair competition which the investor-owned utilities have from public power. We believe this information campaign to be helpful."

One of the holding company's Texas subsidiaries, Central Power & Light, conducted more than 10,000 interviews, doubled its news releases, made 573 film showings, and reached 58,000 people through 271 speeches before civic, church, and other groups in 1963. Tampa Electric's Speakers Bureau scheduled 40 to 50 speeches a month that year. Cleveland Electric's Speakers Bureau reached an audience of more than 76,000 persons in 1963, not counting students reached with literature in school.[20]

The utility message slips into university pronouncements. In 1962, a Columbia University press release, concerning a forthcoming utility management workshop, read:

> For years, government regulation and competition has [sic] been a day-to-day harassment to the management of the privately owned, business managed utility company.
>
> . . . How can these companies compete fairly with each other in the interest of the public and simultaneously resist the continuous inroads of the tax free public ownership?

The press release was not produced by the University news office. In fact, said Columbia's director of university relations, the release "was not produced, so far as I can discover, with the knowledge of the news office. It was not produced with my knowledge. This, of course, is contrary to the organizational plan in the university." [21]

The university official went on to say that the release violated basic principles of journalism, that he did not recall any similar incident during his tenure, and that he would try to see that it did not happen again. The incident recalled similar use of universities by utilities back in the Twenties. The director of the Nebraska Committee on Public Utility Information had pointed up the value of the technique in a letter to his counterpart in Missouri. "The college," he said, "can say things that we can not say, and be believed." [22]

In Elmore, Minnesota (population 1,078), the utility educators used a different technique to get across the same message. On March 28, 1961, Robb M. Winsborough, vice president of Middle West Services, a utility service company, and officials of Interstate Power, which serves portions of Iowa, Illinois, and Minnesota, loaded a bus full of farm families and headed for Interstate Power's Fox Lake generating plant. En route they talked about taxes and played the "Reddy Kilowatt Quiz Game" which featured questions about electricity, rigged heavily in favor of the company.

Minnesota has no state utility regulatory commission. At that time Iowa had none. Interstate Power's rate of return was above average. The farm folks left the bus, though, marveling at the low cost of their light bills and sharing the company officials' anger about utility taxes.

"We thought our bills were high," was one comment, "but we have changed our minds."

"Those taxes are way out of line. Everybody should pay the same taxes," said another.

A third was ready for a rate increase.

"We can see now why your rates have to be higher, paying those taxes," he said.[23]

During the 1964 Presidential campaign, Tampa Electric and Florida Power Corporation arranged for the pro-Goldwater film, "The Welfare State," narrated by Actor Ronald Reagan, to be shown in scores of Florida communities. Earlier, Public Service Company of Oklahoma had diverted some of its engineers to its economics department.[24] They produced and showed civic clubs a 35-minute film on "The American

Economic System," a program developed years ago by Edwin
Vennard, then president of Middle West Services, now manag-
ing director of Edison Electric Institute, and Vice President
Winsborough of Middle West Services.

During the 1950s a high-school text also entitled *The American Economic System* had been published. Reissued with up-
dated charts in 1964, this text includes utilities with ordinary
corporations subject to competition in the marketplace, where
"more new businesses fail than succeed." Students who believe
all they read in *The American Economic System* are primed
to join the movement to abolish the income tax. "Distributing
the income of the wealthy people," it says, "is one of the favorite arguments of the Communists." [25]

And who wrote the text? A teacher, perhaps? An economist?
No, it too was written by Vennard of Edison Electric Institute
and Winsborough of Middle West Services. They told the students that taxes are collected by corporations which turn the
money over to the government, and that "neither the owners
nor the employees of the corporations can have any of this
money." That from the spokesmen for the industry that has
kept hundreds of millions of "tax" dollars—and whose identification with the electric-power industry is nowhere mentioned
in the book.

Chapter 13.

LOOK, JANE, LOOK! SEE THE NICE LOW LIGHT BILL!
—The American Economic Foundation

A contribution of a few hundred dollars from one company to one organization is of no great consequence. A contribution of a few hundred dollars to one organization every year by dozens of companies amounts to a retainer. Contributions of a few hundred or a few thousand dollars each year by dozens of companies to a dozen or more organizations whose means and ends are warmly approved by the John Birch Society, along with interlocking leadership and indirect support through purchase of literature, provide the extremists with strength and resources far beyond that visualized by examining the activities and finances of the John Birch Society alone.

Nationally known companies also give the extremists an aura of respectability that they do not deserve. Electric-utility leaders freely lend their names to these organizations. A spot survey in 1964, by no means complete, showed about 80 instances in which top officials of approximately 50 power companies also served as officials of about a dozen extremist groups.

A description of general characteristics of these extremist organizations is in order before proceeding to more particulars.

Many of the organizations are closely interrelated. They colonize rapidly and multiply geometrically.

Many of them are tax-exempt. Contributions to many, if not most, are deductible from the donor's taxable income.

Their aims are similar. Most of them oppose the income tax, labor unions, civil rights legislation, the antipoverty program, the United Nations, the Supreme Court, and public power. Some of the groups oppose public education.

The extremists tend to reduce the choices of economic systems available to Americans to just two. One is the free-market economy, the other Communism—the former unattainable, the latter repugnant.

These uncharitable groups declare that they are motivated by the purest of patriotic motives. Some assign subversive tendencies, Communist support, or outright Communist direction to those whom they oppose.

Despite their professed Americanism, most of them are less than wholehearted in their support of the profit system. Almost as one voice they have cried out against the efforts to enable the impoverished and the untrained to participate meaningfully in the profit system.

These organizations maintain a maze of communications among themselves and outward to individuals and organizations. One group or a related "colony" may sponsor a nationwide radio program, issue one or more publications (from which reprints with or without attribution are encouraged), sell books, conduct seminars, run a speakers' bureau, direct letter-writing campaigns, train the faithful and the newly converted in special schools, and send magazines and other material free to students.

The education sponsored openly by the investor-owned utilities is the visible top of an iceberg. Indirectly, invisibly, the I.O.U.s carry on their education program through regular contributions by many companies to organizations that take the utility message to all ages, beginning in the elementary schools. For example:

COLUMBUS & SOUTHERN OHIO ELECTRIC COMPANY

215 North Front Street
Columbus 15, Ohio
November 19, 1964

Mr. Morgan S. A. Reichner
Vice President
The American Economic Foundation
51 East 42nd Street
New York, New York 10017

Dear Mr. Reichner:

I am pleased to tell you that the school superintendents in our service area think so well of your manual for teachers in Grades One through Six, "How We Live in Our Town," that we have been forced to order more than 4,000 copies already this year. This means that every elementary teacher will have a copy.

We are also making available to every Junior High School Social Studies teacher your new Junior High School Manual, "Studies in How We Live."

You are to be congratulated on the development of these useful manuals. So far as I know you are the only organization to take action in the lower school grades as well as the High School grades and are, therefore, way ahead of the field. Keep up the good work!

Cordially,

(signed)
John W. Robinson
Supervisor of Information
Public Relations Department [1]

What is the American Economic Foundation, which provided the Ohio utility with literature for the schools? Why does a power company see that every local teacher has A.E.F.'s material?

A.E.F. is a tax-exempt organization founded in 1939 by Fred G. Clark, who is its chairman. Previously he headed the

Crusaders, which through radio programs fought Prohibition and "socialism." Socialism, according to the Crusaders, included the Public Utility Holding Company Act of 1935 and the Tennessee Valley Authority. Clark's method of operation then was to obtain contributions from utility officials and broadcast attacks on the legislation they opposed, after first wiring them to be sure to listen to his program. Officials of Commonwealth Edison (Chicago) and Lord and Thomas, which then handled power-company advertising, each put up $5,000. Lesser amounts came from officials of Iowa Electric Light & Power, Cities Service Power & Light, and utility service companies.[2]

From 1943 to 1965, American Economic Foundation concepts were used in economic training programs for 3½ million hourly-rated workers, foremen, and supervisors in 2,000 corporations, 171 teachers' institutes and workshops involving hundreds of primary and secondary-school teachers, and in community education and discussion group projects throughout the country.

A.E.F. films have been permanently placed in more than 7,000 high schools in 41 states. The foundation promotes textbooks, maintains a speakers' bureau, prepares power-company advertisements, and helps corporations explain financial reports to stockholders and the public. A.E.F. also distributes monthly editorials "for use in whole or in part, with or without byline, in employee magazines, in executive communications and as sermon and classroom material."[3]

The American Economic Foundation introduces children and teachers to an America somewhat different from the country in which they live. According to A.E.F. material, industry is "based on free markets and free enterprise," the "Customer is King," and belief in the Ten Commandments and the Golden Rule permeates the business community, which is burdened by outrageous taxes.

The income tax and role of government is misrepresented in A.E.F. institutes and literature. At a May 1963 teacher institute sponsored by A.E.F. and three Connecticut power companies * together with the schools, teachers were told that the federal government "holds for all practical purposes 52% of the stock . . . in every profitable business."

In a 1963 pamphlet with the ominous title "Destination: Burial?" the Foundation confused income with profit, stating that "the booming cost of government has resulted in tax rates which take 52 cents out of every dollar of corporate income. On top of this federal rate, we must add state and local income, property, excise taxes and other fees." [4]

A.E.F. Chairman Clark's views on the income tax, which was authorized by the Sixteenth Amendment to the Constitution (ratified in 1913), are indicated by his speech to an Eastern Air Lines banquet, reprinted in the *D.A.R. Magazine* in 1962. The title was: "The Socialistic Sixteenth—A National Cancer." [5]

The literature of the American Economic Foundation excludes electric utilities from comparisons showing the advantages they enjoy, or which might lead to a real understanding of them. For example, the "directomat" at the A.E.F.-sponsored Hall of Free Enterprise at the 1964–65 New York World's Fair provided visitors with the answer to any of 120 selected questions. Thirty of the questions dealt with the profits of various industries—petroleum, steel, machinery, aircraft, transportation and communications, and so on. But nobody could ask the directomat about the profits of the nation's largest industry, electric utilities. The profit on sales of every industry carried on the directomat was less than 10%. In contrast, electric utilities enjoyed a profit on sales of 16% in 1964. [6]

Was this omission due to absence of utility officials among the planners of this display? Hardly. The Advisory Council of

* Connecticut Light & Power, Hartford Electric, and United Illuminating.

the Hall of Free Enterprise fairly bristled with the names of presidents of leading electric utilities.

One 1963 A.E.F. publication for schoolchildren, "Studies in How We Live," refers readers to a number of government agencies and private organizations that provide consumer protection or services to individuals. (One of those listed, Reconstruction Finance Corporation, was abolished six years before the booklet was printed.) The students were invited to learn more about the Federal Trade Commission, the Federal Communications Commission, the Interstate Commerce Commission, etc. But nary a word was said about the Federal Power Commission, the Securities and Exchange Commission, or state utility regulatory commissions.

The American Economic Foundation puts great store in what it terms the Ten Pillars of Economic Wisdom. The Ten Pillars, along with several "natural laws," are the "distillation of some 20 years and $5 million of semantic research and testing," according to Chairman Clark.[7] Here, for example, representing about two years of study and half a million dollars, is Pillar Six:

> Because wages are the principal cost of everything, widespread wage increases, without corresponding increases in production, simply increase the cost of everybody's living.

One is tempted to play with the Pillars, to rewrite Pillar Six to read: "Because the cost of electricity is part of the cost of almost everything, widespread overcharges simply increase the cost of everybody's living." After 20 years and $5 million worth of work on them, though, they had better be left alone; the unit cost of production of the materialistic Pillars is already too high.

The John Birch Society thought well enough of the Ten Pillars of Economic Wisdom to include a flyer advertising them with the monthly *John Birch Society Bulletin*. The society and the foundation also draw support from some of the same individuals. A.E.F.'s List of 78 "famous Americans who support the Ten Pillars" includes four persons listed in 1962 by the John Birch Society as members of its national council or endorsers of the society. They are Frank de Ganahl, Dr. E. Merrill Root, Roger Milliken, and T. Coleman Andrews.*

Also among A.E.F.'s 78 "famous Americans" were Hans F. Sennholz, a contributing editor of the John Birch Society magazine, *American Opinion,* and Dr. Ludwig von Mises, a member of *American Opinion*'s editorial advisory committee.[8]

Educators are sometimes approached by A.E.F. through its subsidiary, the National Schools Committee, whose general manager, Morgan S. A. Reichner, is vice president of A.E.F. The committee works directly with teachers and school administrators. A letter from a National Schools Committee official written in January 1965 indicated how contacts are developed:

Mr. Reichner has been in touch with Dr. Woodrow W. Wilkerson, the Virginia State Superintendent of Schools, about the possibility of a statewide project. I believe they plan to meet to work something out at the big school administrators convention in Atlantic City next month.[9]

A.E.F. films and other materials are already permanently placed in 13 Virginia school systems and have been suggested for use on radio and television in some parts of the state. On March 14, 1963, the training director of Union Bag-Camp Paper Corporation at Franklin, Va., wrote A.E.F. executive Louis Milione:

Mr. John C. Parker of this company called today to inform me of your proposal to make available economic information as spot announcements for radio and television. This is a splendid idea. I congratulate you for your diligence in developing additional media to communicate this important subject.

* Andrews recently resigned from the society's national council.

Education of our children in economic and philosophic theory can be accomplished. I am thankful that this is being done in Virginia through our public school systems. Education of the adult population, however, cannot be so easily accomplished. It is, therefore, mandatory that we utilize every avenue of communication to educate and inform our adult population.

In order to achieve balance in the thinking of our citizens, it is imperative that A.E.F. continue its "Economic Fallacy" series. Your proposal to extend the dissemination of economic truths and to expose the fallacies through radio and television is a fine one. With the barrage of "seductive" reasoning being aimed at our population, your work is essential to the health of our nation.

The American Economic Foundation reported to the Internal Revenue Service total income of about $2.3 million during the 1958–62 period. In 1963, the foundation did better than ever before, taking in $799,662.

Large contributors during the 1958–62 period were Robert Donner, a retired steel executive, $69,250; Charles Hook, a former president of the National Association of Manufacturers, $43,055; A. G. Heinsohn, Jr., a textile executive who is on the executive committee of the John Birch Society, $19,540; and DeWitt and Lila Wallace, founders of the *Reader's Digest,* $10,500.[10]

The American Economic Foundation receives massive support indirectly by a variety of methods. Leading magazines make their contributions in the form of free advertising. According to an A.E.F. brochure distributed in 1965:

More than 100 publications, including *Saturday Evening Post, Fortune* and *Reader's Digest* have contributed a total of more advertising space than to any other non-profit project in the nation. However, tax-deductible contributions are required for continuous research to meet the growing demand for educational aids and for promotion of a new motion picture. . . .

The magazine ads are superbly constructed for fund raising. A heart draped in the American flag dominates the full-page A.E.F. advertisement that *Coronet* donated as a public service in its August 1964 issue.

"Send your tax-deductible check," concluded the ad, "to FREE ENTERPRISE . . ." [11]

The American Economic Foundation also benefits from plugs by several national columnists. One of them, John Chamberlain, complained in 1965 that "Clark's show [the Hall of Free Enterprise at the New York World's Fair] . . . has sometimes been hard put to pay the rent." Some corporations dodged contributing to A.E.F., said Chamberlain, by saying they "are already supporting similar economic education programs."

A leading New York public-relations firm, Selvage & Lee, also helps the poor, struggling American Economic Foundation pay the rent. Selvage & Lee's March 10, 1963, release for A.E.F. included one of Clark's appeals for contributions. The release stated that the Hall of Free Enterprise was co-sponsored by A.E.F. and the National Small Business Association with

as cooperating organizations, Junior Achievement, Freedoms Foundation at Valley Forge, Foundation for Economic Education, Christian Freedom Foundation and the Canadian Economic Foundation.

The Foundation for Economic Education warrants a chapter, which follows this one. Brief mention should be made here of two of the other organizations which in cooperation with A.E.F. sponsored the Hall of Free Enterprise.

The founder and president of Christian Freedom Foundation is Howard Kershner. He edits a magazine, *Christian Economics,* which is sent free to about 200,000 ministers, writes a syndicated column sent free to some 700 papers, and has a regular radio program. J. Howard Pew, multimillionaire chairman of Sun Oil, supports the foundation with gifts averaging about a quarter of a million dollars annually during recent years.

Pew is a major contributor to a number of ultraconservative organizations. He has been one of the stockholders in Robert Welch, Inc., which publishes the John Birch Society's magazine, *American Opinion.*

Pew and Kershner share the view that the Protestant clergy is heavily infiltrated with Communists. Kershner, who views the T.V.A. as "socialism" and urban renewal as "Marxism," summarized some of his views in his April 17, 1961, speech at Harding College in Searcy, Arkansas:

> We are driven to the conclusion that evil men in strategic positions with the aid of their dupes, stooges and fellow-travelers have been able to mold public opinion in our country and shape governmental policy along lines that are hurrying us onward to destruction. In a real sense, the Communists have taken over our country and have greatly influenced our major economic, fiscal, military and foreign policies.[12]

One of the other organizations mentioned in the Selvage & Lee release, the Canadian Economic Foundation, distributes American Economic Foundation literature in Canada. According to the Cooperative Press Association of Toronto, the Canadian Economic Foundation "moved into Canada only within the past two years [1962–1963] and is expanding rapidly. It is now preparing to carry its 'economic study materials' into all Canadian schools."

Chairman Clark of the American Economic Foundation told an audience of electric-utility officials in 1961 how A.E.F. and a power company, working together, distributed so much material that "within 18 months, the coverage of the public and parochial high schools in eastern Pennsylvania had almost reached the saturation point." Said Clark:

About ten years ago Mr. Charles Oakes, president of Pennsylvania Power & Light, ran into the training material which has since developed into the "How We Live in America" program. He satisfied himself that it was what he had been looking for and that it had the intellectual traction to secure and hold the interest of the average man who normally was completely disinterested in economics. This enthusiasm was transmitted to his public relations staff and the basic concepts were woven into the company's messages to the public and to its employees.

In 1954, the full high school program was ready for distribution to Mr. Oakes. After careful study of the classroom effectiveness of the material, Pennsylvania Power & Light made the following proposal to the American Economic Foundation:

"You put a field man in our service area. We will team up with the public relations man who is our liaison with the schools. We are not going to stop until the "How We Live in America" program has been introduced to every high school in our area.[13]

Probably no one in the company could say how much this utility-arranged public education cost the customers of Pennsylvania Power & Light. Direct contributions from the utility to the American Economic Foundation show up on the public record sometimes, and as late as 1963 these contributions were considered by the company as part of the cost of serving the customers. The current president of the company, Jack K. Busby, when asked about contributions made in 1963 to a number of organizations, wrote:

In 1963, we contributed to . . . American Economic Foundation ($750), Foundation for Economic Education ($200), National Tax Equality Association ($225), and Southern States Industrial Council ($100). In addition, we purchased the following: "The Bookmailer" ($1), *Spotlight* ($450), and *Freeman* magazine ($40). *Freeman* is published by the Foundation for Economic Education. *Spotlight* is published by the Committee for Constitutional Government. . . .

The above were charged to operating expenses. Upon review, we believe that some of these would more properly have been considered non-operating expense. . . .[14]

A.E.F. Chairman Clark has complained that many businesses do not pay much attention to his material. Investor-owned utilities do, though; the I.O.U.s are different. "I am happy to be able to say that the electric utility group—represented by the people in this room—have shown a high degree of interest in this program," Clark told power-company officials. "More than 50 privately owned power companies have —in one way or another—recognized its importance and done something about it."

There are several ways, in addition to those employed by Pennsylvania Power & Light, by which power companies assist the American Economic Foundation.

In Montana the A.E.F. material was presented to 47 elementary teachers during the fall of 1964 under the sponsorship of the Montana Chamber of Commerce and the Western Montana College of Education at Dillon. The program was a great success, according to the Chamber's newspaper. "The Ten Pillars of Economic Wisdom prepared by the American Economic Foundation should most certainly be as important in our elementary schools as the A, B, C's," one teacher wrote to the Chamber of Commerce. "I see no reason why they should not be in the curriculum after a teacher has had your explanation, sir!" [15]

The Montana Power Company contributes directly to the A.E.F., although it has not itemized the gifts in its annual reports to the Federal Power Commission since 1955—one has to see the reports of the foundation to verify some power-company donations. Perhaps more important to the use of A.E.F. literature in teacher training in Montana are the company's contributions to the Montana Chamber of Commerce, which co-sponsored the teacher institute. Montana Power has strong personal and financial ties with the state Chamber of Commerce. Three past presidents of the chamber sit on the company's board of directors. Each year the company gives thousands of dollars to the state Chamber of Commerce, hiding the contributions in unitemized "miscellaneous general expenses" until required by the Federal Power Commission to be specific.[16]

It is impossible to tell how much utilities give to organizations such as the American Economic Foundation, because reporting requirements of regulatory commissions are inadequate for that purpose and are often disregarded by utilities. The Federal Power Commission's request to Dayton Power & Light to itemize its 1963 donations revealed the utility's $1,500 donation to A.E.F. A similar request to Detroit Edison—whose president, Walker Cisler, was then president of Edison Electric Institute—produced no evidence of his company's contributions to A.E.F. Nevertheless, Detroit Edison had sent A.E.F. Chairman Clark a $500 check in April 1963 as the "first of three annual payments" for the Hall of Free Enterprise at the New York World's Fair and followed it up with a $200 check in September.[17]

Six power companies, in addition to Dayton Power & Light, reported to F.P.C. their contributions to A.E.F. in 1963. Actually, however, 20 power companies contributed to the American Economic Foundation during the first nine months of 1963, according to a report which the American Economic Foundation, as a tax-exempt organization, filed with the Internal Revenue Service.

Substantial utility aid can also be given to A.E.F. through purchase of literature. That was probably the method used by Columbus & Southern Ohio Electric, whose letter to A.E.F. appeared at the beginning of this chapter. In the letter, the utility said it had ordered more than 4,000 copies of a booklet that sells for 50¢ apiece, and was furnishing all junior-high-school social studies teachers with another booklet that sold for 75¢ each. A.E.F.'s literature list stated that those prices quoted apply "only on orders direct from schools and educators." So even if Columbus & Southern Ohio Electric considered itself to be a school or an educator, the bill for the literature amounted to several thousand dollars. The bill did not show in the company's 1964 report to the Federal Power Commission, however. The company itemized $129,414 in "operating expense" contributions, which the Ohio state regulatory commission usually permits to be added to the cost of electricity. No contribution to A.E.F. was listed.[18]

Although tax-exempt organizations such as A.E.F. are required to file annual reports with the Internal Revenue Service, the tax-collecting agency usually discloses only the total contributions reported by tax-exempt organizations. Only Congressional tax committees in closed session, or select committees of the Senate or House, authorized by appropriate resolution, can look at the Internal Revenue Service lists of individual contributors.[19]

Occasionally, however, the public sees the lists of contributors. If such a list is marked as an attachment to the public pages of the return, the I.R.S. may include it in the portion made available for inspection. Thus, for example, the 1963 list of contributors to A.E.F. did become part of the public file, revealing that 24 electric utilities contributed to it during the 1963 fiscal year.

In the hands of a skilled teacher, some of the material distributed by the American Economic Foundation can, in the authors' opinion, be useful in providing students with simple insights into some aspects of American business. Children who believe everything A.E.F. says will eventually be either saddened or angered to learn that the income tax strengthens the United States, and that regulation is often sought by businessmen, whether their product is petroleum or peanut butter, oleomargarine or overshoes, in order to decrease competition. And the kiddies will never, never learn from the American Economic Foundation how utilities differ from lemonade stands and shoe stores, and about all the things Daddy buys for the nice big power company when he pays the electricity bill.

Chapter 14.

GET THE GOVERNMENT OUT OF GOVERNMENT
—The Foundation for Economic Education

For 20 years one of the principal cogs in the I.O.U.s' propaganda transmission system has been the Foundation for Economic Education (FEE) at Irvington-on-Hudson, New York. FEE's early days were described in a September 1946 letter from its founder, Leonard E. Read. He wrote to President W. C. Mullendore of Southern California Edison, a major California power company:

Dear Bill:

I have just returned today after being away for a week—four days of it on Lake Michigan, that being my vacation for this year unless Ag and I can sneak out to California for a week or two in November or December. The pace here has been terrific.

Anyway, I note your two letters. This is in reply to only one of your paragraphs, namely, the one about your concern over our not having more money in the till.

That is a perfectly proper concern but one that, under the circumstances, can hardly be helped. I have felt that I had to bring all aspects of the foundation along together, that I had to conceive a reasonably full plan of procedure, including the acquiring of headquarters, the acquisition of staff, purchase of equipment, the getting under way of a program, the obtaining of trustees, and the financing.

What has been done since March 21, is, even if I do say it, almost phenomenal. Financewise, I had one very bad break, namely, that Carl Byoir, who had promised at least $250,000, was taken out of circulation by what he thought was a heart attack. Having as many bulls by the tail as I have, I have not been able to get out and fill the gap myself.

Anyway, Carl is back on the job, fit as a fiddle, intending to devote most of his time, voluntarily, to the resources of this foundation. While in Chicago yesterday and the day before, and there primarily to make a speech, I did have a chance to talk to one gent, namely Mr. Avery. Believe it or not, I asked him for nothing, but he volunteered $10,000 for Ward's and $10,000 from Gypsum, and will assist with quite a number of other business concerns on whose boards he sits.

Give me 90 more days and I will have my breath and the whole thing in fairly good balance. I had to be a gambler and a risk taker to attempt this damned thing in the first place.

The above is recited only to make your trip across country on the plane without worry.

> Faithfully,
> Leonard E. Read [1]

FEE got off to a fast start. It would have been hard not to, with the backing and purpose it had.

Carl Byoir, who according to Read's letter to the utility president was donating most of his time to FEE, headed one of the nation's leading public-relations firms.

"Mr. Avery," mentioned in Read's letter to Mullendore as a substantial contributor, was Sewell Avery, board chairman of both Montgomery Ward and U.S. Gypsum. He was also on the boards of other major corporations, including Commonwealth Edison (Chicago).

FEE Trustee Mullendore, an associate of Read's from the

days when Read managed and Mullendore sat on the board of the Los Angeles Chamber of Commerce, was well known among electric-utility leaders. He was also a writer and speaker on economic matters.

Read had extensive background in chamber of commerce work and had spent two years as executive vice president of the National Industrial Conference Board.

There were two other factors in FEE's fast start. It was tax-exempt, and it mass-produced pamphlets lauding the doctrine of a free-market economy. Many FEE patrons did not practice that philosophy, but they liked to preach it.

By the end of 1949, 46 corporations and tax-exempt foundations had contributed more than a million dollars to FEE. It had taken in $172,000 by sale of literature. Hundreds of newspapers and magazines had used FEE articles.

Reader's Digest quickly discovered FEE and reprinted its material. The *Digest* was so eager for FEE articles that it asked for advance copies.

"Dear Leonard," Paul Palmer of the *Digest* wrote Read on December 31, 1948, "I am wondering if, in the future, we couldn't get an advance look at your material so that, in case we wished to reprint, we could do so before anyone else? Perhaps you could let me see your pamphlets and other releases in proof?"

The next month A. L. Cole of the *Digest* elaborated on the special interest of the magazine's publisher, DeWitt Wallace:

He [Wallace] said again, as he has several times recently that he is devoting a big part of all his time and effort to this one problem believing that *Reader's Digest* can do an effective and necessary job in educating the mass public, for their own good and for the good of the country, to an understanding of sound economics.[2]

The economic and political philosophy of the Foundation for Economic Education can be gauged from recent articles in

The Freeman, the monthly magazine that FEE bought in 1954. With a circulation of 60,000, it is a major outlet for FEE material, and is distributed free, with emphasis on circulation among college students.[3] Recent *Freeman* articles call for repeal of the income tax, U.S. withdrawal from the United Nations, abolition of public post offices, public education, public roads and public power, and getting the government out of all business, even its own.

The proper role of government is to keep the peace, at home and abroad, according to FEE. Everything else can be decided in the marketplace. "The free market," wrote Read, "is the perfect computer." [4]

From the premise that the free-market, no-government economy solves everything except war and crime flows FEE's solutions to specific problems.

"If government were out of education as its boss—100%— and if we had only free market education," Read wrote in the September 1964 issue, "no child in America would be denied an education any more than any child is presently denied religious instruction or shoes and stockings . . . Literally millions of Americans would like nothing better than voluntarily to finance the education of children of those who might be in unfortunate circumstances." [5]

The income tax horrifies *The Freeman*'s regular contributors. One of them, Admiral Ben Moreell, ranked the income tax and the draft as the "two greatest intrusions on individual freedom in the history of the republic." FEE President Read called for repeal of that "unprincipled" income tax. *Freeman* reviewer John Chamberlain found the income tax "monstrous." [6]

Another thing that *Freeman* writers find objectionable is the federal-state road system. "Government should not be in the creative field of highway construction and ownership," wrote

John C. Sparks. "... The proper role of government should be to defend our nation from outside attack, as a soldier, and defend us from lawlessness from within, as a policeman." [7]

FEE is consistent. Its writers are not beguiled by the notion that only federal government is bad, except for its soldiers. Local government is no good either, except for its cops. Wrote Sparks:

Zoning is an interference with the right of ownership ... Zoning at best is a "respectable" mid-twentieth century form of theft of an owner's right to own. Whenever the right to own is removed, restricted, or eroded in any manner, society declines toward a lower level of economic goods that is matched by a lower level of spiritual and moral values.[8]

FEE President Read cautioned businessmen against saying that they are entitled only to a fair profit. A mere fair profit "connotes egalitarianism." [9] Let the buyer beware!

Despite their belief in the profit system, *The Freeman* authors strongly oppose President Johnson's program to help the poor increase their income. The magazine's managing editor, Paul L. Poirot, termed the war on poverty "a confiscation of the fruits of production." [10]

Those who make the most profit and can submit the highest bids should control what people hear, according to FEE's *Freeman*. Radio and television frequencies should be "disposed of by selling or leasing them to the highest bidder, [thus] there would be no need to use such criteria as proposed or past programming." [11] Another article carried the theme further:

Let broadcasters own the airwaves themselves or lease them from other owners. Let the market pricing system allocate this scarce, valuable, economic resource to the highest bidder with full powers to use his property as he judges best in the conduct of his own business.[12]

And what segment of American society really has it rough, according to *The Freeman?* Why, it's those poor utilities, struggling to "earn profits to survive at all."

Oncoming generations of future leaders have been carefully taught by their economics and other political science instructors to be fundamentally suspicious of A.T.&.T. and other privately-owned utility monopolies.[13]

Admiral Ben Moreell's apologia for the large power companies, *Our Nation's Water Resources—Policies and Politics,* received a rave review by John Chamberlain in *The Freeman:*

The cliches fall like trees in a hurricane in Admiral Moreell's pages. The biggest cliche to bite the dust is the one about the unconscionable private power lobby which is supposed to be mulcting the citizen of hard-earned cash.[14]

FEE's President Read regularly inveighs against the Tennessee Valley Authority in *The Freeman.* He contends that T.V.A. was "founded on violence." His reasoning goes this way:

Suppose that some people decide they want their power and light at a lower rate than the market rate. To accomplish their purpose they forcibly—with guns, if necessary—collect the fruits of your peaceable labor in the form of capital to construct the power plant. Then, they annually use force to take your income to defray the deficits of their operation. . . . What distinguishes [T.V.A.] from that [violent acquisition of capital]? Not a thing, except that in the case of T.V.A. the immoral, aggressive, violent action has been legalized.

Read overlooks the history of T.V.A., a minor point alongside his major premise, which is, baldly, that our republican form of government is immoral. If the creation of the Tennessee Valley Authority by elected representatives—accomplished without guns and with generous compensation for purchased property—is immoral, then our whole concept of government is. He himself says as much.

Who, for instance, ever thinks of T.V.A. as founded on violence? Or social security, federal urban renewal, public housing, foreign aid, farm and all other subsidies, the Post Office, rent control, other wage and price controls, all space projects other than for strictly defensive purposes, compulsory unionism, production controls, tariffs and all other governmental protections against competition? Who ponders the fact that every one of these aspects of state socialism is an exemplification of violence and that such practices are multiplying rapidly? [15]

The increase in the cost of U.S. postage was contrasted with the decreasing cost of private power by *The Freeman*'s managing editor in the February 1965 issue. He concluded that private utilities take better care of consumers than government does.[16] His comparison of the U.S. Post Office to a power company is idle. The utilities operate on a cost-plus basis, by virtue of law; the Post Office also by law carries much of the mail at a deficit. Were each to operate under the other's law, the consumer costs would, of course, be altered substantially. How much more logical it is to compare the rates and costs of an investor-owned utility with one municipally owned. How much better, though, for the purposes of propaganda, to compare an apple to an orange.

A FEE pamphlet, "The T.V.A. Idea," by Dean Russell, was expanded into a book by the same title which is currently distributed by FEE. In the book Russell dismissed as "demagoguery" the claims of power companies' excesses that led to the Public Utility Holding Company Act of 1935 and creation of the Tennessee Valley Authority. He found the electric industry "in great danger of complete nationalization."

Utilities are competitive, he said, because [his emphasis] *"the electric companies must compete with everyone else for the consumer's dollar.*" (Shall we abstain from electricity this year, dear, and go to Bermuda instead?)

Russell also undertook the formidable task of equating electric utilities with bakeries and blacksmith shops. Admitting that the power industry is clothed with the public interest, he added, "so is the baking industry and the shoe industry. In fact, it would be difficult to find any industry that is not 'clothed with the public interest.' " Russell recalled that the old village blacksmith usually had a monopoly in his service area. If his price got too high, a rival shop opened or farmers shod their own horses. Therefore, somehow:

> If any private company produces a desired product or service at a price the consumer is willing to pay, there is no reason why it shouldn't prosper and make a profit. Most private electric companies meet this test. But if any company can't meet this test, it should fail. If the present limited competition among private power companies were made complete by throwing the field open to all comers, private enterprise itself would supply the yardstick for measuring efficiency of operation and fairness of rates in any locality and for any consumer.[17]

Sounds easy, does it not? If you think the light bill is too high, simply get the state legislature and utility commission to make the power company give up its monopoly. Then go borrow a few hundred million dollars and build some high dams and nuclear reactors. And negotiate some power exchanges with other power companies that already have agreements with the company you want to rap on the knuckles with your little yardstick. Be sure, though, that you build enough of your own power plants to take care of any emergency, in case there is another Big Blackout. Buy lots of wire, and offer to install it free, preferably underground, to attract all those customers who are already served by the other company.

T.V.A. is used as a case study in why government should

not be in business in a high-school textbook distributed by FEE, *Understanding Our Free Economy*. Written by FEE's first secretary, Fred R. Fairchild, and Thomas J. Shelly, the text is now in its fourth edition. It includes among "encroachments on free enterprise" the public ownership of land, control over interest rates, government purchase of foreign goods, government guarantee of bank loans, supervision of privately owned banks, and minimum-wage laws.[18] During the 1954–55 school year FEE offered the book, along with Henry Hazlitt's *Economics in One Lesson*, and a collection of FEE essays to high-school principals and teachers. Shelly reported the results of the offer in *The Freeman:*

Altogether, 5,079 principals and teachers requested 6,232 copies of the books offered. After several months, the recipients were asked their opinions of the books and what use they were making of them. More than a third of them have replied to date. Of the first 1,300 replies only 14 were negative; those teachers did not like the books. All the others responded enthusiastically.

In some cases, where the principals or teachers were able to do so, the books are being used as classroom texts; this practice is not extensive because the selection of textbooks often is the prerogative of state, county or district high school boards. But, in practically every case the teachers are recommending the books for collateral reading.

It should be remembered that economics as a separate discipline is not generally included in high school curricula; it is usually merged with other subjects in a course called "social studies." Hence books on economics must come into study by the side door, so to speak.[19]

The teacher who orders literature from FEE is likely to receive material which has the blessings of the John Birch Society. More than half of the 80 books on FEE's literature list, 47 to be exact, are also on the John Birch Society's "approved" list.[20]

FEE's 80 recommended books include seven by Dr. Ludwig von Mises, professor of economics at New York University. Five of Mises' books are also on the John Birch Society approved list; Mises serves on the editorial advisory committee of *American Opinion,* the John Birch Society's monthly magazine. Four of the five books by Columnist Henry Hazlitt that are promoted by FEE are on the J.B.S. approved list. Also on both FEE and J.B.S. lists are works of Clarence Manion, who is head of Manion Forum and a member of the John Birch Society's national council; Admiral Ben Moreell, head of Americans for Constitutional Action; FEE President Leonard Read; *Freeman* Managing Editor Paul Poirot and regular *Freeman* contributors such as Dean Russell, author of *The T.V.A. Idea,* Book Reviewer John Chamberlain and Dr. Hans Sennholz, who is professor of economics at Grove City College (Pennsylvania) and a contributing editor to the John Birch Society's *American Opinion.* Mises and Sennholz and what FEE terms "others of a like caliber" lecture at FEE's summer seminars. There young students and teachers can be warned about organizations such as the Peace Corps, whose programs Sennholz found no different from "similar development projects initiated by the Communist countries." [21]

Since 1962 the John Birch Society has not published the names of its committee of endorsers. Insofar as the society's top officials are known, though, the leadership of the Foundation for Economic Education and of the John Birch Society during recent years has been as interlaced as the two organizations' literature. One FEE trustee is Robert W. Stoddard of Wyman-Gordon, a Massachusetts manufacturing firm, who is a member of the executive committee of the John Birch Society. Another is J. Howard Pew, who has been one of the stockholders of Robert Welch, Inc., the publishing arm of the John Birch Society. A third FEE trustee is Roger Milliken, president of Deering, Milliken and Company, who was listed by the John Birch Society in 1962 as a member of its committee of endorsers.[22]

Another is William Coberly, Jr., president of California Cotton Oil Corporation. Coberly, who also appeared on the John Birch Society's last published committee of endorsers, is a director of Southern California Edison. Coberly's situation is rare; utility officials usually do not involve themselves directly with the John Birch Society. That would be bad form; why risk unfavorable publicity from formal association with an organization receiving close attention from the press? Instead, the utilities use their usual indirect approach. They regularly donate money (sometimes, of course, the customers' money) to organizations whose philosophy and literature generally coincide with that of the Birchers.

Power companies have liberally assisted the Foundation for Economic Education ever since it was established in 1946. Consolidated Edison (New York) gave FEE $40,000 during a four-year period ending in February 1950. During the same early years Detroit Edison gave FEE $12,500; Cleveland Electric Illuminating and Toledo Edison, $3,000 each; Utah Power & Light, $2,000; Virginia Electric & Power, $1,000; smaller amounts came from Ohio Edison, Indianapolis Power & Light, San Diego Gas & Electric, and Pennsylvania Power & Light.[23] Those contributions were reported by FEE or by the companies to the House Select Committee on Lobbying, which held hearings in 1950. However, the investigation by that committee was sharply limited. Fewer than a fourth of the major power companies were asked to furnish information on donations, and some of them declined to answer.

The record of utility contributions to FEE at which the House committee peeked in 1950 has been closed almost lid-tight in the absence of investigations or regulations that put such information in the public record. On college campuses some young professors happily report their opportunity to spend the summer with a power company, with the expense tab paid by that nice foundation on the Hudson. Sometimes a teacher wonders out loud why a utility official who serves on a school advisory board is trying to get FEE literature into the classroom. Occasionally direct contributions to FEE show up on utilities' annual reports to the Federal Power Commission, perhaps after the Commission has specifically requested the company to itemize some vague "miscellaneous" entry.

The breadth of direct utility support for FEE was indicated recently when the foundation's report on contributions for the fiscal year ending in March 1964 was placed in the public files of the Internal Revenue Service.

FEE reported cash contributions from 31 power companies during the year. Southern California Edison had donated $2,800. Southern Cal Ed's former president W. C. Mullendore, who had helped launch FEE, added his personal contribution. So did W. B. Coberly, Jr., the utility's director who is a FEE trustee and who also was on the last-published list of the John Birch Society committee of endorsers. Rochester Gas & Electric and Union Electric each gave $2,000. Contributions of $1,000 each came from San Diego Gas & Electric, New York State Electric & Gas, Columbus & Southern Ohio and the Southern Company, which is the Atlanta holding company controlling Alabama Power, Georgia Power, Gulf Power, and Mississippi Power.

Contributions flowed to FEE from utilities in all parts of the country:

From the East—Long Island Lighting and Central Hudson Gas & Electric, Philadelphia Electric, Pennsylvania Power & Light, West Penn Power, Connecticut's United Illuminating and Connecticut Light & Power, New Jersey's Public Service Electric & Gas.

From the West—Arizona Public Service, Montana Power,

Oklahoma Gas & Electric, Pacific Gas & Electric, Portland General Electric, Washington Water Power.

From the Midwest—Detroit Edison, Ohio Edison, Public Service of Indiana, Indianapolis Power & Light, Kansas Gas & Electric, Iowa Public Service and Interstate Power.

And from the South—Virginia Electric & Power, New Orleans Public Service, Gulf States Utilities.

Chapter 15.

HOW THE OLD GRADS STRUNG ANOTHER TRANSMISSION LINE
—The Intercollegiate Society of Individualists

When M. Stanton Evans, the editor of the *Indianapolis News,* enrolled at Yale during the early 1950s he was, by his own account, "badly in need of help, counsel and information." He wandered into Liggett's drugstore on the corner of York and Elm and chanced upon a copy of *The Freeman.* Then in class a fellow student passed him a card with the names of two organizations written on it.

"These organizations think along lines like yours," Evans was told. "You might want to get on their mailing list." Thus was Evans introduced to the Foundation for Economic Education and its foster child, the Intercollegiate Society of Individualists (I.S.I.).

Through I.S.I., FEE, and *The Freeman,* which was soon to be purchased by FEE, students were able to obtain literature, set up campus libraries, and organize conservative clubs. This all exhilarated young Evans. "The rise of the conservative clubs," he wrote, "has rejuvenated political thinking on college campuses, enlivened once flaccid discussions of issues and produced the first wave of independent thinking in the school since the 1930s."

Independent thinking in the schools? Let's see if it was.

A number of organizations that attract donations from power companies have founder-presidents who learned the trade with a similar established group, then set up their own. The Intercollegiate Society of Individualists is no exception.

In 1953, Frank Chodorov was grinding out copy for *Human Events* and polishing up a new book, *Income Tax: Root of All Evil*. He wrote a *Human Events* column about the need for another organization to attract collegians. Somebody liked the idea and sent in $1,000 for Chodorov's project.[1]

Frank C. Hanighen, who had left *Reader's Digest* and founded *Human Events* in 1944, signed the articles of incorporation for Chodorov's new society. The Foundation for Economic Education offered to keep the files and do mailings for I.S.I. The Intercollegiate Society of Individualists—and Chodorov—were in business.

The thing Chodorov needed next was some collegians. After all, he was 66.

So he picked up some "collegiate" trustees.

One was Adm. Ben Moreell, Washington University (St. Louis), '13.

Another was retired Brigadier General Bonner Fellers. Fellers must have been a collegian. At least he was listed as a member of the national advisory board of Young Americans for Freedom (as well as being on the John Birch Society committee of endorsers.)

Another I.S.I. trustee was Dr. Hans Sennholz. He, at least, taught at a college, served as a lecturer (for American Opinion Speaker's Bureau), and was published in, among other publications, *American Opinion, The Freeman, Human*

Events, and *Christian Economics.* He, too, served on the national advisory board of Young Americans for Freedom.[2]

A new organization ought to have a board of advisers, in addition to trustees. So the Intercollegiate Society of Individualists constructed a board of advisers. There was a slight bobble, however, perhaps natural, in using the lists and office of other organizations. Lists must have gotten mixed up.

At any rate, the seven advisers on the 1962 I.S.I. letterheads were no more collegiate than Admiral Moreell.

Six of the seven Intercollegiate Society of Individualists advisers, however, were affiliated with the John Birch Society.

One of the seven, Clarence Manion, was a J.B.S. national council member.

Four were on the J.B.S. committee of endorsers. They were J. Bracken Lee, the former governor of Utah; Dr. E. Merrill Root, retired professor of English at Earlham College (Indiana), Roger Milliken, a South Carolina textile executive, and Wint Smith, a former Kansas Congressman.

The sixth, Adolphe Menjou, the actor, had been a member of the editorial advisory committee of *American Opinion,* the J.B.S. magazine.

The seventh I.S.I. adviser was 76-year-old Samuel B. Pettingill, a former Indiana Congressman. The grandparents of today's collegians may recall how, as a member of the House Interstate and Foreign Commerce Committee during the 1930s, Pettingill fought on the side of the power companies against the Public Utility Holding Company Act of 1935.[3]

Donations to I.S.I. are tax-deductible. Thus it must file informational returns with the Internal Revenue Service. The reports showed that during fiscal 1962, the Intercollegiate Society of Individualists received nationwide support from one industry—the electric power and light companies.

Twenty-two investor-owned utilities each contributed to I.S.I. during the year. In addition, I.S.I. reported contributions from officials of eight more I.O.U.s in 1962 or in previous years.

The utilities gave the Intercollegiate Society of Individualists more than money. They gave their names, their prestige. They gave them to the organization and to its advisers and trustees. Now the Intercollegiate Society of Individualists could raise money from otherwise hesitant sources.

The I.S.I., laden with uncollegiate Birchers, could point to the support it was receiving from companies that are household names across the country:

Alabama Power, Arizona Public Service, Arkansas Power & Light, Carolina Power & Light, Connecticut Light & Power, Dallas Power & Light, Delaware Power & Light, Indianapolis Power & Light, Kansas Gas & Electric, Minnesota Power & Light, Mississippi Power, Mississippi Power & Light, Montana Power, New Orleans Public Service, Northern States Power (Minnesota), Oklahoma Gas & Electric, the Southern Company (Georgia), Texas Electric Service, Texas Power & Light, Union Electric (Missouri), Utah Power & Light, Washington Water Power.

Chapter 16.

A MULTI-MEGAWATT GENERATOR

—The National Education Program at Harding College

Most corporations and individuals are proud to be identified with colleges. Many electric-power companies, along with other corporations, have given generously to colleges within their service area.

They are rightfully proud of these donations. When investor-owned utilities report to regulatory commissions about their charitable contributions, gifts to colleges frequently lead the list.

But you seldom hear about the I.O.U.s' ties with their favorite institution of learning, Harding College, located near the banks of the Red River at Searcy, Arkansas.

Harding does not specialize in engineering. Electricity is *not* the product that power companies learn how to produce and distribute there.

What is the basic program at Harding? There are two authoritative and, at first glance, seemingly conflicting accounts.

Dr. George S. Benson, who in 1965 stepped down after 30 years as president of the college, but who is still active in its affairs, said his aim is "to move public opinion at the grass roots in the direction of godliness and patriotism." [1]

A utility service corporation—Middle South Services—said Harding is the place to go for company "economic education" programs.[2]

Benson and Middle South Services are not at odds. Dr. Benson equates godliness and patriotism with the particular brand of "economic education" that many utilities seek. The religious and patriotic overtones of the material help in its dissemination. It is easy to sell, and difficult to challenge, economic doctrines that are expertly packaged with the cross and the flag. The job has been done so well that, as *Newsweek* put it, "what M.I.T. [Massachusetts Institute of Technology] is to engineering and Harvard is to law, Harding College is to the far right." [3]

Dr. Benson, who became president of Harding in 1936 after 11 years as a missionary in China, built up the college from a small, indebted school with 200 students to a modern campus with 1,200 students and a good endowment. However, it is the college-related National Education Program, which

Dr. Benson still directs, that put Harding onto the map and into the chips.

The National Education Program at Harding produces films that have been viewed by tens of millions of persons. Dr. Benson sends his weekly column, "Looking Ahead," to 3,000 publications. Another column, "Listen, Americans," goes to about 1,000 industrial employee publications. A monthly *National Program Letter* is also distributed. The National Education Program prepares course outlines for high-school teachers and speeches for busy executives, and distributes tapes and reprints of speeches made on campus.[4]

The National Education Program pours out criticism of federal aid to education, the antipoverty programs, customer-controlled electric-power systems, the United Nations. It wants to fight Communism more, while drastically diminishing the means to fight by doing away with the graduated income tax. Dr. Benson added a new twist to the tax argument during World War II. He urged Congress to tax poor people more in order to make them feel patriotic.[5]

(Despite Dr. Benson's prized "13 personal Awards from Freedoms Foundation at Valley Forge," the Harding College complex has been less than exemplary in tax matters. It failed, seven years in a row, to file with Internal Revenue Service the annual information returns required of tax-exempt organizations. For some time, the college operated a dairy and laundry, in competition with local businesses, without paying property taxes on these commercial facilities. White County, Arkansas, had to take the college to court to get these business enterprises of the college on the property tax rolls.[6])

Among the biggest activities on the Harding campus are the Freedom Forums. The list of organizations which, according to Forum literature, "have sent conferees" to Freedom Forums is unquestionably impressive. There are numerous corporations and schools on the list, a few newspaper and radio stations, some state boards of education and state universities, the

United States Air Force, the United States Army, and the United States Senate. However, some Forum participants apparently "came from" rather than having been "sent by" organizations listed as Freedom Forum participants. There is a difference.

The National Education Program's "Freedom Forum Facts" brochure includes a letter to the National Education Program vice president, retired General William P. Campbell, from another former general, Edwin A. Walker, whose resignation from the Army was preceded by an admonition from higher authority for his use of extremist material in troop indoctrination. General Walker, writing in 1959—the year in which he joined the John Birch Society—told how impressed he was by the Freedom Forum that he attended.

The lecturers at Freedom Forums have included some of the top leaders of the John Birch Society and similar extremist organizations.

Among them are three men named by the John Birch Society as members of its 27-member national council—Clarence Manion, head of Manion Forum; Tom Anderson, former publisher of *Farm and Ranch;* and F. Gano Chance, head of A. B. Chance Company.

Three of the Freedom Forum lecturers have served on America's Future's Textbook Evaluation Committee, on which several right-wing organizations rely for book-banning advice. They are Dr. E. Merrill Root, associate editor of Robert Welch, Inc.'s *American Opinion;* Dr. Anthony Bouscaren; and J. B. Matthews. The latter, who until recently was an associate editor of *American Opinion,* was executive director of the Senate Permanent Investigation Subcommittee when it was headed by Senator Joseph McCarthy (R-Wis.). Matthews resigned from his Senate position after charging that the Protestant clergy were providing substantial support for the Communists.

The list of speakers also includes Dr. Fred C. Schwarz,

founder and president of the Christian Anti-Communist Crusade, and Dr. Howard Kershner, president of the Christian Freedom Foundation. Several of the above speakers have lectured at two or more of the annual forums.[7]

The leaders of the National Education Program and the John Birch Society have spoken well of each other's programs. In a front-page article in his monthly *National Program Letter,* Dr. Benson said that "any American who loves freedom and is willing to work, work, work to protect it can find intelligent direction and companionship in a John Birch Society group." [8]

President Robert Welch of the John Birch Society returned the compliment the following month. Welch wrote:

> Down in Searcy, Arkansas, Dr. George Benson and his associates at Harding College have long been in the forefront of those most ably promoting better understanding and support of the Americanist philosophy and sociological system. One of their most important activities is the National Education Program.[9]

Welch stated that the John Birch Society conceived and arranged for many of the showings of one of the Harding College-produced films, "Communism On The Map": *

> Our people have also been responsible for the production, and then during the past several months for virtually thousands of showings, of a film strip called "Communism On The Map." . . . Full credit for providing the organization, financing, prestige and practical circumstances for such work must go entirely to the National Education Program of Searcy, Arkansas, headed by that great American, Dr. George Benson. But this film strip was conceived, prepared and produced by an ardent member of the John Birch Society, partly from our materials.[10]

---

* A similar version of the film is entitled "Communist Encirclement."

The film, sections of which were taken verbatim from the John Birch Society *Blue Book,* "presents an impression of the United States lying helplessly in the closing jaws of a world Communist conspiracy," according to Cabell Phillips of *The New York Times.*[11]

By 1963, the film had been seen by an estimated 15 million persons. Its showing had often been sponsored by major corporations, including Missouri Power, Iowa-Illinois Gas & Electric, Kansas Gas & Electric, Mississippi Power, Monongahela Power, Pacific Gas & Electric, San Diego Gas & Electric, Southwestern Public Service, Tampa Electric, Texas Power & Light, and West Penn Power.[12]

Determination of direct utility contributions to Harding College or the National Education Program is impossible because of the reluctance of most utilities to report them to regulatory commissions, and inadequate regulations or practices by government agencies to which utilities and tax-exempt organizations report. Three subsidiaries of Middle South Utilities—New Orleans Public Service, Louisiana Power & Light, and Arkansas Power & Light—reported contributions ranging from $1,000 to $2,500 to the National Education Program in 1963.

Through the years, contributions have been reported to the Federal Power Commission by Montana Power and by Washington Water Power, whose board chairman was invited to lecture at Harding. However, in the cases of Southwestern Public Service and Central Illinois Public Service, utility contributions to the National Education Program did not come to light until the Federal Power Commission specifically requested an itemization of a particular account. Even then, Southwestern Public Service did not divulge the size of its donation.[13]

Direct contributions from utilities to Harding's National Education Program may well be insignificant in comparison with the travel expenses of utility public-relations men to Harding, the utilities' purchase of literature, and the time and money spent by utility personnel in developing material in conjunction with the National Education Program people. This expense has been borne by electric consumers for at least 18 years. "Fifteen major electric companies sent people" to the first Freedom Forum in 1949, at which much of the economic education material was developed. That is on the authority of Dr. Benson himself, who went on to laud the power industry for its uncommon support of his endeavors.[14]

From A (Alabama Power) through W (West Penn Power, Wisconsin Electric Power, Wisconsin Power & Light, and Wisconsin Public Service) the power companies have flocked to Harding forums. Forty-nine * of the major investor-owned

* Investor-owned utilities listed by the National Education Program as participants are:

Alabama Power
Arizona Public Service
Arkansas Power & Light
Carolina Power & Light
Central Arizona Light & Power
Central Illinois Light
Central Power & Light (Tex.)
Cleveland Electric Illuminating
Consolidated Edison (N.Y.)
Consumers Power (Mich.)
Dallas Power & Light
Detroit Edison
Empire District Electric (Mo., Okla., Kans., Ark.)
Gulf Power (Fla.)
Houston Lighting & Power
Idaho Power
Indianapolis Power & Light
Interstate Power (Ill., Iowa, Minn., S.D.)
Iowa Electric Light & Power
Iowa Power & Light
Kansas Power & Light
Kentucky Utilities
Louisiana Power & Light
Mississippi Power
Mississippi Power & Light
Missouri Public Service

Montana Power
New Orleans Public Service
Northern States Power
Northwestern Public Service (S.D.)
Oklahoma Gas & Electric
Pacific Gas & Electric
Pacific Power & Light
Pennsylvania Electric
Pennsylvania Power & Light
Public Service Company of Oklahoma
Public Service Company of Colorado
Rochester Gas & Electric
Southern California Edison
Southwestern Public Service (Tex., N.M., Okla., Kans.)
Texas Electric Service
Union Electric (Mo., Ill., Iowa)
Utah Power & Light
Washington Water Power
West Penn Power
West Texas Utilities
Wisconsin Electric Power
Wisconsin Power & Light
Wisconsin Public Service

utilities have participated, as have two of the power industries' other favored educational institutions, the American Economic Foundation and the Foundation for Economic Education. Middle West Services, publisher of the high-school economics text co-authored by its vice president and Edison Electric Institute's Managing Director Edwin Vennard, has been represented at the forums. And so have N. W. Ayer & Son, the agency that handles the I.O.U.s' national advertising, Bozell & Jacobs, which handles the industry's public relations, and Central Surveys and Opinion Research Corporation, which survey public opinion for the utilities.[15]

With that clientele, the Harding campus could stage a convention of Edison Electric Institute.

Chapter 17.

HOW TO FIND REDS UNDER EVERY BED
—The Southern States Industrial Council

> Another U.N. special agency about which the American people know all too little is UNICEF—The United Nations International Children's Fund. Created in 1946 as an adjunct of UNRRA, it has always been and is now completely Communist dominated. Ostensibly working for the relief of needy children in the under-developed lands, UNICEF is in fact a powerful propaganda agency for the worldwide Communist conspiracy.
>
> —From the Southern States Industrial Council's statement of policy, adopted at The Homestead, Hot Springs, Virginia, May 20–22, 1963.[1]

Every Halloween thousands of American children collect money for UNICEF, through which millions of children in other lands receive medical care and food. As the youngsters make their rounds, they are usually well-received. Occasionally the young collectors are rebuffed. They turn away, puzzled, wondering what the man who shut the door meant about "the Communists" when he refused to give to UNICEF.

Most people give gladly to UNICEF. They recall watching UNICEF's great friend, comedian Danny Kaye, on television, as he brought laughter to the eyes of children who could see because of medical care provided by the international agency, which in 1965 received the Nobel Peace Award.

UNICEF is probably the most "American" agency of the United Nations. Herbert Hoover conceived the idea of UNICEF. He urged its establishment in a report after World War II to President Harry Truman, who had asked Hoover to survey world food supplies and needs. UNICEF was established by the United Nations General Assembly in 1947, and its first director was an American proposed by Hoover, Maurice Pate, who headed the agency until his death in 1965. He was succeeded by another American, Henry Labouisse, who had previously served as U.S. Ambassador to Greece and director of the U.S. International Cooperation Administration.

The UNICEF administrative staff consists of 714 persons from 65 countries. Of these, 108 are U.S. citizens; 10 are citizens of countries with Communist governments. In 1964, 120 nations contributed to UNICEF, which rendered assistance in 112 countries. About 3% of UNICEF's aid since 1950 has gone into Communist countries.

Former Presidents Eisenhower and Kennedy strongly supported UNICEF, as former Presidents Hoover and Truman had before them, and as President Johnson does.

One of the strongest Congressional supporters of UNICEF is former Congressman Walter H. Judd (R-Minn.), whose career in government was preceded by service in China as a medical missionary during the Thirties and included his delivery of the keynote speech at the 1960 Republican convention.

As a Congressman, Judd proposed the initial $15-million U.S. Government contribution to UNICEF, with a total of $50 million to be available as other countries matched the U.S. contribution. In a 1962 speech he summarized the international agency's work in these words:

> During the first 15 years of UNICEF's operation, over 148 million children and young adults were vaccinated against tuberculosis in programs aided by UNICEF; over 17 million mothers and children were cured of yaws, a disease of tropical sores; almost 9.7 million mothers and children, victims of trachoma and acute conjunctivitis, were saved from possible blindness; almost 700,000 children and mothers were treated for leprosy; in 1961, alone, about 30 million mothers and children were protected from malaria, and 5.5 million children benefited from the 160 dairies and milk drying plants and the other 19,000 maternal and child health centers which UNICEF has thus far helped to equip.
>
> Our contribution has amounted to $12 million a year these last few years. I don't know any money we have spent anywhere that has done more good and been better administered.[2]

In summary, UNICEF's very existence is due in large part to some of America's most respected citizens, and its accomplishments are marvelous.

Despite the facts, the Southern States Industrial Council (S.S.I.C.) declared, in its policy statement quoted at the beginning of this chapter, that UNICEF "has always been and is now completely Communist dominated" and "is in fact a powerful propaganda agency for the worldwide Communist conspiracy."

What is this Southern States Industrial Council that makes such incredible charges reflecting on America's leadership and many citizens and organizations? Whom else does the Council smear? For whom does the Council speak? Who sustains it?

S.S.I.C. is an industry association formed in 1933, with headquarters in Nashville, Tennessee; it claims a membership of about 2,000 companies that contribute "dues," actually contributions, ranging from $25 to $3,500 a year. S.S.I.C. stated in a 1964 brochure that it is organized as a "non-profit business association and membership dues are tax-deductible." [3]

S.S.I.C. strongly opposed wage and labor legislation enacted during the 1930s. The Council still lobbies, and is registered under the lobbying act. A column by Executive Vice President Thurman Sensing, "Sensing the News," is distributed to more than 1,000 papers and is widely used in the South. The Council also issues the *S.S.I.C. Bulletin.*

S.S.I.C. devotes much time and paper to promulgation of the collective views of its 103 principal officers, who gather annually at Southern resorts to abhor and deplore. S.S.I.C.'s view of UNICEF as a Communist apparatus is but one example of its proclivity to assign sinister motives to those with whom it disagrees.

The civil rights bill approved by the House of Representatives in 1964 was termed "clearly of Communist origin and inspiration" by S.S.I.C.'s board of directors at its 1964 annual meeting. "There is not one of its 11 titles which the Reds could not and do not support," said the directors. "It is an open invitation to violence and the final destruction of this Republic and the freedom of the individual for which it stands." [4]

"Conservatism is Patriotism," according to one of S.S.I.C.'s pamphlets. (More than one million S.S.I.C. pamphlets were distributed in 1964.) The pamphlet, written by Sensing, concludes with a Khrushchev "quote" that has been termed "spurious" by former Central Intelligence Agency Director John McCone. The phony quote, widely used by extremist groups, has the former Soviet premier saying,

we can assist [U.S.] elected leaders in giving Americans small doses of socialism until they suddenly awake to find they have communism.[5]

Sensing is generally supported by the Council's directors. "We wouldn't permit him to write it if we didn't believe it," said Council Vice President J. S. Gregory.[6]

One of the programs that S.S.I.C. considers to be a dose of socialism is federal aid to education, which was well established in the United States 33 years before the birth of Karl Marx.* More recent examples of socialism, according to the Southern States Industrial Council, include the Tennessee Valley Authority, Bonneville Power Administration, and Southwestern Power Administration. S.S.I.C. has long contended that the Rural Electrification Administration should be abolished.

The Southern States Industrial Council's list of officers and directors in 1964 included top officials of 11 utilities, 7 railroads, and a number of non-utility corporations. Although its officers are Southerners, the Southern States Industrial Council is in some respects as non-Southern as the Intercollegiate Society of Individualists is non-collegian. S.S.I.C. consistently receives donations from Northern corporations.

Top contributor during the period from 1958 to 1963 was E. I. du Pont de Nemours of Delaware, which gave $21,000. Some of the other contributors, and the amounts they have given the Council during the six-year period, were Chesapeake & Ohio Railroad (Ohio), $4,500; Firestone Tire & Rubber (Ohio), $4,000; General Motors (Michigan), $3,900; Household Finance (Illinois) $2,900; General Electric (New York), $2,500; Pullman-Standard Car Mfg. (Illinois), $2,500; Champion Spark Plug (Ohio), $2,000 and National Gypsum (New York), $2,000.[8] Some of the above-named corporations do have plants in the South.

---

* The Northwest Ordinance of 1785 reserved a section of every township in many parts of the country for "maintenance of public schools." Congress voted additional federal aid to education, during this period, in the Northwest Ordinance Act of 1787, the Ohio Enabling Act of 1802 and in legislation passed in 1803.[7]

Other companies that are as un-Southern as a snowbank in June also contribute regularly to the Council. That is where the investor-owned utilities north of the Mason-Dixon line come in.

One I.O.U.—un-Southern Idaho Power—voluntarily reports to the Federal Power Commission its contributions to the Southern States Industrial Council. Every year during the decade checked, from 1953 to 1962, Idaho Power sent $250 down to S.S.I.C. in Nashville.[9] However, the Council's bank account is heavy with donations from I.O.U.s that do not report the contributions to the F.P.C.

Twelve of the 35 power companies that responded to the authors' query on utility donations said they gave to S.S.I.C. in 1963.* We had asked 103 investor-owned utilities about their donations to S.S.I.C. and some other organizations. Almost two thirds of the I.O.U.s did not respond to the question. Was there any way to determine whether they supported S.S.I.C.?

In a few cases, yes. Some of the companies belonged to holding companies that file annual reports with the Securities and Exchange Commission. One such holding company is Middle South Utilities of New York. It controls Arkansas Power & Light, Louisiana Power & Light, Mississippi Power & Light, and New Orleans Public Service.

Neither Arkansas Power & Light nor Louisiana Power & Light had answered the query about 1963 contributions. However, Middle South reported to the Commission that each of those subsidiaries had donated to S.S.I.C. in 1963. Middle South said that the S.S.I.C. contributions were for "industrial development."

---

* The 12 companies were Alabama Power, Georgia Power, Gulf Power, Kansas Gas & Electric, Mississippi Power, Mississippi Power & Light, Monongahela Power, New Orleans Public Service, Oklahoma Gas & Electric, Pennsylvania Power & Light, Potomac Edison, and Virginia Electric & Power.

Middle South's report to the Commission also showed that Mississippi Power & Light gave S.S.I.C. $575 in 1963. The Mississippi company told us it gave S.S.I.C. $750 that year. The fourth operating company subsidiary of Middle South, New Orleans Public Service, had told us it gave S.S.I.C. $800 in 1963. However, the report by Middle South to the Securities and Exchange Commission did not list any contribution to S.S.I.C. from New Orleans Public Service during the year.

Thus, in one way or another, all four of the operating company subsidiaries of Middle South Utilities reported contributions to S.S.I.C. In one case, the contribution was not reported to S.E.C. In two cases, the companies did not live up to their nationally advertised claim to answer questions from the public. In the fourth case, the amount of the contribution reported to the Commission was less than the amount subsequently reported to us. (Inasmuch as renowned Harvard is the principal stockholder of Middle South Utilities, perhaps someone on the Harvard campus should offer a course in accounting, new math, or plain old arithmetic for Middle South executives.)

Where else could one find information about donations to S.S.I.C.? At the Internal Revenue Service? No, as a business association, S.S.I.C. does not have to file a public report with the Internal Revenue Service, as the Intercollegiate Society of Individualists and other "charitable" and "educational" tax-exempt organizations must.

There was, however, one other public record to search for clues about electric-utility contributions to the Southern States Industrial Council. As a registered lobby, S.S.I.C. must file quarterly reports with the Secretary of the Senate and the Clerk of the House under the Federal Regulation of Lobbying Act.

Contributors to lobbies do not have to be named unless they donate $500 or more per quarter. Thus companies can each give up to $1,999 per year, in equal quarterly installments, without having their identity or donation revealed.

Knowing the preference of many power companies for making modest annual donations to many organizations, rather than a few large contributions that appear in public reports, we did not expect anything to show in the lobbying reports. We were surprised. These reports did yield more information.

The lobbying reports showed consistent utility support for the Council. Mississippi Power, for example, had contributed a total of $4,500 to the Council from 1958 through 1963.

The lobbying reports showed support for S.S.I.C. from a utility that we had not queried. Kentucky Utilities gave the Council $3,000 during the six-year period.

The reports also showed that Public Service Company of Indiana had contributed $2,900 to S.S.I.C. during the six years.

Public Service Company of Indiana was one of the investor-owned utilities that the authors had asked about its contributions to S.S.I.C. and some other uncharitable organizations. In reply, the president of the company, Carroll H. Blanchar, had (1) not answered the questions asked, (2) delivered a lecture, (3) made unfounded accusations, and (4) enclosed the October 9, 1964, editorial in the *Indianapolis Star* which concluded that ". . . the electric light and power companies not only have the right, but a moral obligation, to educate the public." Blanchar wrote:

While we are vitally concerned with supplying operating information for bona fide regulatory purposes we recognize the dangers of calculated misuse of isolated pieces of information by those who seek to weaken or destroy a segment of the nation's investor-owned business by substitution of government ownership or financing. We see evidence of such misuse in your own frequent attacks which have appeared in the *Congressional Record* and your recent article in *Coronet* magazine * intended to smear the investor-owned utility industry.

* "Are You Being Overcharged on Your Electric Bill?" by the authors, *Coronet*, November 1964, pp. 12–18.

We believe in the economic system which has created a great abundance of goods and services for the people who are this nation. Consequently, we regard it our duty to defend this system against those who are hostile to it and seek to replace it with government ownership.

The authors, of course, had not suggested nationalization of electric power. By his reply Blanchar maintained his company's "freedom *from* information" policy. It was one of the electric utilities that in 1950 refused to furnish the House Select Committee on Lobbying Activities information on "contributions made or membership fees paid by the company to municipal chambers of commerce, to state and local taxpayer's associations, to management and trade associations, and to similar types of organizations." [10] However, Public Service Company of Indiana did report to the House committee its contributions to the National Association of Electric Companies, National Tax Equality Association, Indiana State Chamber of Commerce, Chamber of Commerce of the U.S., and the National Association of Manufacturers.

The Southern States Industrial Council exemplifies an important and often-overlooked fact about the extremist organizations. Many of the extremely uncharitable groups enjoy consistent support year in and year out from major corporations, especially from companies that are part of the nation's largest industry—electric utilities.

Chapter 18.

BOOK REVIEWS FOR THE BIRCHERS
—America's Future

America's Future is one of the offspring of the Committee for Constitutional Government, which is the grandfather of several extremist groups. The genealogy of this clan and some of the family idiosyncrasies were reported in part in the report issued in 1950 by the House Select Committee on Lobbying Activities:

Not only do different groups draw support from common sources but they also frequently share common personnel as well. This tendency is especially marked with respect to interlocking directorates. An analysis of five typical foundations, American Enterprise Association, National Economic Council, Committee for Constitutional Government, Foundation for Economic Education and America's Future reveals that eight men have served as officers, directors, or trustees of at least two of the five organizations. . . .

A final aspect of massed effort by different lobbying groups is perhaps more illusory than real. We refer to the great wealth of seemingly independent groups which are actually created for special purposes by going organizations. The Committee for Constitutional Government has been especially prolific in this regard, having spawned at last count no less than four subsidiary organizations: Fighters for Freedom, America's Future, Constitution and Free Enterprise Foundation, and Features for America. One group specializes in the distribution of literature, another in political action within Congressional districts, a third in syndicated columns and releases, a fourth in contacts with educational institutions. But what appears to be a number of distinct groups is in reality the

Committee for Constitutional Government operating in several different ways. The Committee for Constitutional Government has learned well what has been called the first rule of successful pressure politics: to wit, never admit that it is only you who is talking.[1]

By 1965, 15 years after the House committee made its perceptive report, America's Future had provided the Committee for Constitutional Government with five grandchildren.* The third generation includes—in addition to America's Future's long-established nationwide radio program—a weekly newsletter, book digest, a pamphlet distribution service through which millions of pamphlets have been disseminated, and "Operation Textbook." The latter has sent school board members, teachers, and other interested persons free reviews of "a substantial portion of the 400 social science texts currently in use."

In a pamphlet distributed in 1964, America's Future described its radio program as follows:

"BEHIND THE HEADLINES," a weekly commentary by R. K. Scott, is produced and sponsored by America's Future and programmed over the nationwide facilities of the Mutual network—483 radio stations in metropolitan and grass roots America. Over the past 10 years these commentaries and other dramatic and educational programs have provided a strong antidote to the flood of socialist, collectivist propaganda to which our citizens are constantly exposed. . . .[2]

America's Future's 1964 bibliography of books which it sells, "Readings in Liberty," lists some 80 titles.[3] The books on economics are generally those of the literature list of the Foundation for Economic Education. America's Future's

---

* America's Future and the Committee for Constitutional Government now say they are unrelated. However, although America's Future left its parental home with the Committee for Constitutional Government, it is the same America's Future for which E. A. Rumely, executive secretary of the Committee for Constitutional Government, used to countersign checks.

books dealing with the United Nations and race relations would be read approvingly by the directors of the Southern States Industrial Council. Twenty-four of the books deal with "collectivism and modern liberalism in the United States" or "communism in the United States." A number of the titles are autobiographies by former spies.

One of the books in America's Future's "U.S. Government" series is *Nine Men Against America*,[4] by Rosalie M. Gordon, the editor of the America's Future newsletter. This attack on the Supreme Court was listed as one of the three references to be consulted in the John Birch Society essay contest, "Grounds for the Impeachment of [Chief Justice] Warren." * Founder Robert Welch of the John Birch Society frequently plugged the Gordon book in the J.B.S. *Bulletin* and in 1963 claimed that the society had sold more than 100,000 copies.[5]

Nineteen of the books on America's Future's literature list appear under the heading "schools and education." The flavor of these books is conveyed by some of the titles, *Brainwashing in the High Schools*, *Collectivism on the Campus*, and *The Quiet Betrayal*.

America's Future spelled out in its pamphlet the organization's distrust of American teachers and school officials:

> For a number of years, thoughtful, observant parents have noted that their children have been acquiring, presumably at school, dangerous misconceptions about the American form of government and our economic system. Investigation by various educators and others have shown that certain of the textbooks in popular use in our schools sharply criticize our free enterprise economy, without giving credit for its accomplishments, distort our history, disparage our representative form of government, and impute base

---

* The other references: *Dan Smoot Reports* and *The Supreme Court As An Instrument of Global Conquest* by SPX Associates, which is headed by a retired Air Force Reserve colonel, Tom R. Hutton, who was listed in a 1962 brochure of the John Birch Society as a member of its committee of endorsers.

motives to those who framed our Constitution. Conversely, they create the impression that some form of state socialism or collectivism is more desirable.

Then, in the unkindest cut of all at educators, America's Future said:

... in 1958 there was not a single authoritative source in the United States to which school board members, parents, teachers or other interested individuals could turn for professional, objective information in the textbooks used in their schools. To fill this need America's Future formed a textbook evaluation committee, made up of 16 of the nation's leading educators.

Now where do you suppose America's Future went to find "leading educators" who would be authoritative and objective?

One was Dr. E. Merrill Root, formerly professor of English literature at Earlham College, Richmond, Indiana, author of *Collectivism on the Campus* and *Brainwashing in the High Schools* and associate editor of Robert Welch, Inc.'s *American Opinion.*[6]

Another was Hans F. Sennholz, chairman of the department of economics at Grove City (Pennsylvania) College. Sennholz is a contributing editor of *American Opinion* and available as a speaker through the American Opinion Speakers Bureau.

Another was Charles Callan Tansill, professor emeritus of American history at Georgetown University. He had been one of the judges of the 1961 and 1962 John Birch Society essay contests and had written for *American Opinion.*

Another was Medford Evans, who had formerly been with the department of social sciences at Northwestern State College in Natchitoches, Louisiana. He was a member of the John Birch Society committee of endorsers and is on the staff of *American Opinion.*[7]

A majority of America's Future's 16 "leading educators" were affiliated with the John Birch Society, the uncollegiate

Intercollegiate Society of Individualists, or Young Americans for Freedom.

The literature distributed by America's Future's Textbook Evaluation Committee has been used in scores of communities to sow hate, fear, and suspicion. As a result, some educators have become reluctant to use texts that detail programs or institutions disparaged by the committee—social security, the United Nations, the income tax, customer-owned power systems. Textbook publishers, fearing loss of sales, have changed or deleted sections to mollify the critics. This has led in some states to use of insipid classroom material. The "controversial" matters have been removed, and the student is the poorer for it.

The John Birch Society has no textbook-reviewing apparatus. Instead, it distributes textbook material prepared by America's Future's evaluation committee. The work of this committee has been highly recommended by the society's President Robert Welch. The job that America's Future does even satisfies that exceedingly militant member of the John Birch Society, Robert De Pugh, head of the Minutemen, a group that specializes in weapons collection and preparation for guerrilla warfare. The Minutemen dropped plans to study the suitability of school texts when they discovered that it would duplicate the work of other extremist groups such as America's Future.[8]

America's Future, like the Southern States Industrial Council, had long benefited from corporate contributions and reflected respectability of big names in electric utilities and other industries. The nature and extent of the assistance in earlier years was indicated in 1950 by the House Select Committee on Lobbying, in its inquiry into contributions from business, farm, and labor groups to a number of organizations.

The House committee investigation was limited by two important restrictions. Only a minority of the corporations and farm and labor organizations were asked to submit information, and they were asked to submit it on a voluntary basis.

Forty-nine investor-owned utilities—less than a fourth of the big ones—were among the 173 corporations asked to furnish information about lobbying, contributions, travel expenses, advertising, and maintenance of Washington offices. Of the 49 I.O.U.s, 10 did not respond to some of the committee's questions.* Three did not answer at all.[9]

Delaware Power & Light furnished information to the committee under protest "against the request to furnish such information which obviously is of little consequence to anyone." [10]

The committee's attempt to determine the breadth of support for organizations was further hampered by a provision in the lobbying act that required the organizations to report only those individual contributions exceeding $500. Gifts exceeding that amount were discouraged in order to avoid disclosure; Executive Secretary Edward A. Rumely of America's Future's parent organization, the Committee for Constitutional Government, testified that he frequently returned checks exceeding $490. Contributions of $500 or more were usually accepted as "purchase" orders for literature, which would often be distributed by the Committee for Constitutional Government rather than by the company that gave it the money.[11]

The House committee found that the donations above $500 —to either the Committee for Constitutional Government or to America's Future—averaged more than $1,300 each.

The contributions to America's Future came from Connecticut Light & Power, Delaware Power & Light, Indianapolis Power & Light, and Wisconsin Power & Light—and from some

---

* The ten companies that did not answer some of the committee's questions were Cleveland Electric Illuminating, Florida Power & Light, Indianapolis Power & Light, Northern Indiana Public Service, Pacific Gas & Electric, Pacific Power & Light, Pennsylvania Electric, Public Service of Colorado, Public Service of Indiana and Public Service of Oklahoma.

The three that did not respond at all were Puget Sound Power & Light, Mountain States Power (which in 1954 merged with Pacific Power & Light), and Southern California Edison.

other corporations such as American Can, Armco Steel, Champion Spark Plug, Cities Service, Continental Can, du Pont, Erie Railroad, Gulf Oil, Kennecott Copper, S. S. Kresge, Libbey-Owens-Ford Glass, Eli Lilly, National Dairy Products, Northern Pacific Railway, Republic Steel, Socony-Vacuum Oil, Westinghouse, and Youngstown Sheet and Tube.

Some of the above companies also contributed to America's Future's parent, the Committee for Constitutional Government. At that time, before America's Future came of age, the parent still gave its offspring an allowance of sorts, despite the youngster's independent income. Among the companies that contributed to the Committee for Constitutional Government during the 1947–1950 period were Montana Power, Public Service Electric & Gas (New Jersey), Virginia Electric & Power, Beech Aircraft, Celanese Corporation, Fruehauf Trailer, R. J. Reynolds, and Swift.

Power companies that reported literature purchases from one or both organizations were Carolina Power & Light, Central Power & Light (Texas), Cleveland Electric Illuminating, Kentucky Utilities, Pacific Gas & Electric, Pennsylvania Power & Light, Philadelphia Electric, Public Service of Colorado, Public Service of Oklahoma, Virginia Electric & Power, and Western Massachusetts Electric.

One of the big utility propaganda projects of that postwar period was distribution of John T. Flynn's *The Road Ahead*, which as previously noted * succinctly misstated the status and misread the future of the electric-power industry. The Committee for Constitutional Government had declared that the book "should go to everyone in a position to disseminate ideas" and, if possible, to "every family in the nation."

Money for distribution of *The Road Ahead* or its condensation by *Reader's Digest* was sprayed in several directions. Utilities and other corporations purchased the book or the conden-

* Page 101.

sation by sending checks to the Committee for Constitutional Government, *Reader's Digest*, Edison Electric Institute, or local bookstores. Columbus & Southern Ohio Electric bought its copies of *The Road Ahead* through Fighters for Freedom, which had also been sired by the Committee for Constitutional Government. Pacific Gas & Electric supplemented its distribution of *The Road Ahead* with 16,000 copies of a sermon based on the book and preached by a Presbyterian minister in Nashville, Tennessee.

Recent power-company contributions to America's Future are hard to uncover. It is easy enough to note that among the organization's 13 trustees, listed on a pamphlet about the Textbook Evaluation Committee was the then "president of Edison Electric Institute," Montana Power's President John E. Corette.* Reporting of utility purchases of books, literature, and subscriptions from America's Future and like organizations is not required. America's Future is not a registered lobby, as is the Southern States Industrial Council, so there are no quarterly lobbying reports to check. America's Future's public file at Internal Revenue Service does not include detail on individual contributions (which are tax-deductible), as the reports of the Intercollegiate Society of Individualists usually do.

Thirteen investor-owned utilities ** reported contributions to America's Future in 1962 or 1963, or in both years. A few reported the donations voluntarily to the Federal Power Commission [12] or in response to the authors' query. Others tried their best to keep the contribution secret.

Central Illinois Public Service had stated in its 1962 annual

* The pamphlet was apparently issued in 1958. Corette was still listed as a trustee in September, 1962, but his name does not appear on current America's Future literature or letterheads.

** Alabama Power, Arizona Public Service, Carolina Power & Light, Central Illinois Public Service, Interstate Power (Iowa), Iowa-Illinois Gas & Electric, Jersey Central Power & Light, Metropolitan Edison (Pennsylvania), Mississippi Power, Pennsylvania Electric, Public Service Company of Oklahoma, Southwestern Public Service, and Washington Water Power.

report to the Federal Power Commission that it donated $39,492 for "charitable, social and community welfare." The expenditures were not itemized. F.P.C. requested itemization. In its response the company divided its contributions into two categories, those above $1,000 and those below $1,000.

In the "under $1,000" category the company listed only 10 specific items, totaling $6,190. Those donations included $82.50 for the March of Dimes, $80 for the Heart Fund, $67.50 for Salvation Army, and so on.

There was an eleventh item in the company's "under $1,000" list of contributions. It read: "Various civic activities, school activities, social projects, and so forth." The amount alongside it was $10,512.

The accountants at F.P.C. presumed that the company had reported all donations that should be listed in order to enable the state regulatory commission to decide whether the donations should be billed to the stockholder or the rate-payer. After all, the itemization furnished by the company indicated that it was giving small amounts of money, sometimes less than $100 each, to many worthwhile community activities.

Nevertheless, a member of Congress requested that the Federal Power Commission please ask the company to itemize that $10,512 which it gave to "various civic activities, school activities, social projects, and so forth."

The F.P.C. made the request. The company opened the account to public view.

At first glance the report appeared to be similar to the earlier breakdown. The company had donated to the cornbread and bean festival, high school proms, a beauty contest, and Little League baseball.

Then some larger contributions appeared, of from $100 to $500 each, to different organizations.

There was a whole nestful of uncharitable contributions— to America's Future, the Committee for Constitutional Government, Manion Forum, the Foundation for Economic Education, the American Economic Foundation, *Educational Reviewer,* the National Education Program at Harding College, and the National Tax Equality Association. All of these contributions were considered by the company to be part of its operating expenses.

Another example is Southwestern Public Service, which serves portions of Texas, New Mexico, Oklahoma, and Kansas. That utility had its contributions to the uncharitable organizations listed under an account labeled "General Educational Materials for the Public." Itemization of the account, furnished by the company in response to specific Federal Power Commission request, showed contributions in 1962 to America's Future, the Southern States Industrial Council, Manion Forum, the National Education Program at Harding College, *Dan Smoot Reports,* National Tax Equality Association, Young Americans for Freedom, the Texas Bureau of Economic Understanding, and others. The company did not tell how much it gave to each organization, but its total tab for these "general educational materials for the public" was more than $7,000 that year.

The utility's donations to the extremists fitted in with what had been going on in Amarillo, Texas, where Southwestern Public Service is headquartered. During the early 1960s, "Amarillo had been torn apart by the winds of suspicions," Arnold Forster and Benjamin R. Epstein wrote in *Danger on the Right:*

The permanent damage that could be seen after the storm had subsided is a graphic illustration to the bitter and disruptive effects of Rightist extremism. The climax here had come only after a long, febrile season in which clergymen and teachers had been accused of spreading communism, the libraries and schools had been purged of certain outstanding books, and many a long friendship had been severed by hate.[13]

There was a meeting ground, though, for the neighbors who had been taught to hate each other. Friend and foe alike helped finance the causes of grief—when they paid their electricity bill.

Chapter 19.

GODFATHERS, RELATIVES, AND THE ILL-BEGOTTEN

The most prestigious position in the nation's largest industry is that of president of Edison Electric Institute. The presidency of the investor-owned utilities' trade association changes annually. Many of the companies that have furnished the industry's national leadership have also led the industry in excesses such as the stock option schemes and Project Action. Similarly, national leaders of the power industry are prominent among the utility godfathers of the extremist organizations.

Utility officials are the "big names"—the vice presidents, directors, sponsors, or endorsers. They give their companies' and industry's prestige—and in many cases their customers' unwilling contributions—to the extremists.

A spot survey of connections between the extremists and power-company officials in 1964 showed that 15 key officials of major investor-owned utilities served as endorsers or sponsors of Manion Forum. Among the 15 was Harold Quinton, chairman of Southern California Edison and a former president of Edison Electric Institute.

Nine high officials of I.O.U.s served as vice presidents or directors of the Southern States Industrial Council in 1964. Two of them are former presidents of Edison Electric Institute

—D. S. Kennedy, president of Oklahoma Gas & Electric, and Louis V. Sutton, president of Carolina Power & Light, both directors of S.S.I.C.*

As noted previously, a former president of Edison Electric Institute, President J. E. Corette of Montana Power, served until recently as a trustee of America's Future.

Another intimate association of the electric-power industry and the extremists is revealed in a publication innocently titled *Public Service Magazine.*

This magazine, published in Minneapolis, states in its masthead that it is "independently owned and managed and the owners have no affiliation or connection with any other business, groups, organizations or associations." However, N. W. Ayer & Son, which annually publishes a *Directory* of *Newspapers and Periodicals,* refers to *Public Service Magazine* as a "utility" publication. The facts bear out Ayer's description.

The magazine's origins go back 60 years to the time when utility magnate Samuel Insull incorporated a publishing company and personally purchased the first shares of stock. The company published *Public Service Magazine* and *Public Service Management.*

Ernest Gruening told in *The Public Pays* how this publishing venture expanded and operated:

Later the [publishing] company required additional capitalization which was furnished by other utility officials. The magazine went to public utility officials and employees, to legislators, business executives, college and school teachers, newspaper editors, libraries.

* The other I.O.U. officials who served on the council were President Reeves E. Ritchie of Arkansas Power & Light, President R. Baxter Wilson of Mississippi Power & Light and Assistant to the Chairman P. A. Feringa of New Orleans Public Service, all of them vice presidents of S.S.I.C., and the following members of the S.S.I.C. board of directors:

Chairman of the Board J. J. McDonough of Georgia Power, Vice President William H. Skinner of Kentucky Utilities, Chairman of the Board George S. Dinwiddie of New Orleans Public Service, and President A. R. Watson of Southwestern Public Service.

The company's second magazine had a total circulation of 30,000, of which 26,497 were paid for by the utilities and distributed to a list selected by them.[1]

The survey conducted by the House Select Committee on Lobbying Activity in 1950 showed that power companies were circulating material from *Public Service Magazine*. Of the relatively few companies that answered the questions asked about literature distribution in 1950, six reported using reprints from the magazine.* The titles of the *Public Service Magazine* reprints distributed were: "Encroaching Socialism" and "Hitler Propaganda Technique Proves Its Worth for T.V.A." [2]

Current power-company contributions to *Public Service Magazine* appear to be sunk without a trace in power-company operation expenses, in the form of block subscriptions, the same technique used in the Insull days on which Senator Gruening reported. Contributions to the magazine are not mentioned by utilities in their annual reports to the Federal Power Commission. However, when a Congressional committee or commission with jurisdiction requires a company to itemize certain accounts, such expenditures finally surface.

The Federal Power Commission recently requested Florida Power & Light to itemize more than $400,000 in contributions and other expenses during 1963 which the utility had accounted incorrectly as a lump sum and, also incorrectly, as an operating expense. In response the company still did not itemize more than $125,000 in "public relations," "educational . . ." and "donation" expenditures of less than $1,000 each. Florida Power & Light did, however, report spending more than $1,000 on *Public Service Magazine* subscriptions during the year.[3]

---

* The companies were American Gas & Electric Service (now part of American Electric Power), Central Power & Light (Texas), Connecticut Light & Power, Pennsylvania Power & Light, Southwestern Gas & Electric (now part of Southwestern Electric Power, headquartered in Shreveport, La.), and Texas Electric Service.

Public Service Magazine, which carries no advertising, prints page after page of speeches by power-company officials and articles by the leaders of the utility-supported organizations. When Board Chairman G. L. Andrus of Middle South invoked the phony "Lincoln" quotes before the children of New Orleans, *Public Service Magazine* reprinted his remarks. The speeches of Edison Electric Institute presidents are regularly reprinted in the magazine. The power industry is presented as the harassed hero, out of ammunition, on a precipice above the Tennessee Valley, pressed by angry farmers and townspeople who are closing in on him with pitchforks provided by Uncle Sam, as the Communists dance with delight.

"The motivation of the Rural Electrification Administration and Castro's Cuba appear to be identical," one reads in *Public Service Magazine.* The Southwestern Power Administration is "a story of socialism in action." The utility industry "is not, by any test, a monopoly," T.V.A. should be sold, and electric power should be removed from "the arena of city hall politics" by the simple device of selling city-owned power systems to the I.O.U.s.[4]

For a brief period in 1959, the magazine carried letters to the editor. Most of the letters came from utility officials— Board Chairman Austin D. Barney of Hartford Electric Light, Vice President Robert R. Gros of Pacific Gas & Electric, Del Stone of Iowa Public Service, Lloyd E. Zacharias of Public Service Company of Oklahoma and a junior Carolina Power & Light official. All commented favorably on the magazine. Some saw a need for increasing its distribution. (The letters-to-the-editor department, which started off with a splash as a new section of the magazine, was abruptly discontinued after a few months.)

Public Service Magazine reviews right-wing books, such as *Collectivism Challenges Christianity,* by Verne P. Kaub, a former publicist for Wisconsin Power & Light. This book, ac-

cording to *Public Service Magazine,* "laid much of the ground-
work for examination of the activities of collectivist-minded
clergymen." [5]

The magazine reprints material from the Southern States
Industrial Council, American Economic Foundation, the Foun-
dation for Economic Education, Harding College, and the
Industrial News Review. It carries articles by Admiral Ben
Moreell, President Willis E. Stone of the Liberty Amendment
Committee (which seeks abolition of the income tax) and
Thomas J. Anderson, a member of the national council of the
John Birch Society who until recently published *Farm and
Ranch.*

Such reprinting of sister organizations' articles is a characteristic of a number of utility-supported publications. Thus,
for example, the Foundation for Economic Education's *Freeman* has carried articles by the leaders of most of the other
groups, favorable reviews of their books, or plugs for their
publications. In this manner, the *Freeman* has assisted Manion
Forum (Clarence Manion), the Intercollegiate Society of Individualists (Frank Chodorov), Americans for Constitutional
Action (Admiral Ben Moreell), the American Economic Foundation (Fred Clark), *Dan Smoot Report,* the Southern States
Industrial Council (Thurman Sensing) and America's Future
(Dr. Merrill Root).

Periodicals recommended by the John Birch Society included *Christian Economics* (Christian Freedom Foundation),
Human Events, The Freeman (Foundation for Economic Education), *Manion Forum Newsletter, Dan Smoot Report,* and
America's Future.[6] (The latter two periodicals bear the same
name as their companion radio programs.) The society, which
has promoted literature of the American Economic Foundation, has also suggested that the Intercollegiate Society of Individualists (Frank Chodorov) is worthy of support.[7]

It is obvious that many organizations, interrelated, well-
organized, spewing out a steady stream of their own and each

other's material, can sow distrust and fear in millions of minds —all the more so when this complex is inextricably tied to what is politically and economically the most powerful industry in the country.

As Senator Barry Goldwater told the leaders of the power industry, at the 1959 Edison Electric Institute convention, "You operate in every state in the Union except Nebraska. I know of no other industry with this same advantage. You have responsible representatives in almost every Congressional district who are, or should be, well acquainted with local officials and opinion leaders."

Goldwater suggested to the utility leaders that they "select a top official to handle [politics] as his primary responsibility . . . since politics now is one of the most important activities that confronts you." [8]

When this coordinated, calculating clan goes into action, the public and political leaders of both parties are virtually helpless in stemming the stream of hate literature that flows into practically every community in the country. During the 1964 Presidential campaign, the chairman of the Republican National Committee and the chairman of the Republican Governors' Conference vainly attempted to discourage distribution of what the latter called "smut" literature.[9] One of the books which the chairman of the Republican governors' conference put in this category was *None Dare Call It Treason*, by John A. Stormer.

Distribution of the book was being promoted by the John Birch Society, America's Future, and the Southern States Industrial Council. The Southern States Industrial Council, in its August 1, 1964, *Bulletin*, "highly recommended" as "election-year reading" the Stormer * book and *A Texan Looks at Lyndon, A Study in Illegitimate Power*, by J. Evetts Haley. The

---

*During recent months, Stormer has frequently been featured by Carl McIntire, whose Twentieth Century Reformation Hour is broadcast over more than 600 stations.

Haley book was also on the G.O.P. "smut" list. Both books, said the S.S.I.C. *Bulletin,* were available "at greatly reduced prices for larger quantities."

America's Future sent out free copies of Stormer's book "with our compliments through the generosity of one of our donors."

"Millions of copies of this book have been sold," wrote America's Future's President R. K. Scott, "and judging from the continuing demand, it is quite likely that this figure will continue to grow." [10]

And the contrived demand for such smut will continue to grow, until America looks beyond the Birchers to their backers.

PART IV

WHAT TO DO ABOUT IT

Chapter 20.

REGULATION

Utilities in many states have a hidden advantage over their customers. As the Florida Public Service Commission succinctly put it, "the public provides public utilities, through *rates,* with such experts as the public utilities may require to protect the utilities' rights, but the public, through *taxes,* does not provide adequate funds for its own protection." [1]

The expertise paid for by utilities through rates is invisible; the regulatory commission budget, when funded by taxes, is fair game for any "economy"-minded legislator who wishes to cut the budget or stop an increase, and the material supplied him by the rate-financed utility experts will make his case sound good before a public indoctrinated by utility propaganda.

About three fourths of the states finance a part or all of the cost of state regulatory commissions through special fees or taxes paid by the utilities regulated. Most of these states, however, impose statutory limitations upon the amount that may be assessed. [2] In those states, legislators who want to provide the commission with a bigger budget have to change the

227

law. It is no easy task to win such battles against the utility lobby, which is often the strongest one in the state capital.

Nor is it realistic to expect too much assistance for the consumer from the Federal Power Commission. Its jurisdiction is limited; its staff has never recovered from the studied enervation accomplished during the Eisenhower administration. Despite the rejuvenation of the Commission under former Chairman Joseph C. Swidler, its electric-power staff in 1965 was smaller than in 1949. During those 16 years the industry grew threefold, and its interstate transactions increased at an even more rapid rate.[3]

Competition keeps consumer prices in line with producer costs in free-enterprise businesses. In monopolies, regulation is supposed to provide a similar cost-price adjustment. Yet the public investment in regulation is ridiculously low, with consequent ineffectiveness.

The entire budgets of all the state regulatory commissions —with their jurisdiction over many industries besides electric utilities—plus the budget of the Federal Power Commission amount to six tenths of 1% of the annual revenue of only the 34 largest investor-owned electric utilities. A dollar a year from each family in the United States would double the annual budget of all the state regulatory commissions and the F.P.C. That would be a good investment for those families who now are overcharged $60 per year in their electricity bill. It might help reduce some of the other utility bills, too, such as extra monthly charges for a colored telephone.

The electric consumer is caught in a vicious circle. He cannot obtain adequate rate reductions because many regulatory commissions do not have the staff or inclination to reduce rates, due to the political and propaganda activities of the utilities, which are designed to prevent adequate rate reductions. Where can the circle be broken?

There is no easy answer. There are, however, many ways

to approach the problem, at each level of government and through consumer organizations.

If a state commission can not or will not make a strong case for consumers in a rate hearing, municipalities can. That is what Miami, Florida, has done, using its city attorney's staff and a utility consultant. In Miami, important assistance came from the *Miami Herald,* which told its readers in a series of articles and editorials about the real world of utilities and the overcharges paid by Miami residents. The experience led Miami's City Attorney, John R. Barrett, to the conclusion late in 1965 that vigilance and cooperative action on utility rate matters by municipalities are of overriding importance in obtaining reasonable rates.

An Iowa mayor went a step further. "We should be militantly helping other cities establish municipal electric systems," said Mayor Maurice TePaske of Sioux Center, Iowa, which is served by a municipal system. Mayor TePaske cited, as other city officials have, the financial benefits of city ownership of utilities, which can mean the difference between stagnation and growth.[4]

Counties can help keep tab on utilities through establishment of utility commissions. Although lacking regulatory powers, such county commissions can enter rate proceedings, as the pint-sized Arlington, Virginia, County Public Utilities Commission did.*

A state may represent the interest of utility customers through an agency other than an ill-equipped regulatory commission—perhaps through a people's counsel, the Attorney General, or a state legislative council. In Massachusetts, the chairman of the Consumers' Council, an official state agency, recently proposed establishment of a commission to investigate "the laws of the Commonwealth and their organizations;

* The role of the Arlington commission was described in Chapter 4, pp. 37-40.

the availability of electric energy, including atomic or other sources, and the manner best suited to make such energy available to the people of the state, and necessary steps to see that transmission or wheeling arrangements are available to public and private electric systems to best serve the needs of the people and industry of the state." [5]

The Massachusetts council chairman, Dr. John J. Reid, suggested that the commission be composed of eight members of the legislature, the heads of the state Public Utilities Department, Department of Commerce, and Consumers' Council, and six persons appointed by the governor, including a member of AFL-CIO, an official of a private power company, and a manager of a municipal electric system. This approach has much to commend it, in that the utilities themselves put through the basic regulatory laws in many states. (Massachusetts was not one of them, however.) It is high time for representative state groups to evaluate the results of the utilities' handiwork and suggest ways to bring consumer and industry interests into balance.

However, legislators who attempt to get better utility laws or appropriations for an adequate commission staff can expect utility-inspired opposition. The governor appoints the utility commissions in two thirds of the states, thus the gubernatorial election often decides the orientation of a majority of the commission. With an unparalleled apparatus for getting their message into community organizations and media, utilities can swing elections. And they do.

The federal government can help in rate regulation in ways other than through the established regulatory commissions. And it should. After all, Uncle Sam is the biggest utility customer of all. Since 1944, a small public-utilities division, located at first in the Treasury Department and now in General Services Administration, has represented U.S. government interest in some rate proceedings. During its first decade of operations, this group, averaging 10 persons, saved the federal government at least $15 million in actual out-of-pocket cost of utility services—about $20 for each $1 spent on the entire operations of the division.[6]

As to the principles of regulation, perhaps the most salutary improvement would be abolition of the "water over the dam" rule * by which overcharges are not refunded. The Public Service Commission of Wisconsin developed the concept of retaining control over excess earnings above the allowed rate of return. That was at least a modification of the "water over the dam" rule. The excess could not be distributed as dividends. It could, however, be used by the utility, which would thus require less capital from rate-payers or investors.

The Federal Power Commission has required gas pipeline companies to refund overcharges, and the savings to consumers have been substantial. One of the F.P.C. gas cases, involving El Paso Natural Gas, was disposed of through a settlement which resulted in a $155-million refund and an annual rate reduction of $30 million. The refunds went from the pipeline companies to the gas companies, thence in part to the ultimate consumer. The El Paso settlement involved four successive rate increases starting in 1954 and involving a total of $80 million per year of rate increases being collected by the pipeline company subject to refund.[7]

In the El Paso case the company initiated rate increases; the Commission could question their reasonableness and provide, as it did, for refund. An electric utility, though, with steadily decreasing costs, does not have to go to a commission for a rate increase.

The refund idea is understandably unpopular among utilities and has been represented as a terribly expensive way to roll back prices for each consumer by a few dollars. (Yet the El Paso rebate alone amounted to two and a half times the

* Described in Chapter 4, pp. 36-37.

annual budgets of the Federal Power Commission and all the state regulatory commissions combined.) *Empire Trust Letter,* published by the New York bank, considered the gas refund as obnoxious as and analogous to a situation where government would require a shoe store to refund part of the price to the shoe purchaser, plus interest, after the shoes have worn out.[8] That argument by Empire Trust overlooks the substantial differences between competitive shoe stores and monopoly utilities, the most significant being the utilities' entitlement to have the public contribute to its revenues at rates set to assure profit. Refund of overcharges, for electricity as well as for gas and other utility products or services, is simply the consumers' side of the coin. And it's time to flip it.

One of the most substantial ways to improve utility regulation is through increased use of electronic data processing. Ten years ago utility trade literature told of company losses due to poor handwriting; penned data was simply illegible.[9] One utility official suggested a nationwide handwriting course. Today the national penmanship is probably worse than ever—machines have replaced many of the pens. The power industry along with most others is becoming computerized.

From allocating electricity in distant states, or a neighboring country, to accounting for expenses and sending out bills, the machine does most of the work. Ohio Power, for example, recently opened its Computer Center in Canton, an electronic power-control system combining accounting, billing, engineering, and management information and retrieval. Edison Electric Institute has suggested a uniform national coding system to enable utilities to order directly from manufacturers and secure emergency materials from neighboring systems, all by computer. Utility workshops stress the seemingly limitless application of electronic data processing in utility operations.[10]

Vice President Frank Twohy of a utility financial consulting firm, Wainwright and Ramsey, recently described the adaptability of electronic data processing to utility accounts:

> Distribution of charges is a relatively simple function. Because of this sorting ability, sequences of major, intermediate and minor groupings can be utilized for detailed or summary review. With all accounting transactions in machine use form (this is *after* entry into the electronic system), the analytical possibilities are limitless and of tremendous value. In preparing the analytical journals or ledgers, the identification of the transaction can be part of the analytical report so as to permit detailed audit and review of those transactions which must be or should be authenticated.[11]

In other words, a modern utility will have no difficulty and, in fact, find it easy and economical to enter its transactions so that a regulatory commission can almost immediately determine the expenses and revenue of the company and project actual rate of return. There need not be the time lapse in which the "water over the dam" principle takes effect; the facts that justify rate adjustments can be made available promptly to the utility, the commission, and the public.

Use of electronic data processing could also ease the difficulty that some utilities seemingly have in reporting their contributions and propaganda expenses in sufficient detail to permit regulators to determine whether the costs should be borne by the stockholders or rate-payers. As things stand now, some utilities slip those expenses into one account, some into another, perhaps in a "dues," or "subscriptions," or "industrial development" account. When the F.P.C. asks a utility to itemize a particular account, the utility is not about to divulge non-operating expenditures that happen to be in another account. It's like playing the old game, "Button, button, who's got the button?"—and the regulatory commission is always it.

The F.P.C. could now ask all utilities how much it gave to a particular organization and what account it was put in—but only if the Commission first received the requisite approval from the Budget Bureau to put the same questions to more than nine utilities. If the Budget Bureau turned to its utility advisory committees for advice on procedure, the negative results are predictable—only investor-owned utilities are represented on the committees. Alerted by the request, the I.O.U.s could push the buttons that put the heat of manufactured public opinion on regulators who try to illuminate the utilities' murky accounts.

The Federal Communications Commission is encouraging the telephone industry to computerize information needed for regulatory purposes.[12] The Federal Power Commission is using computers to a limited extent. The major consumer concern in application of electronic data processing to regulation will, of course, be in seeing that costs and revenue are properly programmed into the computer.

Electronic data processing offers a logical, economical way to expedite and simplify utility regulation. A nation with the know-how to project and direct a satellite millions of miles out in space, and to call an election with only 2% of the vote in, can easily compute and regulate the bounds of a fair rate of return for an industry whose control is based on its accounting system. Old-fashioned accounting systems belong on the shelf, alongside the Aladdin kerosene lamp. The success of the new technique, from the customers' viewpoint, depends on the regulators and the extent to which they receive insistent support from the public and legislators.

The utilities' rate of return, indeed the power industry's entire financial structure, needs examination. The industry constantly, naturally, presses for even greater increases in the rate of return. Meanwhile, the gap between the theoretical commission-"allowed" rates of return and the actual rates of return grows ever wider.

Editor Francis X. Welch of *Public Utilities Fortnightly* writes about "the comfortable old rut of 6% of cost base" [13] as if utilities actually earned that modest a return. Actually most regulators permit utilities to earn above 7%, often above 8% or 9%, some more than 10%. Because of the increase in low-cost debt financing by utilities, tax benefit accruals and retained earnings, and because of the growing practice of using retained overcharges for construction, rather than financing construction through sale of securities, the return on common stock of many utilities exceeds 15%.

In one instance, a company with a rate of return of a mere 6.91% earns a return on common stock equity of 20.83%.[14] That is certainly no reflection on the company; its management is perhaps more astute than that of most others. It is good business to finance utilities principally through cheap, long-term mortgage bonds and debentures rather than through sale of stock; the trend should be encouraged. The objection to curtailment of stock sales could well come from some of the utilities themselves. They have found stockholder mailing lists "conducive to establishment of the most beneficial political climate" through distribution of political literature. And in Michigan, in the words of the secretary of Consumers Power— yes, that's the name of the investor-owned utility—use of stockholder mailing lists has helped attain "understanding, if not enthusiastic approval, of higher electric rates." [15]

Regulators must look beyond the theoretical "allowed" rate of return to the actual return on common stock equity to find the real earnings of a utility. Then, according to the landmark *Bluefield* and *Hope* decisions of the Supreme Court, the regulators must look about for other business undertakings with risks corresponding to those of utilities, and allow the utilities corresponding returns. A public utility, said the Court in the *Bluefield* case, is entitled to such rates as will permit it to earn a return "equal to that generally being made at the same time and in the same part of the country on investments and in other business undertakings *which are attended by corresponding risks and uncertainties.*" In the *Hope* case the Court said "the return to the equity owner should be *commensurate with return in other enterprises having corresponding risks.*" [16] [Emphasis added.] Unfortunately, the courts have not indicated how comparable risk can be determined, and the regulators have found no business undertakings as risk-free as electric utilities, because there are none.

The *Bluefield* and *Hope* cases provide the foundation for modern-day regulation. Volumes have been written about them. They permit broad latitude in determining the reasonableness of the return to the utility and its owners.

In addition, the *Hope* decision permits state commissions to adopt any rate-base method that state courts will approve. Thus state commissions gained greater power and responsibility in selection of regulatory methods.[17] The electric utilities have seen to it that the methods adopted have shifted the regulation from themselves to their customers, and reduced their own risk to zero.

During good times—when other enterprises fail at the usual rate of 13,500 a year—during recessions, and during depressions, utility earnings hold steady. The last financial failure of a power company was long before the *Hope* decision in 1944.

True, many utility advertisements give the industry the *appearance* of risk. And many power companies have during the past decade adopted the remunerative status symbols of risk enterprises, restricted stock option plans. But the utility books tell a different story from what the industry ads say. The return to the utility equity owners has risen above that of most business enterprises that are subject to the perils of the marketplace. The difficult doctrine of the Supreme Court has not been applied.

Chapter 21.

COMPETITION

Competition in the distribution of electricity cannot apply in the usual manner where a customer has a choice of two or more companies from which to buy the product. It is possible to achieve a degree of competition when consumers can select their heat supplier from different companies—an electric utility, a gas utility, or an oil supplier. This kind of peripheral competition can lead to lower rates for heating, if not for other purposes.

The trend here, however, is toward increased acquisition by the electric utilities of markets formerly held by the fossil fuels, except in those areas convenient to water transportation, where oil heat is still competitive, and in communities close to natural-gas fields. In this heating competition "oil has lost steadily and substantially," summarized Resources for America's Future, Inc., in 1963:

On the whole, oil heating seems to have lost, year after year, at least one third of the replacement market. This trend, coinciding with a declining share in heating equipment for new homes, a drying up of the coal-to-oil replacement demand, and projected below-average population growths in those areas where oil has had its strongest foothold, does not suggest a reversal in the decline of oil heating.[1]

The electric utilities took the lighting business away from the gas utilities half a century ago and are probably on their way toward domination of the heating industry as well. In 1962, 1.6 million homes were electrically heated. *Electrical*

World's recent survey foresees six million electrically heated homes by 1970. At Edison Electric Institute's 1963 convention, President Donald C. Cook of American Electric Power said that the industry's goal of predominance in heating is not only feasible but highly probable.[2]

The competition for the heating market is keen in some areas; this benefits the consumer. But half of the customers served by the investor-owned electric utilities cannot benefit from this heating competition because their electric company and their gas company are the same corporation. A combination utility is understandably reluctant to promote one of its products to the disadvantage of the other.*

With many gas companies already in its tent, the mammoth electric industry is now moving into the field of the second largest industry, petroleum refining. The electric battery-powered automobile, rechargeable from house current, has already appeared in commercial models. General Electric is developing an electric-powered vehicle suitable for short hauls close to home—the kind of trips that account for half of all automobile travel. GE's vehicle will accommodate two seated adults with space for children and packages, have a range of 30–40 miles, and be inexpensive in comparison with the cost of a Volkswagen.[3] The top speed of GE's transporter—20 miles per hour—will restrict its use, but acceleration has been no problem for American engineers. In October 1966, General Motors unveiled an electric battery-powered Corvair which accelerated from zero to 60 miles an hour in 16 seconds—the same rate as gasoline-powered models.

Electricity's superiority over alternative energy sources is bound to hasten widespread use of electric cars. Pollution from internal-combustion engines "is so serious and is growing so fast," the President's Science Advisory Committee reported

* Major investor-owned electric-natural gas combination companies are listed in Appendix F, p. 285.

late in 1965, "that an alternative non-polluting means of powering automobiles, buses and trucks is likely to become a national necessity." [4]

Electricity has another big advantage over gasoline. Gasoline costs a service station the same amount no matter when the attendant pumps it into the tank. Electricity is different; the most costly electricity is that generated during hours of peak use, and the cheapest is that generated during off-peak hours, usually at night, when the electric plant is operating below capacity.

Electric car batteries can be most conveniently charged overnight, permitting utilities to obtain more sales and revenue without buying new equipment. With an electric car, you don't have to stop by the filling station and fumble for a credit card. You simply drive on home, plug a cord from the battery into a household outlet and let Reddy Kilowatt, Willie Wired Hand,* or the municipal power system fill 'er up while you sleep. No bother about bills from gasoline companies, either. The cost of running your car, electrifying the house, and perhaps heating and cooling it, too, will all be in the bill from the power company.

In a few communities, the electric utility also provides water and telephone service. If the advice of the power industry's leading trade publication is heeded, the power companies will be moving further into the water business. *Electrical World*'s suggested excuse for moving into yet another field is what it termed a "new threat" unveiled by President Johnson in 1964.

The President, in a speech to a college audience, had told of the heartening prospect for increasing the nation's water supply by desalting ocean water. He said that the tremendous heat needed for generating nuclear power could, at the same time, desalinize water.

---

* Reddy Kilowatt and Willie Wired Hand are the cartoon symbols of, respectively, investor-owned electric utilities and rural electric cooperatives.

This combination nuclear-power-desalinization process described by the President was developed principally by the Atomic Energy Commission, upon the suggestion of Senator Clinton P. Anderson (D-N.M.). As chairman of the Senate Interior Committee, he was familiar with the steam temperature requirements of effective desalinization plants. As a member of the Joint Committee on Atomic Energy, he learned that the steam that came off electrical turbines in nuclear reactors is about the same temperature as that needed in the desalinization process. Anderson suggested to the Atomic Energy Commission that the processes be combined, and the combination was found to be practical.

The investor-owned utilities could not very well argue that the new nuclear-power-desalinization process, which the President spoke of, was exclusively theirs. Taxpayers have contributed about $1.5 billion to federal research on the civilian nuclear-power program and have also put up most of the money—$55 million—that has gone into research and development in desalinization.

Development of the nuclear-power-desalinization process was good news for America. Yet *Electrical World* saw in it only an "insidious" threat of competition for the investor-owned utilities from the combination plants.

"The alternative," said *Electrical World*, "is for electric utilities to assume a responsible role in the supply of potable water."

The *Electrical World* editorial appeared just before June 1964 graduation ceremonies around the country. The magazine encouraged utility leaders who might be making commencement addresses to use these occasions to attack the President's offer to share with all the world the U.S. breakthrough in economic nuclear power and water desalinization:

Electric utilities in all susceptible areas must lose no time in facing this new attack. They must fight water with water and assertions with facts. Commencement platforms should not be over-looked; they can be an important channel in campaigns for getting all the pertinent facts before all the people.[5]

The investor-owned utilities cannot be held accountable for the unfulfilled desires of a trade publication to have them enter another major utility field. Nor should expansion of the electric industry into competition with gasoline be discouraged. On the contrary, use of electric batteries in vehicles should be encouraged, not only for health reasons, but also for the competitive benefits that should reduce the price of gasoline, especially in those sections of the country that are saddled with unfair pricing systems. The point is, because electricity is unique, essential, and marvelous, the industry has grown until it overshadows any other. The shadow is growing longer, and the loose rein of control over the industry on which all persons depend the most slackens more.

Power that has accumulated in so few hands within the industry, among persons not subject to the democratic process, is used for purposes of mind manipulation unforeseen by legislators who granted the utilities extraordinary power. The power is used for undue personal and corporate enrichment, at the expense of dependent customers. How can this mushrooming monopoly be contained?

Separation of the 77 combination electric-gas utilities would permit competition among suppliers of heat, if not electricity, in practically all areas of the country. However, the only way in which a degree of competition with its salutary effect on prices can be injected into electric power is through the indirect competition and example offered by the customer-controlled power systems. Most of the big power battles in Congress involve this point. Here's why:

Many of the consumer-controlled systems do not generate all or even any of their own electricity. Instead, they buy it at wholesale from the federal government, which does not retail electricity, or from the investor-owned utilities. Public bodies and cooperatives have preference right to purchase federally generated power. Congress granted the preference long ago as a means toward obtaining widespread use and low cost of power and to prevent complete monopolization.

The preference does not relate to the cost of federally generated power. The private industries and investor-owned utilities that buy some 22% of the federal power output * pay the same price as the public and co-op systems that have first call. Nor does the preference clause assure any wholesale purchaser that there will be additional power for its expanding needs.[6]

Even if federally generated wholesale power is available to the public and co-op distribution systems, they still cannot necessarily serve their customers. First they must get the power into their service area, over one of the big transmission lines, and step down the voltage so it can be sent over their smaller distribution lines.

Most of the big transmission lines are owned by the investor-owned utilities. If the transmission line serving a co-op or municipal is owned by an I.O.U., the latter may agree, for a price, to transmit the power to the distributing co-op or city system. If the I.O.U. does not want to sell the power to the public system or the co-op—well, it's as if a chain food store that was engaged in both the wholesale and retail business refused to

---

* Generation of power by the federal government is declining relatively— from 15% of the nation's total during the 1950s to 13%. It may decline more still, because most federal power generation is hydroelectric and there are not many good dam sites on which either the federal government or a private utility has not already put a dam. Then, too, the growing demand for preservation of wild rivers, fish spawning grounds, and other river-related resources will probably result in construction of fewer dams which, from an engineering viewpoint, are feasible. Thus, if federal generation of power is to regain and maintain the percentage of the market it once had, the power will have to be generated by some other methods. These might include, to the horror of *Electrical World,* combination desalinization-nuclear-power plants.

sell to a small retail grocer, who was unable to buy wholesale anywhere else. The small grocer's customers would have to get their bread and beans from the big store, instead.

Thus, as Federal Power Commissioner Charles R. Ross put it bluntly, "it is the parties who control the transmission, the arteries of the industry, that control the destiny of the millions of rate-payers of this nation."

". . . There has to be some method," he said, "under which the retail sellers . . . can be guaranteed the right to use these facilities at a reasonable cost. Otherwise, these very same retail sellers will be at the absolute mercy of the owners of the transmission systems." [7]

Practically every session of Congress, there are battles over two fundamental issues—producing enough federal power so that customer-controlled power systems, most of them small, can buy at least part of their power supply through exercise of the preference clause, and second, providing access for them to transmission lines so the purchasers can transmit the power home.

In 1965, despite the united opposition of the investor-owned utility lobby, Congress authorized and voted initial funds for the Dickey-Lincoln Dam on the St. John River in Maine. Unless the I.O.U. lobby blocks construction, New England, the highest-cost power region in the nation, will for the first time have a federal hydroelectric project, by which the performance of the investor-owned utilities can be judged and from which low-priced wholesale power can be purchased by public and co-operative systems, provided I.O.U.s agree to reasonable transmission agreements—or the federal government constructs a transmission line.

It does not make sense to construct costly duplicating transmission lines, any more than it would to string small distribution lines to your house from two different companies. A prohibition against construction of a duplicating federal transmission line frequently has been written into the appropriations affecting the U.S. Bureau of Reclamation. This provision, dating from 1952 and referred to as the Keating Amendment, goes beyond prevention of duplication, however. It prohibits the Bureau of Reclamation from building a transmission line to serve preference customers in areas where investor-owned utilities have agreed to wheel the power. Whether or not the I.O.U.'s transmission service is adequate or the price reasonable, the federal government cannot build a transmission line anywhere in the area.

As a consequence, some customer-controlled power systems have been unable to obtain the power to which they are entitled from the I.O.U. on whose transmission they depend. In other cases, the investor-owned utilities have charged them far above the cost of transmission, far more than it would have cost to construct another transmission line.

In California, where a T.V.A.-sized investor-owned utility, Pacific Gas & Electric, had a monopoly on transmission lines, municipal power systems were charged millions of dollars more than an additional transmission system for them would have cost. On the other hand, the Sacramento Municipal Utility District built its own eight-mile transmission line and will, as a consequence, save a staggering $200 million over a 50-year period.[8]

The power-distribution systems that cannot get wholesale power at reasonable rates are in the same fix that Englishmen were in back in the 17th century when ferryboat operators overcharged them, leading Lord Hale to lay down the basic rule of regulation. Today, obtaining electricity is more important than crossing a river, and no utility ought to be permitted to gouge the customers who must have power. The goal of power transmission in America today, whether reached through negotiation, regulation, or legislation, must be to permit all electricity, whether produced by Reddy Kilowatt, Uncle Sam,

Willie Wired Hand or the city light plant, access for the same fare onto the transmission highways.

Some of the transmission grids being put together by investor-owned utilities have shown little enthusiasm for including other types of power systems. One such grouping is Mid-Continent Area Power Planners (MAPP), covering a 10-state area, whose formation was announced in 1963.

MAPP excluded the Bureau of Reclamation, which markets a substantial amount of power in the Midwest, from all initial planning. *St. Louis Post-Dispatch* reporter Rufus Terral asked MAPP Chairman Earl Ewald, the executive vice president of Northern State Power (Minnesota) whether municipals would be accepted as members. The response was negative. That, said Ewald, "would require too many members on committees."

"MAPP is predominantly political in nature and obstructionist in purpose," editorialized the *St. Louis Post-Dispatch.* "It emerges as a hastily pasted together paper grid . . . that . . . could eventually be used to force many of the 600 municipal systems, 77 of them in Missouri alone, into selling out to the companies." [9]

Another power pool, WEST (Western Energy Supply and Transmission Associates), formed in the fall of 1964 by 10 I.O.U.s serving parts of nine Southwestern states, specifically excluded rural electric cooperatives and federal power suppliers.[10] WEST did originally include municipals, however, and now cooperates with co-ops and federal power systems.

In sharp contrast with the lack of some needed transmission lines, duplication of the smaller distribution lines is common in many parts of the nation. Drive into America's rural heartland and you see the front lines of the closest thing to real competition that exists in the power industry. The fight is real, the battlefield marked by utility poles going up across the street from those of another power supplier, or miles of lineless poles that serve no customers, extending deep into the territory of another power system.

Rural electrics seek and investor-owned utilities oppose state legislation that would establish territorial boundaries for rural electric cooperatives. The I.O.U.s usually win these state legislative battles. Thus in most states the fringe areas of competitive service are no-man's-land. Customers are served by whichever power supplier can secure and hold a beachhead or launch a successful invasion.

As in genuine war, cost is inconsequential to a power company bent on destroying its competitors. Alabama Power spent more than half a million dollars building lines across the street from those of the 800-member Covington Electric Co-op in Samson, Alabama. The Co-op sought an injunction. The Alabama Supreme Court ruled late in 1964 that a cooperative has no right to relief where a power company begins to construct lines and facilities within a town served by a co-op.

California Electric Power showed no interest in serving Death Valley, which it had a long-standing certificate to serve, until the Amargosa Valley co-op asked for a certificate to serve the area. Then California Electric Power turned over its rights in Death Valley to Southern California Edison, which rushed crews into the area. Southern California Edison admitted to the California Public Utilities Commission that it would lose $25,000 a year serving Death Valley—a bargain price for stopping a customer-owned power system.

Close associations with other industries pay off for the investor-owned utilities in territorial disputes. South Louisiana Electric Cooperative of Houma, Louisiana, had a line 50 feet from a small plant operated by Transcontinental Gas Pipe Line Corporation. The co-op offered to serve the industry. The pipeline company declined the offer and asked Louisiana Power & Light to serve it instead. Unlike the co-op, the I.O.U. did not have any distribution lines in the area—its nearest were 15 miles away. So the I.O.U. brought in some mobile generators to serve the pipeline company and a Shell Oil plant, which also had declined co-op service. Then, at a cost of hundreds of thousands of dollars, the utility acquired right-of-way and built lines and a substation to serve the industrial loads in co-op territory.

In 1964, Texas Electric Service started selling power to an oil company in an area served by Lone Wolf Electric Cooperative since 1947. Texas Electric officials said the oil company insisted on obtaining service from the investor-owned utility.

Hiram Walker & Sons, a distillery, asked Western Illinois Electric Co-op to provide additional electric service, then reneged after investor-owned Union Electric complained. The Illinois Commerce Commission upheld the co-op's right to provide the power, but the appeal had cost the co-op more than $10,000.

Similarly, American Telephone and Telegraph asked the Egyptian Electric Cooperative Association to serve a microwave site at Walsh, Illinois, then reversed itself and told the co-op that Illinois Power would serve the site. The co-op had a line at the site and could have provided service for $1,500, about one tenth the cost to Illinois Power for bringing in a line.

In Florida, elementary safety rules seemed secondary to a utility in its eagerness to invade co-op territory. In 1962, construction started on a new gymnasium at the Shadeville school, which Talquin Electric Co-op has served since 1948. The co-op had put its lines outside the playground area to avoid a hazard to children. Florida Power Corporation decided it should serve the new gym. So it strung a line from two miles away directly down the center of the play area, to the gymnasium. The school as well as the co-op protested, and the company rolled up its line.

In these border skirmishes between I.O.U.s and co-ops there are even night forays into "enemy" territory. One November

day in 1962, a crew from a North Carolina co-op surveyed
lines needed to serve homes under construction within the
co-op's territory near Gastonia. That night a crew from Duke
Power, with searchlights, built a section of line near where the
homes would be built. The co-op protested and the company
agreed to take down the lines, presumably by daylight.[11]

The power-company line crews, probing into a competi-
tor's territory, are the infantry in the fights between power suppliers. The utility public-relations people concentrate on a
more sophisticated counter-intelligence approach. Their mission: to create a climate in which a city or co-op will sell its
power system to an I.O.U. The usual pattern of a sellout
campaign was described by Mayor Benjamin Friedman of
Taunton, Massachusetts:

1. A power company selects a victim. . . .

2. A quiet campaign is launched to win over one or more city
councilmen who will side with the power company or elect ones
who will. This gives the power company a source of inside information.

3. Suddenly a carefully selected "citizens committee" is formed
which gives advice to one and all on how the municipal utility
should be operated, with an "expert authorities" report that recommends that the city should let the power company take over the
system on its own terms.

4. The "citizens committee" circulates a petition and presents it
to the city officials, demanding that they "invite" the power company to submit an offer to lease the electric system.

5. The "citizens committee" puts on a membership drive to
get a large number of people to high pressure the city officials into
"inviting" a buy-out proposal by a power company or at least a
lease-out proposal on the most attractive terms. A referendum
date is set.

6. The power company comes out in the open with an offer
to lease the system, promising lower rates, 30 years franchises,
etc.; but no mention is made as to where the city will get the ad-

ditional money for the general fund when it loses its electric system.
Power company employees and hired workers then descend like
locusts on the city, urging all the voters to vote in favor of their
proposal. Ads will appear; the air will be filled with radio and TV
commercials; the mails will be used to swamp the voters with
letters; and cocktail parties will be given for citizens. The idea is
to dazzle the people with promises of some sort of electrical para-
dise. The city operation will be belittled and lied about.

7. At the time of the election, a spirited campaign will be waged
by the power company by a well directed organization and campaign, doing all that is possible to win the election.[12]

During the six-year period from 1958 through 1963, there
were at least 28 municipal elections on sellout or lease-out of
city-owned power systems to investor-owned systems. In 14
instances, sellout or lease-out was approved. Officials of five
cities refused the company proposal without putting the matter
to referendum. In one city (Bloomington, Illinois), officials
sold the municipal system despite four previous votes against
selling by city residents.

Mayor Friedman could have added an eighth step to the sellout campaign: If you can't buy now, try later. Power-company
persistence sometimes pays off. Voters of Dunkirk, New York,
turned down Niagara Mohawk's purchase proposal in 1950,
narrowly approved a much higher offer in 1957. Residential
rates went up within a year after the purchase and have risen
again since.

In 1957, the voters of Winnetka, Illinois, narrowly defeated
a purchase proposal by Commonwealth Edison, which offered
$3.4 million for Winnetka's municipal system. That $3.4
million would have produced an annual income of about
$114,000 for the city, only about half the plant's annual earn-
ings. In 1964, the Winnetka plant earned $466,000, about
four times as much as it would have realized annually had it
sold out.

It is a different story in nearby Woodstock, Illinois. Twice that community rejected overtures from Commonwealth Edison, then, in 1960, Woodstock sold its power system to the I.O.U. Since the sale, rates have increased. So have Woodstock's local taxes. Woodstock received $627 in taxes from Commonwealth Edison in 1964, in contrast with the $80,000 it obtained in revenue and street-lighting service during the last year of municipal operation. Mayor Frances Kuhn, late in 1965, told how sale of the power plant hurt her city:

> The company said the old plant building would be worth $150,000; we managed to get $30,000 for it. The company was going to put its substation in the city limits so we would get taxes on it. They didn't. We have fewer residential street lights, the lights on our Christmas display in the town square—which the city electric department used to put up and light free—have been cut in half and it still costs us money ... And we need a new city hall, but where is the money coming from? [13]

Woodstock had sold the goose that laid the golden eggs. What is even more important, the yardstick of competition in the supply of electric power was whittled down by Woodstock's sale, and by similar sellouts around the country.

Monopoly abhors competition; through the years even the threat of competition has forced significant rate reductions. For example:

Item. Some years ago Consolidated Edison, serving New York City, reduced its rates even though the courts had overturned a rate reduction ordered by the Public Service Commission. Why did Con Ed cut the rates anyhow? Because Mayor Fiorello La Guardia was going ahead with plans for a municipal yardstick plant in New York City (which, of course, has not yet materialized).

Item. Potomac Electric, serving Washington, D.C., once agreed to a sliding scale formula which reduced its residential rates twice as fast as those in the U.S. as a whole, because the company faced the prospect of a federal hydroelectric dam (which has not been built) at Great Falls on the Potomac River.

Item. The Hill County Electric Cooperative in Montana used to be dependent on Montana Power for its wholesale power supply. The company charged the co-op 9½ mills per kilowatt-hour and refused to transmit to the co-op power from a federal Bureau of Reclamation line to which the company had access. When Congress voted funds for a transmission line to serve the co-op, Montana Power immediately slashed its rates to the co-op almost in half, from 9½ mills to 5½ mills. The company's rate cut had been too long delayed, though, and Hill County Electric Cooperative soon got power direct from the Bureau of Reclamation.

Item. In 1962, Georgia Power paid the city of Rome, Georgia, $50,000 for its agreement "not to establish a municipal electric system in competition with" the company.[14]

A strong, competitive public power yardstick helps investor-owned utilities. Look at the record of the nine big investor-owned utilities bordering the Tennessee Valley Authority. Their annual common stock earnings in 1963 were 12 times higher than they had been in 1937–1939, when the Federal Power Commission first published financial data.* Common stock earnings of all major power companies increased but fivefold during this period—less than half as much.[15] T.V.A. is required by Congress to charge "the lowest possible rates" consistent with a financial policy that will make the power system "self-supporting and self-liquidating." The adjacent investor-owned utilities had cut their rates to look good alongside T.V.A. And they had discovered, to the surprise of some com-

---

* The companies are Alabama Power, Appalachian Power, Arkansas Power, Carolina Power & Light, Duke Power, Georgia Power, Kentucky Utilities, Mississippi Power, and Mississippi Power & Light.

pany officials, that a low-rate policy is good business. This elementary fact holds true for investor-owned utilities within T.V.A. territory as well. "We are a private power company, but completely pro-T.V.A.," President Lawrence Howard of Franklin (Tennessee) Power & Light said recently. "We buy power wholesale from T.V.A. and sell power retail at T.V.A.'s lowest rate . . . and make money all the time." [16]

President Howard will never get invited to make such straightforward comments before the Edison Electric Institute. The value of the yardstick of competition, and commonsense principles of pricing, have escaped the giants of the power industry.

Thomas Edison and Benjamin Franklin would both be pleased, however, to see how their product is merchandised by little old Franklin Power & Light.

Chapter 22.

INFORMATION

Early on a spring morning in 1964, Chairman James A. Washington of the District of Columbia Public Utilities Commission walked into his office at 1625 "I" Street N.W. prepared to discuss utility affairs with the public. He had invited 86 civic and citizens' associations to an informal discussion of the way the Commission regulates electric, telephone, gas, and taxicab industries in the nation's capital.

The initial response to the invitation had indicated that the meeting would not have to be switched to a larger room to accommodate the crowd. Only four of the 86 organizations had even responded to his letter. Perhaps, though, other groups that had been invited would appear.

As it turned out, the meeting could have been held in a taxicab. Only one organization—the Palisades Citizens Association—sent a delegation . . . three persons.[1] Seemingly, the public did not care what the Commission did.

The experience of the District of Columbia Commission is not exceptional; it is typical. The public is apathetic about utility services.

It is not because the public does not care about overcharges in the utility bills. Rather, the consumers usually do not know about them, or how to get rid of them.

They didn't learn in school how utilities differ from risk enterprises. They haven't read in the papers about the growing spread between the cost and the price of electricity. They have been lulled by the incessant utility advertisements into the belief that power companies are taxpaying, competitive free enterprises that somehow, despite Big Government, manage to make and market electricity at bargain rates. And some consumers have been cowed by the propaganda of the extremist organizations financed in part by investor-owned utilities. Is it unpatriotic, un-American, they wonder, to criticize the I.O.U.s?

The public needs to know why power companies never fail, nor fail to make a profit, why their profits often exceed those of risk industries, why consumers do not get refunds of overcharges, how the utilities keep taxes, and how restricted stock options dilute the equity of ordinary electric-utility stockholders.

The public needs to know what is in the rate bases on which the utility gets its percentage, what retainers and extremist organizations are on the utility payroll that is met by the customers, how much the actual rate of return exceeds the rate of return "allowed" by the regulatory commission.

The public needs to know why the return on common stock

is often double the rate of return, how hundreds of millions of dollars in tax-free dividends are distributed by utilities, how millions of dollars worth of capital are obtained from customers by the utilities and retained.

In short, the Big Blackout on utility operations needs to be lifted and the picture of the electric-power business projected —right side up—in the classroom, in the press, and in the precincts.

Appendix A.

CUMULATIVE R.E.A. LOANS TO COMMERCIAL POWER COMPANIES AS OF JUNE 1, 1966 *

Name & Address of Borrower	Total Loans Approved	Date of First Loan	Date Repaid
Arkansas Power & Light Pine Bluff, Ark.	$ 523,000	9/8/37	10/30/44
Central Iowa Power Des Moines, Iowa	5,617	9/24/35	11/8/46
Earl W. Baker Utilities Bethany, Okla.	185,721	11/23/35	1/8/51
Fidelity Gas Minneapolis, Minn.	556,577	4/16/46	
Florida Power St. Petersburg, Fla.	164,500	10/24/35	1/4/51
Florida Public Service St. Petersburg, Fla.	47,690	5/21/36	1/20/44
Georgia Power & Light St. Petersburg, Fla.	107,406	10/24/35	1/3/51
Kentucky Rural Electric Louisville, Ky.	1,774	10/1/35	7/3/41
Louisiana Ice & Electric Alexandria, La.	50,000	3/22/39	4/4/41
Louisiana Rural Electric Pineville, La.	8,447,000	12/31/48	
Missouri Gen. Utilities Rolla, Mo.	35,110	9/21/36	9/1/45
Montana-Dakota Utilities Minneapolis, Minn.	5,043,072	3/2/49	
New York State Elec. & Gas Ithaca, N.Y.	1,863,618	3/21/38	12/1/43
Ocracoke Power & Light Ocracoke, N.C.	30,731	5/12/37	Foreclosed
Ohio-Midland Light & Power Canal Winchester, Ohio	6,242,532	4/29/48	5/16/62

* Source: Rural Electrification Administration, U.S. Department of Agriculture.

Name & Address of Borrower	Approved Total Loans	Date of First Loan	Date Repaid
Pamlico Ice & Light Englehard, N.C.	32,196	12/1/37	5/2/50
Public Service Co. of Ind. Indianapolis, Ind.	430,000	11/9/38	12/31/41
Sheridan Suburban Electric Sheridan, Wyo.	78,700	6/30/39	7/24/47
Stonewall Electric Albuquerque, N.M.	134,498	1/16/41	11/30/50
Stonewall Electric Trinidad, Colo.	100,000	5/18/39	9/26/46
Suburban Electric Dunlap, Ill.	81,173	9/24/35	9/15/38
Tidewater Elec. Service West Point, Va.	192,886	4/25/36	5/27/47
Tide Water Power Wilmington, N.C.	131,277	8/24/35	3/31/52
Utility Services Hoisington, Kans.	5,784	3/31/37	4/14/44
White Mountain Power Meredith, N.H.	200,000	5/26/49	
Total number borrowers: 25	$24,690,862		

Twenty of the power companies have retired their R.E.A. loans in full. Four are still active R.E.A. borrowers, and one has been foreclosed. The Louisiana Rural Electric Corporation has repaid $1,155,678 in principal and $1,043,167 in interest; the Fidelity Gas Company has repaid $539,533 in principal and $111,971 in interest; the White Mountain Power Company has repaid $69,628 in principal and $47,341 in interest; and the Montana-Dakota Utilities Co. has repaid $1,751,986 in principal and $1,149,297 in interest. The loan to the Ocracoke Power & Light Company was foreclosed by R.E.A. 12/28/44, at a loss of $37,230. This included $30,731 principal and interest of $6,499.

Note: Two-percent-interest R.E.A. loans are also made to both investor-owned and cooperative telephone systems. As of Jan. 1, 1966, R.E.A. had made 620 loans to investor-owned telephone companies and 225 loans to customer-owned telephone cooperatives.

Appendix B.

MAJOR ELECTRIC-UTILITY HOLDING COMPANIES AND ELECTRIC-UTILITY SUBSIDIARIES *

ALLEGHENY POWER SYSTEM, New York, N.Y.

Cumberland Valley Electric, Mercersburg, Pa.
Monongahela Power, Fairmont, W.Va. (which controls and operates)
   Marietta Electric, Marietta, Ohio,
   Monterey Utilities, Monterey, Va., and
   West Maryland Power, Oakland, Md.
Potomac Edison, Frederick, Md. (which controls and operates)
   Northern Virginia Power, Winchester, Va.,
   Potomac Light & Power, Martinsburg, W.Va., and
   South Penn Power, Waynesboro, Pa.
West Penn Power

AMERICAN ELECTRIC POWER, New York, N.Y.

Appalachian Power, Roanoke, Va.
Indiana & Michigan Electric, Fort Wayne, Ind.
Kentucky Power, Ashland, Ky.
Kingsport Power, Kingsport, Tenn.
Ohio Power, Canton, Ohio
Wheeling Electric, Wheeling, W.Va.

CENTRAL & SOUTHWEST, Wilmington, Del.

Central Power & Light, Corpus Christi, Tex.
Public Service Co. of Oklahoma, Tulsa, Okla.
Southwestern Electric Power, Shreveport, La.
West Texas Utilities, Abilene, Tex.

DELAWARE POWER & LIGHT, Wilmington, Del.

Eastern Shore Public Service Company of Maryland
Eastern Shore Public Service Company of Virginia

* *Source: Directory of Electric Utilities* (New York: McGraw-Hill, 1965).

EASTERN UTILITIES ASSOCIATES, Boston, Mass.

Blackstone Valley Electric, Pawtucket, R.I.
Brockton Edison, Brockton, Mass.
Fall River Electric Light, Fall River, Mass.

GENERAL PUBLIC UTILITIES, New York, N.Y.

Jersey Central Power & Light, Morristown, N.J.
Metropolitan Edison, Reading, Pa.
New Jersey Power & Light, Morristown, N.J.
Pennsylvania Electric, Johnstown, Pa.

MIDDLE SOUTH UTILITIES, New York, N.Y.

Arkansas Power & Light, Pine Bluff, Ark.
Louisiana Power & Light, New Orleans, La.
Mississippi Power & Light, Jackson, Miss.
New Orleans Public Service, New Orleans, La.

NEW ENGLAND ELECTRIC SYSTEM, Boston, Mass.

Granite State Electric, Lebanon, N.H.
Massachusetts Electric, Boston, Mass.
Narragansett Electric, Providence, R.I.
New England Power, Boston, Mass.

OHIO EDISON, Akron, Ohio

Pennsylvania Power, New Castle, Pa.

PHILADELPHIA ELECTRIC, Philadelphia, Pa.

Conowingo Power, Elktown, Md.
Philadelphia Electric Power, Philadelphia, Pa.
Susquehanna Electric, Philadelphia, Pa.
Susquehanna Power, Philadelphia, Pa.

SOUTHERN COMPANY, Atlanta, Georgia

Alabama Power, Birmingham, Ala.
Georgia Power, Atlanta, Ga.
Gulf Power, Pensacola, Fla.
Mississippi Power, Gulfport, Miss.

TEXAS UTILITIES, Dallas, Tex.

Dallas Power & Light, Dallas, Tex.
Texas Electric Service, Fort Worth, Tex.
Texas Power & Light, Dallas, Tex.

UNION ELECTRIC, St. Louis, Mo.

Missouri Edison, Louisiana, Mo.
Missouri Power & Light, Jefferson City, Mo.

UTAH POWER & LIGHT, Salt Lake City, Utah

Western Colorado Power, Montrose, Colo.

WISCONSIN ELECTRIC, Milwaukee, Wis.

Wisconsin Michigan Power, Appleton, Wis.

RATE OF RETURN AND RETURN ON EQUITY
OF MAJOR ELECTRIC UTILITIES

Service Area	Company	Rate of Return				Return on Equity		
		1961	1962	1963	1964	1962	1963	1964
Ala.	Alabama Power	7.11	7.08	7.01	7.33		13.13	14.41
Tenn., Va., W.Va.	Appalachian Power	6.73	7.55	7.40	7.36		19.35	16.78
Ariz.	Arizona Public Service	6.65	6.63	6.23	5.83		10.18	10.64
Ark., Mo.	Arkansas-Missouri Power [1]	6.23	7.63	7.38	7.81		13.03	14.21
Ark., La., Mo., Tenn.	Arkansas P. & L.	6.53	6.64	6.84	7.22		12.56	13.87
N.J.	Atlantic City Electric	7.00	6.69	6.75	6.63		13.17	13.91
Md.	Baltimore G. & E.	6.91	6.61	6.83	7.07		10.92	11.34
Me.	Bangor Hydro-Electric	6.73	6.98	6.98	6.98		11.66	11.88
S.D., Wyo.	Black Hills P. & L.	7.75	7.09	6.95	6.49		12.46	10.12
R.I.	Blackstone Valley G. & E.	11.38	10.74	11.18	9.00		14.41	11.95
Mass.	Boston Edison [2]	6.70	6.88	7.24	7.07		10.70	10.87
Mass.	Brockton Edison	7.78	7.95	9.63	8.73		12.26	12.87
Ariz., Calif., Nev., Ore., Utah	California Pacific Utilities	6.01	5.28	5.66	6.56		8.64	10.20
Mass.	Cambridge Elec. Light	7.75	7.84	8.22	8.05		10.58	10.61
Mass.	Cape & Vineyard Electric	7.23	7.88	7.84	8.59		10.62	12.21
N.C., S.C.	Carolina P. & L.	6.73	6.88	6.98	7.39		12.83	13.26
N.Y.	Central Hudson G. & E.	6.43	6.46	6.48	6.63		11.10	12.23
Ill.	Central Illinois E. & G.	8.58	8.58	8.73	9.66		18.86	20.51
Ill.	Central Illinois Light	6.30	7.57	8.12	8.10		13.51	14.09
Ill.	Central Illinois Pub. Serv. [3]	8.25	8.35	8.87	9.00		17.50	17.76
Kans.	Central Kansas Power	6.20	6.54	6.42	7.33		10.40	12.12

260

State	Company						
La.	Central Louisiana Electric	8.15	8.46	8.71	8.90	15.18	15.85
Me.	Central Maine Power	5.95	6.02	6.12	6.29	9.92	10.26
Tex.	Central P. & L.	8.02	8.63	8.75	9.00	16.60	17.15
N.Y., Vt.	Central Vermont Pub. Serv.	6.05	6.03	6.07	6.38	10.29	11.74
Wyo.	Cheyenne Light, Fuel & Power	9.82	8.65	8.05	7.15	4.60	9.91
Ohio	Cincinnati G. & E.	8.07	7.28	7.53	8.07	14.38	15.78
Ariz., Idaho, Vt.	Citizens Utilities	7.24	7.38	9.44	10.28	4.28	11.39
Ohio	Cleveland Elec. Illuminating	7.13	6.91	7.02	7.48	13.12	13.59
Ohio	Columbus & Southern Ohio Electric [4]	6.86	5.91	6.69	6.85	12.90	12.83
Ill.	Commonwealth Edison	7.84	7.85	7.89	8.15	13.17	13.14
Ind.	Commonwealth Edison of Indiana	6.11	6.91	6.65	6.68	11.69	11.20
N.M., Tex.	Community Public Service	8.65	9.14	9.08	9.34	15.54	17.32
Conn.	Connecticut L. & P.[5]	6.69	6.71	6.65	6.75	10.64	11.57
Md.	Conowingo Power	4.89	4.90	5.65	4.99	7.86	7.16
N.Y.	Consolidated Edison of N.Y.	5.36	5.40	5.18	5.48	7.76	8.16
Wis.	Consolidated Water Power	8.63	7.28	2.61	3.84	2.12	2.89
Mich.	Consumers Power	6.82	6.73	6.98	7.51	12.75	13.42
Tex.	Dallas P. & L.	7.40	7.98	9.33	8.44	17.08	14.72
Ohio	Dayton P. & L.[6]	7.40	7.52	7.55	8.16	12.30	13.34
Del.	Delaware P. & L.	6.42	6.73	7.21	7.48	15.84	15.50
Mich.	Detroit Edison	6.84	7.08	7.43	7.92	12.16	12.85
N.C., S.C.	Duke Power	6.78	7.54	6.98	7.41	11.03	11.78
Pa.	Duquesne Light	7.42	7.51	7.67	7.93	16.07	16.35
Md.	Eastern Shore Pub. Serv. of Md.	6.12	4.80	5.18	5.44	5.76	6.29
Mich.	Edison Sault Electric	9.31	9.59	9.43	10.00	16.63	17.45
N.M., Tex.	El Paso Electric	8.36	8.98	9.20	9.52	18.98	18.74
Ill., Ky.	Electric Energy	3.53	3.56	3.51	3.52	3.90	4.12
Ark., Kans., Mo., Okla.	Empire District Electric	7.13	7.88	8.07	8.22	15.93	13.48
Mass.	Fall River Elec. Light	7.04	8.16	9.59	7.44	9.42	7.74
Mass.	Fitchburg G. & E. Light	7.01	7.03	6.83	6.98	8.70	9.08

261

See page 267 for notes.

| | | | Rate of Return | | | | Return on Equity | |
Service Area	Company	1961	1962	1963	1964	1963	1964
Fla.	Florida Power	7.54	8.08	7.87	7.91	14.88	13.74
Fla.	Florida P. & L.	7.74	8.32	8.31	8.72	13.29	13.70
Ga.	Georgia Power	6.88	7.26	6.94	7.35	14.27	14.97
Vt.	Green Mountain Power	6.57	6.79	6.76	6.76	10.98	12.33
Fla.	Gulf Power	7.36	7.59	7.73	8.18	14.72	15.36
La., Tex.	Gulf States Utilities	6.97	7.56	7.41	7.54	14.29	14.38
Conn.	Hartford Elec. Light	5.73	6.15	7.03	6.93	12.44	13.70
Mass.	Holyoke P. & E.	10.39	5.83	5.71	6.00	6.73	7.09
Mass.	Holyoke Water Power	10.03	7.30	7.61	8.03	10.11	9.91
Colo.	Home L. & P.	7.56	7.51	8.01	8.62	11.75	12.65
Tex.	Houston Lighting & Power	7.50	8.62	9.45	9.97	15.91	16.08
Idaho, Nev., Ore.	Idaho Power	6.14	5.83	6.45	6.62	11.21	11.93
Ill.	Illinois Power	8.24	8.58	9.18	8.99	17.73	18.62
Ind.	Indiana-Kentucky Electric	3.67	3.65	3.64	3.62	*	
Ind., Mich.	Indiana-Michigan Electric	6.05	6.55	6.91	7.43	20.83	22.27
Ind.	Indianapolis P. & L.[7]	7.95	8.31	8.26	8.53	16.00	15.61
Ill., Iowa, Minn., S.D.	Interstate Power	7.51	7.30	7.14	7.18	13.07	13.53
Iowa	Iowa Electric L. & P.	7.73	8.06	8.06	7.95	15.08	14.30
Ill., Iowa	Iowa-Illinois G. & E.	7.70	7.51	8.14	8.70	15.69	16.08
Iowa	Iowa P. & L.	6.14	6.17	6.28	6.28	14.99	15.01
Iowa, S.D.	Iowa Pub. Serv.	6.99	7.06	7.36	7.25	15.89	13.84
Iowa	Iowa Southern Utilities	7.08	7.99	8.09	8.07	13.54	14.43
N.J.	Jersey Central P. & L.	6.80	6.52	6.94	7.03	10.65	11.15
Kans., Mo.	Kansas City P. & L.	6.69	7.00	7.31	7.36	14.26	13.18
Kans.	Kansas G. & E.	6.74	7.02	7.50	7.56	13.19	12.84
Kans.	Kansas P. & L.	7.80	8.03	8.12	9.14	14.13	14.73

* Indiana-Kentucky Electric, a wholly-owned subsidiary of Ohio Valley Electric, reported no net income.

Kentucky Power	Ky.	7.85	9.90	9.62	8.01	11.04	13.93
Kentucky Utilities	Ky., Tenn.	7.72	7.85	8.08	8.37	13.02	13.88
Kingsport Power	Tenn.	6.49	6.94	6.31	6.53	9.19	10.09
Lake Superior District Power	Mich., Wis.	6.78	6.89	6.81	6.92	8.94	9.39
Long Island Lighting [8]	N.Y.	6.97	6.72	6.41	7.09	10.93	12.02
Louisiana P. & L.	La.	7.25	7.31	7.40	7.89	14.94	15.75
Louisville G. & E.	Ky.	8.00	8.13	8.10	8.56	12.46	12.88
Madison G. & E.	Wis.	7.42	7.25	7.50	7.43	9.13	9.74
Maine Public Service	Me.	7.44	7.03	8.00	6.85	13.10	10.43
Marietta Electric	Ohio	5.98	5.95	6.35	6.56	6.21	6.48
Massachusetts Electric [9]	Mass.	7.87	5.80	5.43	5.39	6.45	6.40
Metropolitan Edison	Pa.	7.23	7.10	7.32	7.63	12.00	12.91
Michigan G. & E.	Mich.	9.43	8.40	9.04	9.03	16.05	15.70
Minnesota P. & L.	Minn.	6.08	6.26	6.27	6.39	13.98	13.67
Mississippi Power	Miss.	7.64	8.11	7.88	7.78	15.78	14.69
Mississippi P. & L.	Miss.	6.88	6.97	7.13	7.21	13.90	14.42
Missouri Edison	Mo.	7.60	7.70	7.25	7.79	10.66	14.21
Missouri P. & L.	Mo.	6.62	7.44	7.21	7.44	15.24	16.96
Missouri Pub. Serv.	Mo.	5.82	6.14	6.17	6.70	11.64	12.33
Missouri Utilities	Mo.	6.23	6.80	7.36	6.51	10.19	12.66
Monongahela Power	W.Va.	6.96	7.18	7.31	7.32	14.00	14.01
Montana-Dakota Utilities	Mont., N.D., S.D., Wyo.; Canada	5.34	5.42	6.42	6.52	10.72	10.73
Montana Power	Idaho, Mont., Wyo.	9.78	10.12	10.24	10.92	17.54	17.49
Montaup Electric	Mass.	5.79	5.64	6.85	5.85	9.00	6.67
Nantahala P. & L.	N.C.	5.72	9.20	9.88	10.12	11.29	11.43
Narragansett Electric	R.I.	4.96	4.77	4.84	5.18	6.59	8.09
Nevada Power [10]	Nev.	8.39	7.79	8.21	8.23	14.94	14.27
New Bedford G. & E.	Mass.	7.54	8.12	7.87	7.20	9.43	8.86
New England Power	Mass., N.H., Vt.	4.51	5.95	6.52	6.46	11.43	10.89
New Hampshire Electric	N.H.	6.49	6.51	6.08	6.05	6.44	6.49

263

See page 267 for notes.

Service Area	Company	Rate of Return				Return on Equity	
		1961	1962	1963	1964	1963	1964
N.J.	New Jersey P. & L.	6.85	6.66	6.82	6.75	12.33	11.89
N.M.	New Mexico Elec. Serv.	9.29	9.25	9.57	9.99	13.01	12.66
La.	New Orleans Pub. Serv.	10.88	12.27	13.04	13.17	12.86	12.82
N.Y.	New York State E. & G.	6.91	6.78	6.67	6.77	11.78	12.40
R.I.	Newport Electric	7.28	7.13	7.56	8.30	11.74	13.37
N.Y.	Niagara Mohawk Power	5.66	5.85	5.82	5.82	11.12	11.38
Ind.	Northern Indiana Pub. Serv.	8.59	8.38	8.37	8.81	16.22	16.38
Minn., N.D., S.D.	Northern States Power (Minn.)	7.44	8.05	8.34	8.07	14.81	15.23
Wis.	Northern States Power (Wis.)	6.55	6.63	6.54	6.60	5.70	7.16
Va.	Northern Virginia Power	5.36	5.51	5.35	5.46	5.37	5.47
S.D.	Northwestern Pub. Serv.	8.13	7.29	8.97	8.57	16.36	17.83
Ohio	Ohio Edison	7.32	6.96	7.33	7.93	14.26	14.72
Ohio	Ohio Power	6.59	6.77	7.26	7.47	20.27	19.41
Ohio	Ohio Valley Electric	4.15	4.13	4.14	4.10	8.00	8.00
Ark., Okla.	Oklahoma G. & E.	6.75	7.47	8.04	8.13	16.58	17.03
Va.	Old Dominion Power	5.19	5.70	5.26	5.13	6.17	5.97
N.Y.	Orange & Rockland Util.	6.43	6.45	6.52	7.00	11.34	13.89
Minn., N.D., S.D.	Otter Tail Power	5.93	6.14	6.77	6.39	11.76	12.26
Calif.	Pacific G. & E.	6.21	6.47	6.43	6.29	11.36	11.86
Calif., Idaho, Mont., Ore., Wash., Wyo.	Pacific P. & L.[11]	6.19	6.45	6.39	6.12	13.85	11.56
N.Y., Pa.	Pennsylvania Electric	7.13	6.71	7.06	7.07	13.27	12.74
Pa.	Pennsylvania Power	7.56	8.10	8.40	7.94	16.76	15.47
Pa.	Pennsylvania P. & L.	6.51	6.47	6.63	6.77	13.01	13.16
Pa.	Philadelphia Electric	6.27	6.44	6.55	6.93	11.76	11.95
Mass.	Plymouth County Electric	6.90	7.45	7.85	8.22	9.39	10.22
Ore.	Portland General Electric[12]	6.50	6.94	6.75	6.27	12.46	11.67
Md.	Potomac Edison	7.81	7.95	7.87	7.21	16.67	13.14

State	Company						
D.C., Md., Va.	Potomac Electric Power	6.98	6.73	6.97	6.62	9.92	10.45
W.Va.	Potomac L. & P.	6.28	6.19	6.01	5.97	6.31	6.32
Colo.	Public Service of Colo.[13]	7.83	7.48	7.68	7.66	11.95	12.84
Ind.	Public Service of Ind.	6.48	6.78	7.06	7.47	13.42	13.85
Me., N.H., Vt.	Public Service of N.H.	5.68	6.41	5.98	5.96	10.17	10.49
N.M.	Public Service of N.M.	7.95	8.09	8.11	8.07	13.74	13.39
Okla.	Public Service of Okla.	7.17	7.44	8.00	7.99	15.93	15.97
N.J.	Public Service E. & G.	7.01	7.22	7.14	7.04	12.22	12.25
Wash.	Puget Sound P. & L.	6.38	6.28	5.36	5.37	6.86	7.16
N.Y.	Rochester G. & E.	6.20	6.65	7.12	7.10	11.07	12.01
N.J.	Rockland Electric	6.75	6.52	7.24	7.34	10.37	12.15
Pa.	Safe Harbor Water Power	5.12	5.09	5.06	5.10	7.28	7.22
Mo.	St. Joseph L. & P.	8.05	8.06	8.23	7.86	11.82	11.13
Calif.	San Diego G. & E.	6.39	6.30	6.31	6.13	9.61	10.65
Ga.	Savannah E. & P.	7.48	7.22	7.37	7.96	14.33	14.91
Calif., Nev.	Sierra Pacific Power	8.83	7.99	8.92	7.55	16.31	14.42
S.C.	South Carolina E. & G.[14]	7.68	7.87	7.45	7.49	15.94	15.77
Pa.	South Penn Power	6.62	5.69	7.10	5.96	7.04	5.93
Calif., Nev.	Southern California Edison	6.71	6.61	6.64	6.55	12.60	11.98
Ala.	Southern Elec. Generating	7.67	7.97	7.94	7.72	12.96	12.40
Ind.	Southern Indiana G. & E.	6.71	6.95	7.63	8.41	13.81	14.53
Ark., La., Okla., Tex.	Southwestern Elec. Power	7.82	8.48	9.23	8.91	16.59	16.91
Tex.	Southwestern Elec. Serv.	6.74	6.76	7.13	7.28	15.01	13.35
Kans., N.M., Okla., Tex.	Southwestern Pub. Serv.	7.24	8.01	8.35	8.56	17.72	18.26
Wis.	Superior Water, L. & P.	7.65	7.47	8.05	7.25	9.66	10.04
Fla.	Tampa Electric	7.64	8.33	8.92	8.89	18.88	17.93
N.C., Tenn.	Tapoco	5.64	5.88	7.63	6.83	6.98	6.38
Tex.	Texas Elec. Serv.	8.38	8.85	9.00	8.59	17.92	16.79
Tex.	Texas P. & L.	8.51	9.06	9.67	10.22	20.73	19.48
Ohio	Toledo Edison	6.32	6.81	6.78	7.11	15.25	13.37

265

See page 267 for notes.

Service Area	Company	Rate of Return				Return on Equity	
		1961	1962	1963	1964	1963	1964
Ariz.	Tucson G. & E.	7.85	8.32	7.48	7.69	12.81	13.29
Ill., Iowa, Mo.	Union Electric	6.61	6.60	6.47	6.66	13.87	14.67
Ky.	Union Light, Heat & Power	6.48	5.93	6.04	6.77	7.47	9.42
Pa.	United Gas Improvement	5.77	5.40	5.43	6.13	8.84	9.01
Conn.	United Illuminating [15]	7.22	7.19	7.52	7.45	11.75	11.84
Idaho, Utah, Wyo.	Utah P. & L.[16]	6.17	6.20	6.33	5.65	9.59	9.73
N.C., Va., W.Va.	Virginia E. & P.	7.02	7.41	7.26	7.20	14.30	13.64
Idaho, Mont., Wash.	Washington Water Power	6.09	6.01	5.93	6.26	9.32	9.87
Pa.	West Penn Power	7.33	7.57	7.23	7.43	16.13	15.61
Tex.	West Texas Utilities	9.28	9.48	9.40	9.72	17.38	17.62
Colo.	Western Colorado Power	4.83	4.64	4.72	4.95	4.82	5.12
Kans.	Western Light & Telephone	7.07	7.56	8.20	7.95	11.38	15.24
Mass.	Western Mass. Electric	6.78	7.52	7.14	7.54	10.31	10.37
Colo.	Western Power & Gas [17]	7.26	7.41	8.25	7.57	17.34	14.80
W.Va.	Wheeling Electric	5.89	5.65	5.40	5.86	7.05	9.30
Wis.	Wisconsin Elec. Power	6.06	6.12	6.42	6.70	10.07	9.98
Mich., Wis.	Wisconsin Michigan Power	5.94	6.15	6.08	5.95	7.49	10.16
Wis.	Wisconsin P. & L.[18]	7.25	7.16	7.40	7.36	10.17	10.56
Mich., Wis.	Wisconsin Pub. Serv.	7.42	7.93	8.16	7.31	12.80	12.53
Mass.	Yankee Atomic Electric [19]	3.40	6.39	6.99	7.48	9.62	10.41

See page 267 for notes.

Notes for Appendix C.

1 Company acquired all properties of Arkansas Utilities Co. as of June 29, 1961, and the Elaine Utilities Co., Inc., as of Nov. 26, 1962.

2 The company reports depreciation for combined utilities. Rate of return for electric utility based on allocation of depreciation to electric plant on the basis of gross average electric plant to gross average total plant.

3 Company acquired Illinois Electric & Gas Co. as of Dec. 1, 1962, through merger.

4 Return reflects acquisition of certain electric transmission and distribution facilities from Ohio-Midland Light & Power Co. as of Apr. 27, 1962.

5 Company acquired the Housatonic Public Service Co. as of May 1, 1961, and the Mystic Power Co. as of Apr. 30, 1963.

6 Prior to 1964, the company reported depreciation for combined utilities. See note 2.

7 Company acquired Mooresville Public Service Co., Inc., as of May 31, 1961, through merger.

8 Long Island Lighting Co. acquired Patchogue Electric Light Co. through merger June 1, 1964.

9 Formerly Worcester County Electric Co., which as of Jan. 1, 1961, acquired through merger Attleboro Electric Co., Northampton Electric Lighting Co., Northern Berkshire Electric Co., Quincy Electric Co., Southern Berkshire Power & Electric Co., and Weymouth Light & Power Co. Subsequently, on Jan. 19, 1961, Worcester County Electric Co. changed its name to Massachusetts Electric Co. Acquired Lynn Electric Co., Merrimack-Essex Electric Co., and Suburban Electric Co., as of Sept. 1, 1962, through merger.

10 Formerly Southern Nevada Power Co., which as of Feb. 14, 1961, acquired Elko Lamoille Power Co. Subsequently, on May 26, 1961, Southern Nevada Power changed its name to Nevada Power Co.

11 Company acquired the California Oregon Power Co. through merger, and electric and water properties of Southern Wyoming Utilities Co. as of June 21, 1961, and Mar. 11, 1961, respectively.

12 Additional provision for depreciation reported as other interest expense is deducted from net operating revenue. 1961, 1962, and 1963 returns are adjusted to reflect this charge.

13 Company acquired Colorado Central Power Co. as of Dec. 29, 1961, through merger. Return reflects full year operation of the acquired company.

14 Company acquired its subsidiary, South Carolina Generating Co., through merger Oct. 31, 1963.

15 As of May 1, 1961, company acquired from the Housatonic Public Service Co. the electric business, associated properties and assets in the towns of Ansonia, Derby, and Shelton, Conn.

16 Company acquired its subsidiary Telluride Power Co. Mar. 15, 1963.

17 Formerly Central Electric & Gas Co., which on May 1, 1961, acquired through merger Southern Colorado Power Co., and the name of surviving company changed to Western Power & Gas Co.

[18] The company charges to depreciation expense an amount equivalent to the estimated reduction in Federal income taxes under sec. 167 of the 1954 Internal Revenue Code. The amount reported was for combined utilities.

[19] Company commenced commercial operations July 1, 1961.

Source: *Statistics of Electric Utilities in the United States, 1964, Privately Owned* (Washington, D.C.: Federal Power Commission, 1965), pp. 651–2 (rate of return) and 701–4 (service areas). Return on equity computed from data in above volume and in companion 1963 edition according to the following formula:

Average proprietary capital minus average preferred stock equals *average (common stock) equity.*

Net income plus provision for deferred income taxes, minus dividends declared on preferred stock, equals *return on (common stock) equity.*

Return on (common stock) equity divided by *average (common stock) equity* equals *rate of return on (common stock) equity.*

Appendix D.

TAX BENEFITS OF UTILITY COMPANIES

Table 1. Amounts Collected from Consumers for Taxes but Not Paid as Taxes (as of Dec. 31, 1964)—Privately Owned Electric Utilities, Classes A and B *

Company	Attributable to Accelerated Amortization (Section 168 of 1954 Internal Revenue Code)	Attributable to Liberalized Depreciation (Section 167 of 1954 Internal Revenue Code)	Total
Alabama Power	$ 17,070,173	$ 21,647,007	$ 38,717,180
Alaska Elec. L. & P.	—	17,297	17,297
Alpena Power	—	288,196	288,196
Appalachian Power	38,446,674	8,851,851	47,298,525
Arizona Pub. Serv.	3,492,827	—	3,492,827
Arkansas P. & L.	11,644,633	10,927,559	22,572,192
Atlantic City Electric	2,315,204	1,637,446	3,952,650
Black Hills P. & L.	—	1,141,000	1,141,000
Boston Edison	4,760,524	14,523,493	19,284,017
Boston Gas	—	2,303,484	2,303,484
Brockton Edison	—	955,718	955,718
California-Pacific Util.	—	520,855	520,855
Cambridge Elec. Light	—	1,107,170	1,107,170
Cape & Vineyard Electric	—	799,459	799,459
Carolina P. & L.	14,187,731	2,794,943	16,982,674
Central Hudson G. & E.	1,604,109	1,263,541	2,867,650
Central Illinois E. & G.	1,388,741	3,893,777	5,282,518
Central Illinois Light	1,434,300	7,661,100	9,095,400
Central Illinois Pub. Serv.	583,000	9,324,700	9,907,700
Central Kansas Power	475,347	224,653	700,000
Central Louisiana Electric	4,221,381	4,420,808	8,642,189
Central Maine Power	10,152,343	—	10,152,343
Central P. & L.	6,945,100	12,319,300	19,264,400
Central Vermont Pub. Serv.	437,269	—	437,269
Cincinnati G. & E.	16,587,094	6,982,378	23,569,472

* Source: Federal Power Commission Form 1.

Company	Attributable to Accelerated Amortization (Section 168 of 1954 Internal Revenue Code)	Attributable to Liberalized Depreciation (Section 167 of 1954 Internal Revenue Code)	Total
Citizens Util.	159,984	722,441	882,425
Cleveland Elec. Illuminating	29,839,000	—	29,839,000
Columbus & Southern Ohio Elec.	6,522,500	6,300,100	12,822,600
Commonwealth Edison	12,290,000	75,955,000	88,245,000
Commonwealth Edison of Ind.	720,000	5,035,000	5,755,000
Community Pub. Serv.	—	2,074,478	2,074,478
Connecticut L. & P.	5,318,301	—	5,318,301
Consolidated Edison of N.Y.	18,203,627	—	18,203,627
Consumers Power	17,109,381	46,394,469	63,503,850
Dallas P. & L.	7,297,221	—	7,297,221
Delaware P. & L.	6,231,035	4,221,357	10,452,392
Detroit Edison & Subs.	22,263,662	45,767,332	68,030,994
Duquesne Light	7,232,869	2,819,860	10,052,729
Eastern Shore Pub. Serv. of Md.	237,855	1,027,004	1,264,859
Eastern Shore Pub. Serv. of Va.	—	164,698	164,698
Edison Sault Electric	—	576,281	576,281
El Paso Electric	2,437,941	3,699,148	6,137,089
Empire District Electric	993,897	2,003,807	2,997,704
Fall River Elec. Light	—	420,351	420,351
Fitchburg G. & E. Light	—	361,616	361,616
Florida Power	10,266,948	15,242,986	25,509,934
Florida P. & L.	17,100,504	—	17,100,504
Florida Pub. Util.	—	469,272	469,272
Georgia Power	19,667,703	25,002,899	44,670,602
Gulf Power	3,783,092	4,648,685	8,431,777
Gulf States Util.	5,542,175	20,179,019	25,721,194
Hartford Elec. Light	6,880,268	—	6,880,268
Hawaiian Electric	—	6,650,182	6,650,182
Hilo Elec. Light	—	858,120	858,120
Holyoke Power & Elec.	—	37,167	37,167
Holyoke Water Power	—	1,813,999	1,813,999
Home L. & P.	—	290,536	290,536
Houston Lighting & Power	11,149,280	—	11,149,280

Company	Attributable to Accelerated Amortization (Section 168 of 1954 Internal Revenue Code)	Attributable to Liberalized Depreciation (Section 167 of 1954 Internal Revenue Code)	Total
Idaho Power	3,601,300	9,540,209	13,141,509
Illinois Power	6,751,000	16,254,304	23,005,304
Indiana & Michigan Electric	38,957,920	10,757,938	49,715,858
Indianapolis P. & L.	6,075,300	6,777,700	12,853,000
Iowa Elec. L. & P.	2,282,600	6,373,500	8,656,100
Iowa-Illinois G. & E.	550,060	5,832,674	6,382,734
Iowa P. & L.	5,816,733	5,737,398	11,554,131
Iowa Pub. Serv.	1,379,787	4,210,270	5,590,057
Iowa Southern Util.	967,700	2,106,700	3,074,400
Kansas City P. & L.	10,201,031	8,898,608	19,099,639
Kansas P. & L.	2,435,645	7,483,708	9,919,353
Kauai Elec.	—	8,244	8,244
Kentucky Power	351,996	2,560,092	2,912,088
Kentucky Util.	1,957,534	7,737,600	9,695,134
Kingsport Util.	8,654	134,685	143,339
Lockhart Power	—	137,200	137,200
Long Island Lighting	10,364,060	—	10,364,060
Louisiana P. & L.	9,943,568	10,709,678	20,653,246
Maine Pub. Serv.	293,984	—	293,984
Marietta Electric	16,100	312,450	328,550
Massachusetts Electric	—	455,000	455,000
Maui Elec.	—	332,949	332,949
Michigan G. & E.	31,500	963,400	994,900
Minnesota P. & L.	7,204,300	—	7,204,300
Mississippi Power	3,585,683	4,445,875	8,031,558
Mississippi P. & L.	6,325,729	5,823,299	12,149,028
Missouri Edison	—	55,000	55,000
Missouri P. & L.	—	170,000	170,000
Missouri Pub. Serv.	1,191,747	—	1,191,747
Monongahela Power	5,066,900	5,151,000	10,217,900
Montana-Dakota Util.	1,114,063	2,691,365	3,805,428
Montana Power	2,907,079	3,534,188	6,441,267
Montaup Electric	—	1,415,347	1,415,347
Mt. Carmel Pub. Util.	—	196,143	196,143
Nantahala P. & L.	2,165,575	—	2,165,575
Nevada Power	1,853,208	1,571,576	3,424,784

Company	Attributable to Accelerated Amortization (Section 168 of 1954 Internal Revenue Code)	Attributable to Liberalized Depreciation (Section 167 of 1954 Internal Revenue Code)	Total
New Bedford Gas & Ed. Light	—	1,372,253	1,372,253
New England Power	10,641,300	1,138,400	11,779,700
New Orleans Pub. Serv.	—	7,200,000	7,200,000
New York State E. & G.	7,538,900	—	7,538,900
Niagara Mohawk Power	17,300,000		17,300,000
Northern Indiana Pub. Serv.	138,139	17,161,337	17,299,476
Northern States Power (Minn.)	7,202,400	2,688,000	9,890,400
Northern Virginia Power	78,200	163,900	242,100
Northwestern Pub. Serv.	—	1,300,700	1,300,700
Ohio Edison	23,819,388	12,866,177	36,685,565
Ohio Power	58,879,114	6,888,970	65,768,084
Oklahoma G. & E.	10,530,000	4,098,000	14,628,000
Old Dominion Power	—	277,200	277,200
Orange & Rockland Util.	3,353,181	—	3,353,181
Pacific G. & E.	72,787,443	—	72,787,443
Pacific P. & L.	44,089,794	—	44,089,794
Pennsylvania Electric	7,990,730	—	7,990,730
Pennsylvania Power	3,871,960	—	3,871,960
Pennsylvania P. & L.	14,222,789	—	14,222,789
Philadelphia Electric	17,981,251	—	17,981,251
Plymouth County Electric	—	364,345	364,345
Portland General Electric	12,417,740	—	12,417,740
Potomac Edison	4,323,600	496,400	4,820,000
Potomac L. & P.	586,800	196,200	783,000
Public Service of Colo.	9,572,287	5,654,343	15,226,630
Public Service of Ind.	18,639,000	17,213,000	35,852,000
Public Service of N.H.	4,253,011	—	4,253,011
Public Service of N.M.	2,656,846	1,756,578	4,413,424
Public Service of Okla.	14,774,000	9,440,000	24,214,000
Public Service E. & G.	16,505,455	22,397,266	38,902,721
San Diego G. & E.	—	1,626,181	1,626,181
Savannah E. & P.	—	2,934,178	2,934,178
Sierra Pacific Power	—	2,595,843	2,595,843
South Carolina E. & G.	15,694,000	8,103,900	23,797,900
South Penn Power	48,000	—	48,000
Southern California Edison	50,804,171	—	50,804,171

Company	Attributable to Accelerated Amortization (Section 168 of 1954 Internal Revenue Code)	Attributable to Liberalized Depreciation (Section 167 of 1954 Internal Revenue Code)	Total
Southern Elec. Generating	—	8,583,681	8,583,681
Southern Indiana G. & E.	2,078,470	3,482,090	5,560,560
Southwestern Elec. Power	3,758,900	8,667,400	12,426,300
Southwestern Elec. Serv.	—	135,233	135,233
Southwestern Pub. Serv.	11,271,187	4,770,549	16,041,736
Tampa Electric	—	11,010,000	11,010,000
Tapoco	157,830	—	157,830
Texas Elec. Serv.	13,371,460	—	13,371,460
Texas P. & L.	14,137,425	—	14,137,425
Toledo Edison	6,992,000	3,945,000	10,937,000
Tucson G. & E.	—	5,126,127	5,126,127
Union Electric	17,415,000	3,511,000	20,926,000
Union Light, Heat & Power	428,896	—	428,896
United Illuminating	1,567,000	—	1,567,000
Upper Peninsula Power	26,000	1,338,834	1,364,834
Utah P. & L.	697,000	—	697,000
Virginia E. & P.	34,793,076	—	34,793,076
Washington Water Power	9,756,817	—	9,756,817
West Penn Power	13,263,000	—	13,263,000
West Texas Util.	2,447,900	4,595,900	7,043,800
Western Light & Telephone	2,418,800	975,100	3,393,900
Western Massachusetts Elec.	1,164,800	3,623,200	4,788,000
Western Power & Gas	—	2,060,425	2,060,425
Wheeling Electric	746,330	127,286	873,616
Yankee Atomic Electric	—	2,819,700	2,819,700
Total	$1,067,585,839	$711,424,338	$1,779,010,177

274   *Appendixes*

Table 2. Power Companies' Investment Tax Credit Generated Through 1964 *

Alabama Power	$ 3,282,656
Alaska Elec. Light & Power	31,791
Alpena Power	19,511
Appalachian Power	1,852,316
Arizona Public Service	4,174,000
Arkansas-Missouri Power [1]	130,854
Arkansas Power & Light	1,230,016
Atlantic City Electric	1,637,300
Baltimore Gas & Electric [1]	2,644,439
Bangor Hydro Electric	165,289
Black Hills Power & Light	160,610
Blackstone Valley Electric	123,271
Boston Edison	1,480,274
Boston Gas [1]	295,208
Brockton Edison	113,587
California-Pacific Utilities	121,346
Cambridge Electric Light	171,145
Cape & Vineyard Electric	102,304
Carolina Power & Light	1,932,090
Central Hudson Gas & Electric	492,261
Central Illinois Electric & Gas	184,000
Central Illinois Light [1]	812,036
Central Illinois Public Service [1]	1,160,000
Central Kansas Power [1]	78,232
Central Louisiana Electric [1]	641,656
Central Maine Power	664,134
Central Power & Light	1,103,000
Central Vermont Public Service	257,858
Cheyenne Light, Fuel & Power [1]	76,655
Cincinnati Gas & Electric [1]	1,909,583
Citizens Utilities [1]	180,437
Cleveland Electric Illuminating	1,718,629
Columbus & Southern Ohio Electric	952,178
Commonwealth Edison	6,483,471
Commonwealth Edison of Indiana	248,911
Community Public Service [1]	394,307
Concord Electric	29,950
Connecticut Light & Power [1]	1,800,000
Connecticut Valley Electric	11,934
Conowingo Power	72,800
Consolidated Edison of N.Y.	14,915,000

* Source: F.P.C. *Statistics of Electric Utilities in the U.S., Privately Owned, 1964.*
[1] Amounts shown relate to all utility properties of the company.

Consolidated Water Power [1]	3,868
Consumers Power [1]	5,859,859
Dallas Power & Light	1,653,321
Dayton Power & Light	819,458
Delaware Power & Light [1]	775,528
Detroit Edison and subsidiaries	2,697,482
Duke Power [1]	3,758,288
Duquesne Light	1,164,141
Eastern Shore Public Service (Md.)	190,089
Eastern Shore Public Service (Va.)	84,726
Edison Sault Electric [1]	68,251
El Paso Electric	460,997
Electric Energy	3,976
Ellenville Electric	7,832
Empire District Electric [1]	273,650
Exeter & Hampton Electric	32,954
Fall River Electric Light	58,002
Fitchburg Gas & Electric Light [1]	67,405
Florida Power	2,613,536
Florida Power & Light	4,340,813
Florida Public Utilities [1]	84,673
Georgia Power [1]	5,880,390
Granite State Electric	47,805
Green Mountain Power [1]	128,562
Gulf Power	421,085
Gulf States Utilities	2,511,104
Hartford Electric Light	1,368,000
Hawaiian Electric	1,302,236
Hilo Electric Light	128,401
Holyoke Power & Electric	2,206
Holyoke Water Power	12,206
Home Light & Power	62,606
Houston Lighting & Power	1,739,527
Idaho Power	603,800
Illinois Power [1]	3,091,000
Indiana & Michigan Electric [1]	2,912,786
Indianapolis Power & Light [1]	481,500
Interstate Power [1]	697,000
Iowa Electric Light & Power	540,891
Iowa-Illinois Gas & Electric [1]	688,731
Iowa Power & Light [1]	886,000
Iowa Public Service	778,927
Iowa Southern Utilities [1]	249,800
Jersey Central Power & Light	1,491,700
Kansas City Power & Light [1]	1,694,489
Kansas Gas & Electric	493,000

Kansas Power & Light [1]	1,201,489
Kauai Electric	47,271
Kentucky Power	853,226
Kentucky Utilities	1,059,000
Kingsport Power	71,605
Lake Superior District Power	90,893
Lockhart Power	54,062
Long Island Lighting	2,536,100
Louisiana Power & Light	1,338,401
Louisville Gas & Electric [1]	931,100
Madison Gas & Electric	407,000
Maine Public Service	107,741
Marietta Electric	47,900
Massachusetts Electric	1,252,738
Maui Electric	48,882
Metropolitan Edison	1,077,800
Michigan Gas & Electric [1]	103,500
Minnesota Power & Light	320,627
Mississippi Power	576,809
Mississippi Power & Light	636,726
Missouri Edison	100,000
Missouri Power & Light	245,000
Missouri Public Service [1]	373,890
Missouri Utilities [1]	193,524
Monongahela Power	579,300
Montana-Dakota Utilities [1]	1,646,334
Montana Power	445,800
Montaup Electric	15,669
Mt. Carmel Public Utility	6,650
Nantahala Power & Light	33,354
Narragansett Electric	428,965
Nevada Power	916,326
New Bedford Gas & Edison Light [1]	138,623
New England Power	1,772,727
New Hampshire Electric	55,662
New Jersey Power & Light	518,700
New Mexico Electric Service	31,163
New Orleans Public Service	867,000
New York State Electric & Gas	1,669,000
Newport Electric	41,421
Niagara Mohawk Power	2,710,000
Northern Indiana Public Service [1]	3,045,000
Northern States Power (Minn.)	2,526,500
Northern States Power (Wis.) [1]	255,000
Northern Virginia Power	101,000
Northwestern Public Service [1]	222,000
Ohio Edison	1,492,855
Ohio Power	1,875,369

Ohio Valley Electric	885
Oklahoma Gas & Electric	2,020,830
Old Dominion Power	52,000
Orange & Rockland Utilities	366,193
Otter Tail Power	674,000
Pacific Gas & Electric [1]	12,763,279
Pacific Power & Light	3,230,715
Paul Smith's Electric L. & P. & R.R.	14,198
Pennsylvania Electric [1]	1,793,300
Pennsylvania Power	659,500
Pennsylvania Power & Light	1,737,425
Philadelphia Electric	2,897,000
Plymouth County Electric	51,882
Portland General Electric	2,411,560
Potomac Edison	302,100
Potomac Electric Power	4,241,482
Potomac Light & Power	144,200
Public Service of Colo.	2,213,205
Public Service of Ind.	996,824
Public Service of N.H.	406,708
Public Service of N.M. [1]	797,383
Public Service of Oklahoma	897,520
Public Service Electric & Gas	7,307,181
Puget Sound Power & Light	1,273,592
Rochester Gas & Electric	691,000
Rockland Electric	102,000
Rumford Falls Power	14,651
Safe Harbor Water Power	1,611
St. Joseph Light & Power [1]	168,965
San Diego Gas & Electric [1]	1,826,175
Savannah Electric & Power	152,268
Sherrard Power System	18,573
Sierra Pacific Power	936,124
South Beloit Water, Gas & Electric	3,778
South Carolina Electric & Gas	1,496,811
South Penn Power	72,200
Southern California Edison	8,058,500
Southern Indiana Gas & Electric [1]	353,200
Southwestern Electric Power	1,180,000
Southwestern Electric Service	62,157
Southwestern Public Service	1,916,963
Superior Water, Light & Power	55,139
Susquehanna Power	578,000
Tampa Electric	1,439,859
Tapoco	8,229
Texas Electric Service	1,982,000
Texas Power & Light	2,330,000

Toledo Edison [1]	1,100,514
Tucson Gas & Electric	676,270
Union Electric	3,094,000
Union Light, Heat & Power [1]	239,117
United Gas Improvement [1]	478,506
United Illuminating	533,703
Upper Peninsula Generating	802,934
Upper Peninsula Power	150,082
Utah Power & Light	1,912,599
Vermont Electric Power	24,087
Virginia Electric & Power	7,203,000
Washington Water Power	558,455
West Penn Power	1,817,000
West Texas Utilities	439,581
Western Colorado Power	53,722
Western Light & Telephone [1]	800,800
Western Massachusetts Electric [1]	369,094
Western Power & Gas [1]	268,200
Wheeling Electric	96,898
White Mountain Power	62,447
Wisconsin Electric Power	1,298,300
Wisconsin Michigan Power	277,300
Wisconsin Power & Light [1]	1,097,000
Wisconsin Public Service [1]	1,121,000
Wisconsin River Power	91
Yadkin	128,172
Yankee Atomic Electric	19,299
Total	$237,486,248

Table 3. Tax-Free Dividend Payments by Power Companies, 1954–63 *

Power Company	Tax-Free Dividends Paid, 1954–1962 **	Tax-Free Dividends Paid, 1963	% of Dividend Tax-Free, 1963	Total Tax-Free Dividends Paid Since 1954
Arizona Pub. Serv.	$ 6,463,289	$ 5,100,000	75%	$ 11,563,289
Atlantic City Elec.	11,086,766	4,098,793	65.7%	15,185,559
Brockton Edison	1,260,641	814,053	71.37%	2,074,694
Calif. Elec. Power [1]	12,144,854	3,200,208	95.7%	15,345,062
Calif. Ore. Power [2] (C)	17,799,341	—	—	17,799,341
Calif. Ore. Power (P)	534,583	—	—	534,583
Central Hudson G. & E.	7,482,181	554,579	14.96%	8,036,760
Central Louisiana Elec.	7,224,564	961,234	19.3%	8,185,798
Central Maine Power	4,812,492	—	—	4,812,492
Connecticut L. & P.	10,826,051	3,617,061	30%	14,443,112
Connecticut Power [3]	1,340,731	—	—	1,340,731
Consolidated Edison	—	18,705,147	33.8%	18,705,147
Detroit Edison	83,033,850	3,454,551	10%	86,488,401
Duquesne Light	8,714,376	1,141,879	6.68%	9,856,255
El Paso Elec.	2,958,458	—	—	2,958,458
Essex County Elec.[4]	565,796	—	—	565,796
Fall River Elec. Light	912,043	110,067	15.29%	1,022,110

279

* Compiled by Consumers Information Committee on Resources and Energy (formerly Electric Consumers Information Committee), 1346 Connecticut Ave. N.W., Washington, D.C.
** Not all companies paid tax-free dividends in all years from 1954 through 1962.
See page 282 for numbered notes.

Power Company	Tax-Free Dividends Paid, 1954–1962 **	Tax-Free Dividends Paid, 1963	% of Dividend Tax-Free, 1963	Total Tax-Free Dividends Paid Since 1954
Fitchburg G. & E. Light	235,936	71,280	16.71%	307,216
Florida Power	760,396	—	—	760,396
Florida Pub. Util.	222,724	—	—	222,724
Gulf State Util.	8,535,997	—	—	8,535,997
Hartford Elec. Light	18,390,311	1,685,440	32%	20,075,751
Haverhill Elec.[5]	176,474	—	—	176,474
Idaho Power	10,036,031	3,000,379	45%	13,036,410
Illinois Power (C)	3,201,000	—	—	3,201,000
Illinois Power (P)	1,877,064	—	—	1,877,064
Interstate Power	1,189,634	173,012	4.7%	1,362,646
Lawrence Elec.[5]	466,917	—	—	466,917
Lowell Elec. Light	522,886	—	—	522,886
Maine Pub. Serv.	528,048	119,779	17.3%	647,827
Merrimack-Essex Elec.	2,649,636	—	—	2,649,636
Missouri Pub. Serv.	339,300	—	—	339,300
New England Elec. Sys.	28,537,997	4,237,802	26.62%	32,775,799
New England Power (P)	347,568	—	—	347,568
Niagara Mohawk Power	72,944,524	7,672,800	23%	80,617,324
Oklahoma G. & E.	10,161,303	—	—	10,161,303
Orange & Rockland Util.	519,295	993,671	35.46%	1,512,966
Pacific G. & E.	38,894,663	15,531,265	27.5%	54,425,928
Pacific P. & L. (C)	59,398,056	12,774,080	88%	72,172,136
Pacific P. & L. (P)	8,788,658	—	—	8,788,658

Portland Gen. Elec.	18,571,683	4,510,176	66.4%	23,081,859
Potomac Elec. Power	—	4,275,771	14%	4,275,771
Public Service E. & G.	—	5,131,863	13.51%	5,131,863
Public Service of Ind.	25,340,454	—	—	25,340,454
Public Service of N.H.	10,147,547	1,497,453	37.33%	11,645,000
Puget Sound P. & L. (C)	—	5,274,109	91.73%	5,274,109
Puget Sound P. & L. (P)	—	273,412	21.52%	273,412
Rockland L. & P.[6]	2,783,439	—	—	2,783,439
Sierra Pacific Power	—	381,243	24.53%	381,243
South Carolina E. & G.	—	1,244,431	18%	1,244,431
Southern Berkshire P. & E.[7]	190,646	—	—	190,646
Southwestern Elec. Serv.	1,644,594	201,237	47.92%	1,845,831
Southwestern Pub. Serv.	9,382,321	753,662	7.5%	10,135,983
Suburban Elec.	1,480,291	—	—	1,480,291
Union Elec.	54,986,681	9,482,768	42%	64,469,449
Utah P. & L.	7,308,063	187,428	2.9%	7,495,491
Virginia E. & P.	4,062,107	—	—	4,062,107
Washington Water Power	30,400,577	2,665,253	46.08%	33,065,830
Weymouth L. & P.[7]	435,990	—	—	435,990
Worcester County Elec.	5,117,085	—	—	5,117,085
Totals	$617,735,912	$123,895,886		$741,631,798

See page 282 for numbered notes.

Sources: For % of dividend payments considered tax-free by companies, Prentice-Hall's "Capital Adjustments" and Moody's "Public Utilities" services. For total dividend payments, company reports to F.P.C. Dividend payments are those made on common stock, except where noted. Where company paid tax-free dividends on both common and preferred, each is identified. (C) On common stock. (P) On preferred stock.

[1] Merged with Southern California Edison Co. Dec. 31, 1963.
[2] Merged with Pacific Power & Light, 1961.
[3] Merged with Hartford Electric Light, 1956.
[4] Name changed to Merrimack-Essex, 1957.
[5] Merged with Merrimack-Essex, 1957.
[6] Name changed to Orange & Rockland Utilities, 1958.
[7] Merged with Massachusetts Electric, 1961.

Appendix E.

ELECTRIC UTILITIES WHOSE SECURITIES ARE SUBJECT TO JURISDICTION OF THE FEDERAL POWER COMMISSION

I. States in which F.P.C. has jurisdiction because there is no state commission with power to regulate security issues by public utilities:

State	*Companies Affected & State of Incorporation (in paren.)*
S.D.	Black Hills Power & Light (S.D.)
Minn.	Minnesota Power & Light (Minn.) Northern States Power (Minn.) Otter Tail Power (Minn.)
Tex.	Community Public Service (Tex.) * Dallas Power & Light (Tex.) El Paso Electric (Tex.) Gulf States Utilities (Tex.) * Houston Lighting & Power (Tex.) * Southwestern Elec. Serv. (Tex.) * Texas Elec. Service (Tex.) * Texas Power & Light (Tex.)
Iowa	Iowa Elec. Light & Power (Iowa) Iowa-Illinois G. & E. (Iowa) Iowa Power & Light (Iowa) Iowa Pub. Service (Iowa) Iowa Southern Utilities (Del.)

* These companies are jurisdictional according to the Federal Power Commission. The companies, however, maintain they are not jurisdictional, and they have not sought F.P.C. approval of their security issues.

Special situation: Holyoke (Mass.) Water Power is subject to F.P.C. regulation of security issues because provisions of its charter exclude it from Massachusetts public-utility regulation.

II. Companies incorporated in one state but operating in another (excepting those otherwise exempt):

    Idaho Power (inc. in Me.; op. in Idaho)
    Interstate Power (inc. in Del.; op. in Ill., Iowa, Minn.)
    Iowa Southern Utilities (inc. in Del.; op. in Iowa)
    Kansas Gas & Elec. (inc. in W.Va.; op. in Kans.)
* Consumers Power (inc. in Me.; op. in Mich.)
* Detroit Edison (inc. in N.Y.; op. in Mich.)
    Citizens Utilities (inc. in Del; op. in Ariz., Idaho, Vt.)
    Montana-Dakota Utilities (inc. in Me.; op. in Mont., N.D., S.D., Wyo.)
    Pacific Power & Light (inc. in Me.; op. in Calif., Idaho, Mont., Ore., Wash., Wyo.)
    Northwestern Pub. Service (inc. in Del.; op. in S.D.)
    Western Power & Gas (inc. in Del.; op. in Colo.)

Source: Federal Power Commission, 1965.

Appendix F.

INVESTOR-OWNED
ELECTRIC-NATURAL GAS
COMBINATION UTILITIES *

(Note: A number of the companies operate in more states than the one
under which they are listed.)

Arizona

Arizona Public Service
Tucson Gas, Elec. Light & Power

Arkansas

Arkansas-Missouri Power

California

Pacific Gas & Electric
San Diego Gas & Electric

Colorado

Public Service Co. of Colorado
Western Power & Gas

Connecticut

Connecticut Light & Power
Hartford Electric Light

Delaware

Delaware Power & Light

Florida

Florida Public Utilities

Illinois

Central Illinois Electric & Gas
Central Illinois Light
Central Illinois Public Service
Illinois Power
Mount Carmel Public Utility
South Beloit Water, Gas & Elec.

Indiana

Northern Indiana Pub. Serv.
Southern Indiana Gas & Elec.

Iowa

Interstate Power
Iowa Elec. Light & Power
Iowa-Illinois Gas & Elec.
Iowa Power & Light
Iowa Public Service
Iowa Southern Utilities

Kansas

Central Kansas Power
Kansas Power & Light
Western Light & Telephone

Kentucky

Louisville Gas & Electric
Union Light, Heat & Power

Louisiana

Central Louisiana Electric
New Orleans Public Service

Maryland

Baltimore Gas & Electric

* Source: Federal Power Commission, 1965.

285

Massachusetts

Boston Gas
Fitchburg Gas & Elec. Light
New Bedford Gas & Ed. Light

Michigan

Consumers Power
Michigan Gas & Electric

Minnesota

Northern States Power (Minn.)

Missouri

Missouri Edison
Missouri Power & Light
Missouri Public Service
Missouri Utilities
St. Joseph Light & Power
Union Electric

Montana

Montana Power

Nevada

Sierra Pacific Power

New Jersey

Public Service Elec. & Gas

New York

Central Hudson Gas & Elec.
Consolidated Edison of N.Y.
Long Island Lighting
New York State Elec. & Gas
Niagara Mohawk Power
Orange & Rockland Utilities
Rochester Gas & Electric

North Dakota

Montana-Dakota Utilities
Otter Tail Power

Ohio

Cincinnati Gas & Electric
Dayton Power & Light
Toledo Edison

Oregon

Calif.-Pacific Utilities

Pennsylvania

Philadelphia Electric
United Gas Improvement

South Carolina

South Carolina Elec. & Gas

South Dakota

Northwestern Public Service

Texas

Community Public Service
Gulf States Utilities

Vermont

Citizens Utilities

Virginia

Virginia Electric & Power

Washington

Washington Water Power

Wisconsin

Madison Gas & Electric
Northern States Power (Wis.)
Superior Water, Light & Power
Wisconsin Michigan Power
Wisconsin Power & Light
Wisconsin Public Service

Wyoming

Cheyenne Light, Fuel & Power

Appendix G.

NET INCOME AS PERCENTAGE OF INVESTED CAPITAL OF THE 35 MAJOR ELECTRIC UTILITIES, 1965 *

Utility	Percentage	Utility	Percentage
Allegheny Power System	12.8	Northern Indiana Public Service	12.5
American Electric Power	14.9	Northern States Power (Minn.)	10.0
Baltimore Gas & Electric	11.2		
Central & Southwest	14.3	Ohio Edison	12.9
Commonwealth Edison	12.3	Pacific Gas & Electric	9.8
Consolidated Edison	7.3	Pacific Power & Light	10.1
Consumers Power	11.3	Pennsylvania Power & Light	10.5
Detroit Edison	12.2	Philadelphia Electric	10.7
Duke Power	11.4	Potomac Electric Power	9.5
Florida Power & Light	11.7	Public Service Electric & Gas	10.9
General Public Utilities	10.7	Public Service of Colorado	10.1
Gulf States Utilities	10.8	Public Service of Indiana	11.4
Houston Lighting & Power	16.0	Southern	11.7
Illinois Power	13.8	Southern California Edison	10.0
Long Island Lighting	10.5	Texas Utilities	14.3
Middle South	12.4	Union Electric	10.8
New England Electric System	9.2	Virginia Electric & Power	11.5
Niagara Mohawk	9.7	Wisconsin Electric Power	9.8

* Source: *Fortune,* July 15, 1966, pp. 260–1.

NOTES

PART I. THE OVERCHARGE IN THE LIGHT BILL

Introduction

(Pp. 1–4)

[1] Data on monthly rates for 500 kilowatt-hours and usage of electricity from *Typical Electric Bills, 1965* (Washington, D.C.: Federal Power Commission, 1966), and from authors' correspondence in May 1966 with state commissions having jurisdiction over utilities mentioned.

[2] Boston-Seattle tax comparison from "Estimated Burden of Taxes for a Family of Four Owning a Residence and an Automobile in the 21 Largest Cities of the United States for Fiscal Year 1966" (Washington, D.C.: D.C. Department of General Administration, Finance Office, Sept. 1965).

[3] "The Fortune Directory," *Fortune*, Aug. 1965, p. 178; *Statistics of Electric Utilities in the United States, 1964, Privately Owned* (Washington, D.C.: Federal Power Commission, 1965).

[4] Estimate of $11 billion possible annual savings from *National Power Survey* (Washington, D.C.: Federal Power Commission, 1964), Part I, p. 4.

Chapter 1. WHAT'S WHAT AND WHO'S WHO

(Pp. 4–20)

[1] Data on rates and usage from *Typical Electric Bills, 1965* (Washington, D.C.: Federal Power Commission, 1966).

[2] Organization of the power industry from *National Power Survey* (Washington, D.C.: Federal Power Commission, 1964), Part I, pp. 15–26.

[3] Sales of federal wholesale power in fiscal 1963 from *Rural Electric Fact Book* (Washington, D.C.: National Rural Electric Cooperative Association, 1965), pp. 34, 100.

[4] Statistics on growth and size of power industry from *National Power Survey*, Part I, pp. 10, 11, 51, 151; *Comparison of Coal-Fired*

and Nuclear Power Plants for the T.V.A. System (Chattanooga, Tenn.: Tennessee Valley Authority), June 1966.

⁵ James River veto message by President Theodore Roosevelt, *Congressional Record,* 60th Cong., 2d Sess., Jan. 15, 1909, XLIII, Part 1, pp. 978–80.

⁶ Statistics on use and cost of electricity in other countries from *World Power Data* (Washington, D.C.: Federal Power Commission, 1963); Aug. 20, 1965, letter to Senator Lee Metcalf (D-Mont.) from F.P.C. Chairman Joseph C. Swidler.

⁷ Investment in power industry from *Edison Electric Institute Pocketbook of Electric Utility Statistics* (New York: Edison Electric Institute, 1965), p. 31, and *National Power Survey,* p. 11. Investment in nuclear development from Senator John Pastore, chairman, Joint Congressional Committee on Atomic Energy, "25 Years of Nuclear Progress," *General Electric Forum,* VII, No. 3 (July–Sept. 1964), p. 7.

⁸ Rate differentials and consumption of electric energy by class of customers in 1960 is discussed by Paul J. Garfield, Ph.D., and Wallace F. Lovejoy, Ph.D., in *Public Utility Economics* (Englewood Cliffs, N.J.: Prentice-Hall, 1964), p. 150.

⁹ Average residential rates acording to type of supplier from *Statistics of Electric Utilities in the United States, 1963, Publicly Owned,* and *Statistics of Electric Utilities in the United States, 1963, Privately Owned* (Washington, D.C.: Federal Power Commission, 1965); "More Power at Lower Cost," *Public Power,* Jan. 1966, p. 23.

¹⁰ Reports on benefits from municipal electric plants from *Jacksonville* (Fla.) *Municipal Yearbook, 1963–1964* (Jacksonville: City of Jacksonville, 1964), and program for dedication of Jacksonville City Coliseum, Nov. 24, 1960.

¹¹ Reports on benefits of municipal electric plants appear in *Proceedings of the 21st Annual Convention,* American Public Power Association (Washington, D.C., 1964). See within "Public Power in the Land of Lincoln Serves a Grateful Community," an address by V. Y. Dallman, Sr., editor emeritus, *Illinois State Register;* "How Public Power Benefits Nebraska," an address by Clarence J. Wittler, president, board of directors, Loup River Public Power District; an address by J. Dillon Kennedy, commissioner of utilities, Jacksonville, Fla., and president (in 1964) of the American Public Power Association. The reports by Dallman, Wittler, and Kennedy were all made in Jacksonville, Fla., on May 12, 1964.

¹² Utility taxes, as a percentage of revenue, from *Statistics of Electric Utilities in the United States, 1963, Privately Owned,* and *Statistics of Electric Utilities in the United States, 1963, Publicly Owned;* and "More Power at Lower Cost."

¹³ Comparison of rates and taxes of Seattle City Light and Puget

Sound Power & Light from report by John M. Nelson, superintendent, Seattle City Light, *Proceedings of the 21st Annual Convention* of the American Public Power Association (1964), pp. 197–99.

[14] Rural electric cooperative taxes, as percentage of revenue, *Rural Electric Fact Book,* p. 91.

[15] Statistics on miles of line, percentage of customers and sales, and customers per mile of line from Department of Agriculture, Rural Electrification Administration, *Rural Electrification Looks to the Future,* Mar. 1964, p. 5; *Rural Electric Fact Book,* pp. 108–115; address by Norman M. Clapp, Administrator, Rural Electrification Administration, before Western Conference of Public Service Commissions, Aug. 29, 1966, Glacier National Park, Mont.

[16] Data on comparative interest payments from Norman M. Clapp, administrator, Rural Electrification Administration, speech before Minnesota Association of Electric Cooperatives, Minneapolis, Feb. 15, 1965.

[17] John C. Satterfield, president (in 1961), American Bar Association, speech in Indianapolis, quoted in *An Indiana R.E.M.C. Power Primer* (Indianapolis: Indiana Statewide Rural Electric Cooperative, Inc., 1964), p. 12.

[18] W. W. Lynch, president, Texas Power & Light, "Not By Chance . . . ," *Public Utilities Fortnightly,* June 6, 1963, p. 70.

[19] I.O.U. capital structure from *National Power Survey,* Part I, p. 19.

[20] Investor-owned utility ownership data from *The Electric Utilities* (New York: Merrill Lynch, Pierce, Fenner & Smith, 1964), p. 3.

[21] Stock holdings based on 1961 annual reports from companies to Federal Power Commission, published as *Top Stockholders of Private Power Companies* (Washington, D.C.: Electric Consumers Information Committee, 1963). See also Gene Smith, "Utility Owners Hard to Detect," *New York Times,* Aug. 11, 1963, Section 3, p. 1.

[22] "Aldermanic Committee Investigating Holyoke Water Power Stock Ownership Asks Further Study on Many Aspects of Their Probe," *Holyoke* (Mass.) *Transcript-Telegram,* Sept. 1, 1964; "Aldermanic Committee Report on Holyoke Water Power Company Stock Ownership," city of Holyoke, Mass., 1964.

[23] Proxy voting patterns determined by authors' analysis of annual reports by electric utilities for 1963 to Federal Power Commission (Form 1 reports, p. 106).

[24] U.S., Congress, Senate, Subcommittee on Antitrust and Monopoly of the Committee on the Judiciary, *Interim Report, Monopoly in the Power Industry,* 83d Cong., 2d Sess., 1955 (although hearings held in 1954), pp. 13–14. See especially the testimony of James T. Stietenroth, former chief financial officer, Mississippi Power & Light.

[25] Donald S. Kennedy, president, Oklahoma Gas & Electric, "How

O.G.&E. Approached Antitrust Settlements," *Electrical World,* July 8, 1963, pp. 29–31.

[26] Letter from R. E. Kerns, secretary, Oklahoma Gas & Electric to Vic Reinemer, Mar. 19, 1965.

Chapter 2. I.O.U.s—INVESTOR-OWNED UTILITIES— ARE DIFFERENT

(Pp. 20–25)

[1] Comparative profit percentages from tables published by First National City Bank of New York, 1925–1964; *Fortune,* Aug. 1965, p. 178; *Federal Reserve Bulletin,* July 1965; *E.C.I.C.* (Electric Consumers Information Committee) *Newsletter,* Aug. 13, 1965; *Statistics of Electric Utilities in the United States, 1964, Privately Owned,* and *Statistics of Electric Utilities in the United States, 1963, Privately Owned* (Washington, D.C.: Federal Power Commission, 1964 and 1965).

[2] Everett C. McKeage, former chairman, California Public Utilities Commission, *Public Utility Regulatory Law* (New York: Vantage Press, 1956), pp. 27–29.

[3] *Re Hope Natural Gas Co.,* 44 PUR (NS) 1, 24 (1942); *Colorado Interstate Gas Co.* v. *F.P.C.* and *Canadian River Gas Co.* v. *F.P.C.,* 324 U.S. 581, 601 (1945); *Panhandle Eastern Pipeline* case, 324, U.S. 635.

[4] *The Failure Record Through 1964* (New York: Dun & Bradstreet, 1964), p. 3.

PART II. HOW IT GOT THERE: HOW THE CONSUMER IS REGULATED

Chapter 3. LOGJAMS, AND THE REGULATORY LAPSE

(Pp. 26–33)

[1] Edwin L. Mason, chairman, Florida Public Service Commission, quoted from testimony before the Committee on Commerce of the United States Senate, *Exemption of Certain Public Utilities from Federal Power Commission Jurisdiction, S. 218,* 89th Cong., 1st Sess., 1965, pp. 111–12.

[2] Sir Matthew Hale, Lord Chief Justice of the King's Bench, *De Jure Maris* (circa 1670), *A Collection of Tracts Relative to the Law of England* (Dublin: Printed for E. Lynch, W. Colles, *et al.,* 1787), I, 6.

[3] Munn *v.* Illinois, 94 U.S. 113 (1877).

[4] James River Veto message by President Theodore Roosevelt, *Con-*

gressional Record, 60th Cong., 2d Sess., Jan. 15, 1909, LXIII, Part 1, pp. 978–80.

[5] For detail on pre-World War I attitudes toward licensing of hydroelectric sites see hearings before Senate Committee on Public Lands in H.R. 16673, Water Power Bill, 63d Cong., 3d Sess., 1914, especially colloquy between Senator John D. Works (R-Calif.) and John D. Ryan, president of Montana Power, p. 719, and testimony of Gifford Pinchot, pp. 225–49.

[6] Federal Power Act, originally enacted as Federal Water Power Act, approved June 10, 1920 (41 Stat. 1063, 16 U.S.C. 791–823).

[7] Public Utility Holding Company Act of 1935, approved Aug. 26, 1935 (49 Stat. 838, 16 U.S.C. 791a–825r).

[8] Samuel Insull's corporate connections from Arthur Schlesinger, Jr., *The Crisis of the Old Order* (Boston: Houghton Mifflin, 1957), p. 255.

[9] Data on state regulatory commissions from *State Commission Jurisdiction and Regulation of Electric and Gas Utilities* (Washington, D.C.: Federal Power Commission, 1960); "Selected Statistics, 1961," *Public Utilities Fortnightly,* Dec. 20, 1961, pp. 888–89; Hong N. Kim, Ph.D., and June Kysilko, Research Paper No. 65.3b, *State Regulatory Commissions* (Washington, D.C.: National Rural Electric Cooperative Association, Feb. 1966); "Report of the Committee on Secretarial Offices," 1963 and 1964 editions (Washington, D.C.: National Association of Railroad and Utilities Commissioners); scope of California regulatory responsibility by Everett C. McKeage, former chairman, California Public Utilities Commission, *Public Utility Regulatory Law* (New York: Vantage Press, 1956), pp. 105–106.

[10] "P.S.C. Is Checking Rates of PEPCO, Gas Company," *Washington Post,* Mar. 5, 1965, p. B1.

[11] "Maryland P.S.C. Called Ineffective," *Washington Post,* Oct. 9, 1963, p. B1.

[12] Data on infrequency of electric rate cases from *An Outline of Electric Utility Regulation by States* (New York: Clark, Dodge & Co., 1965).

[13] Rate and earnings data from *Utilities—Electric: Industry Survey* (New York: Standard & Poor's, July 18, 1963), pp. U8–U29; Owen Ely, "Financial News and Comment," *Public Utilities Fortnightly,* Mar. 14, 1963, p. 45.

Chapter 4. THE RATE OF RETURN

(Pp. 33–41)

[1] Rates of return from *Statistics of Electric Utilities in the United States, 1963, Privately Owned* (Washington, D.C.: Federal Power Commission, 1965), pp. 651–52.

[2] The U.S. Fish and Wildlife Service counted 51 whooping cranes in 1966, including seven in captivity. ("Whooping Cranes Start Migration to Northern Nesting Grounds," Fish and Wildlife Service release, Apr. 8, 1966.)

[3] List of states in which electricity is most or least costly is based on average monthly bills for 500 kilowatt-hours of residential service from *Typical Electric Bills* (Washington, D.C.: Federal Power Commission, 1964), p. viii.

[4] Information on overcharges, 1956–62, by Ronnie J. Straw, economist, National Rural Electric Cooperative Association, "Report on Overcharges of 106 Major Electric Utilities" (Washington, D.C.: National Rural Electric Cooperative Association, 1965).

[5] VEPCO (Virginia Electric & Power) episode from Record #4336, Supreme Court of Appeals of Virginia, *Board of Supervisors of Arlington County* v. *VEPCO,* Case #11788; "Virginia Electric Sees Record 1st Quarter Net," *Wall Street Journal,* Mar. 7, 1960, p. 21; letter to VEPCO shareholders, June 20, 1961; "County to Push VEPCO Probe," *Northern Virginia Sun,* Aug. 12, 1963, p. 1; "State Confirms VEPCO's Profits Exceed the Authorized Level," *Washington Post,* Sept. 21, 1963, p. C1; letter from Ernest M. Jordan, Jr., assistant engineer, Virginia State Corporation Commission, to Vic Reinemer, Feb. 14, 1964; interviews with officials of Arlington County Public Utilities Commission.

[6] Florida episode from article by Lewis W. Petteway, "Florida's Regulatory Climate," *Public Utilities Fortnightly,* May 9, 1963; *Statistics of Electric Utilities in the United States, 1963, Privately Owned;* files of *Miami Herald,* 1964–65, especially series of articles by Juanita Green reprinted as booklet, *Your Utility Bill Too High?*

[7] Public Utilities Commission of California, *Pacific Telephone and Telegraph,* Case 7409, Decision 67369, June 11, 1964; Supreme Court of California, *Pacific Telephone and Telegraph Company* v. *Public Utilities Commission,* 401 P. 2d 353, Apr. 28, 1965.

Chapter 5. THE OPERATING EXPENSES

(Pp. 42–49)

[1] Edwin Vennard quote from Edwin Vennard and Robb M. Winsborough, *The American Economic System* (Chicago: Middle West Service Company, 1964), p. 72.

[2] Utility professor quoted on difference in taxation of utilities and other businesses is Martin T. Farris, Ph.D., professor of economics, Arizona State University, in "Tax Reductions and Utility Rates," *Public Utilities Fortnightly,* Aug. 27, 1964, p. 31.

[3] President J. E. Corette of Montana Power, quoted in "The Electric

Utility Executives' Forum," *Public Utilities Fortnightly,* June 4, 1964, p. 120.

4 M. S. Handler, "Utilities Pressed to Share Tax Gain," *New York Times,* June 18, 1964, p. 47.

5 Testimony of Secretary of the Treasury C. Douglas Dillon before Senate Finance Committee, *Revenue Act of 1962, H.R. 10650, Part I,* 87th Cong., 2d Sess., Apr. 2, 1962, pp. 86–87, 123–27.

6 U.S., Congress, House, Ways and Means Committee, *Revenue Act of 1963, H.R. 8363,* 88th Cong., 1st Sess., Sept. 13, 1963; U.S., Congress, Senate, Finance Committee, *Revenue Act of 1964, H.R. 8363,* 88th Cong., 2d Sess., Jan. 28, 1964; *Congressional Record,* Feb. 4–7, 1964, CX, Part 2, pp. 1828–2393 *passim.*

7 Thomas M. Venables, Ph.D., economist, National Rural Electric Cooperative Association, "The Power Company Tax Bonanza Grows," *Rural Electrification,* Jan. 1964; J. D. Brown, assistant general manager, American Public Power Association, "Companies Win Tax Fight," *Public Power,* Mar. 1964, pp. 13–14; Brown, "Power Companies Get Federal Tax Favors," *Public Power,* Apr. 1964, pp. 20–22; "Power Companies' Tax Favors Growing," *Public Power,* Apr. 1965, pp. 26–28; Dr. Robert Eisner, professor of economics, Northwestern University, "Depreciation Under the New Law," *Harvard Business Review,* Jan.–Feb. 1955, pp. 66–74; Federal Power Commission press release, "Electric and Gas Utilities Had Accumulated More than \$2.1 Billion in Deferred Income Taxes at End of 1963, F.P.C. Reports," Feb. 4, 1965, and "Federal Tax Favors to Companies Grow," *Public Power,* June 1966, pp. 14–15.

8 Tax-free dividends by I.O.U.s were compiled annually by Consumers Information Committee on Resources and Energy (formerly Electric Consumers Information Committee) by dividing total dividends, as reported by each company to the Federal Power Commission, by the percentage considered tax-free, as listed in Prentice-Hall's *Captital Adjustments* and Moody's *Public Utilities Services.*

9 Utility taxes as percentage of revenue from *Edison Electric Institute Pocketbook of Electric Utility Statistics* (New York: Edison Electric Institute, 1965), p. 12.

10 Martin Farris, Ph.D., *op. cit.,* p. 36.

11 Data on shifts in utility financing from Donald C. Cook, president, American Electric Power, "Financing Electric Utility Industry Growth," *Public Utilities Fortnightly,* June 4, 1964, pp. 65–73; Federal Power Commission press release 14046, Sept. 28, 1965.

12 Edwin Vennard, *The Electric Power Business* (New York: McGraw-Hill, 1962), p. 83.

13 Data on increasing use of internal cash generation for utility financing from Research Study, Goodbody & Co., Oct. 23, 1963; Wil-

liam F. Craig, assistant vice president, Irving Trust, "Cash Flow Growth and Its Impact on Financial Planning for Electric and Gas Companies," *Investment Dealers' Digest,* June 1, 1964, pp. 40–42.

Chapter 6. GIVE—TO THE CHARITY OF *THEIR* CHOICE

(Pp. 49–59)

¹ William C. MacInnes, president, Tampa Electric, "It's Never Too Late for Tampa Electric," *Investment Dealers' Digest,* June 1, 1964, pp. 56–58; "Tampa Electric," report by F. S. Smithers & Co., New York, Nov. 2, 1964; report of Tampa Electric to Federal Power Commission, 1963 (Form 1 report, p. 304); *Statistics of Electric Utilities in the United States, 1963, Privately Owned* (Washington, D.C.: Federal Power Commission, 1965), p. 652.

² Listed donations from companies' Form 1 annual reports to Federal Power Commission.

³ List of states that permit deduction of utility contributions as operating expenses, as compiled by telephone utilities, appears in Federal Communications Commission's "Rulemaking Proceeding 419, American Telephone and Telegraph, United States Independent Telephone Association," along with the arguments of the utilities and supporting letters from charitable and educational organizations. The request to list contributions as operating expenses was initiated by A.T.&T. Feb. 19, 1963, and denied by the F.C.C. June 12, 1963. USITA's appeal for reconsideration was denied by the F.C.C. Jan. 1, 1964. Previous attempts by the telephone industry to change accounting regulations of donations are recorded in F.C.C. Docket 11402 (1956). Decisions on allowance of contributions in various states are listed in *PUR Digest, 2d Series, Expenses,* 46. See also "F.C.C. Rules Gifts Not Business Expense," *Public Utilities Fortnightly,* Aug. 1, 1963, p. 43.

⁴ United Gas Pipe Line Company, F.P.C. Opinion 428, Docket RP 63–1, May 14, 1964.

⁵ Francis X. Welch, "Pages with the Editor—Charitable Contributions by Utilities," *Public Utilities Fortnightly,* July 2, 1964, p. 6.

⁶ National Industrial Conference Board study summarized in "Where Do Donations Go?" *Electrical World,* Dec. 16, 1963, pp. 119–22.

⁷ Ray E. Untereiner, former member, California Public Utilities Commission, "Duties of a Commissioner," *Public Utilities Fortnighly,* Aug. 28, 1958, pp. 312–13.

⁸ Public Utilities Commission of California, Pacific Telephone and Telegraph, Case 7409, Decision 67369, June 11, 1964.

⁹ *Remarks by J. K. Horton, president, Southern California Edison Company, before The New York Society of Security Analysts, June 3, 1965,* Southern California Edison, pp. 14–15.

[10] Order 276, Dec. 18, 1963, Docket R-226, Federal Power Commission; proposed accounting revision by F.P.C., Docket R-226, Dec. 19, 1962.

[11] Letter from F.P.C. Chairman Joseph C. Swidler concerning audit cycle and inclusion of political expenditures as operating expenses to Senator Metcalf, Mar. 12, 1965.

[12] William J. Powell, chief, division of systems, Federal Power Commission, "The Case for the Regulatory Accountant," *Public Utilities Fortnightly,* Jan. 7, 1965, pp. 36–47.

Chapter 7. THE RATE BASE

(Pp. 60–72)

[1] George N. Steinhauer, assistant vice president, Mountain States Telephone and Telegraph, *New Concepts and Current Issues in Public Utility Regulation* (Denver: Peerless Publishing Company, 1963), p. 246.

[2] *An Outline of Electric Utility Regulation by States* (New York: Clark, Dodge & Co., 1965).

[3] Juanita Green, "State Without Rate Base for Two Key Utilities," *Miami Herald,* Nov. 15, 1964.

[4] Details on audit backlog in *1965 Annual Report* (Washington, D.C.: Federal Power Commission), p. 96.

[5] Suggestions for rate base expansion from William F. Craig, assistant vice president, Irving Trust, "Cash Flow Growth and Its Impact on Financial Planning for Electric and Gas Companies," *Investment Dealers' Digest,* June 1, 1964, pp. 40–42.

[6] The price-fixing conspiracy is described by Richard Austin Smith, "The Incredible Electrical Conspiracy," *Fortune,* Apr. and May 1961, and by John G. Fuller, *The Gentlemen Conspirators* (New York: Grove Press, 1962). See also U.S., Congress, Senate, Subcommittee on Antitrust and Monopoly, Committee on the Judiciary, *Administered Prices: Identical Bidding (T.V.A.),* 86th Cong., 1st Sess., 1959, Part XIII.

[7] Press release by Tennessee Valley Authority, "Statement by T.V.A. on Purchase of Turbogenerator from C. A. Parsons & Co., Ltd., England," Feb. 27, 1959.

[8] "What Price National Security?" advertisement by General Electric, *Los Angeles Times,* Feb. 27, 1959, Part 1, page 16.

[9] Statements by J. C. Moller and William S. Peterson at Los Angeles City Council hearing, March 3, 1959; Ralph Cordiner, chairman of the board, General Electric, U.S., Congress, Senate, Subcommittee on Antitrust and Monopoly, Committee on the Judiciary, *Administered Prices, S.215,* 86th Cong., 1st Sess., 1959, Part II, p. 5644; Representative

Chet Holifield (D-Calif.), "American Managed Prices Versus Foreign Competition—Facts Regarding Governmental Purchase of Generating Machines," *Congressional Record,* July 20, 1959, CV, Part 2, pp. 13728–30.

[10] Federal Power Commission Accounting Release AR-1, Dec. 30, 1961.

[11] "Buyer-Seller Relationships Are in for a Change," *Electrical World,* Dec. 30, 1963, p. 56.

[12] William H. Dinsmore, "Dear Stockholders: Everything Looks Rosy . . . ," *Harper's,* Mar. 1965, pp. 134–35.

[13] Letter from Chairman Joseph C. Swidler of the Federal Power Commission to Senator Lee Metcalf, Nov. 5, 1965, and Enclosure 722; Internal Revenue Service Ruling 64-224, July 24, 1964.

[14] Remarks by Senator Philip A. Hart (D-Mich.) upon introducing S. 2479, a bill to amend Section 4 of the Clayton Act, U.S., *Congressional Record,* 89th Cong., 1st Sess., Aug. 30, 1965, CXI (Daily Record), pp. 21383–84; U.S., Congress, Joint Committee on Internal Revenue Taxation, *Staff Study of Income Tax Treatment of Treble Damage Payments under the Antitrust Laws,* Nov. 1965.

Chapter 8. STOCK OPTIONS—WHIPPED CREAM
ON THE DESSERT

(Pp. 72–91)

[1] Edwin Vennard, *The Electric Power Business* (New York: McGraw-Hill, 1962), p. 53.

[2] J. E. Corette, president, Montana Power, "Results of Complete Government Ownership and Control," *Public Service Magazine,* Dec. 1958, p. 7.

[3] Stock option windfalls from Form 4 reports to Securities and Exchange Commission by individual utility officials.

[4] Executive salaries from "Paycheck Race Is Still on a Treadmill," *Electrical World,* Dec. 7, 1964, pp. 31–34; American Public Power Association, "Survey of Executive Salaries and Fringe Benefits of Local Publicly Owned Electric Utilities," Sept. 1963.

[5] *Moody's Handbook of Widely Held Common Stocks* (2d ed.; New York: Moody's Investors Service, Inc., 1964).

[6] The Federal Trade Commission investigation, lasting seven years and filling 84 volumes, was printed as U.S., Congress, Senate Document 92, *Utility Corporations,* 70th Cong., 1st Sess., 1928. The summary report is Part 71-A.

[7] Wendell Willkie, president, Commonwealth & Southern, testimony before House Committee on Interstate and Foreign Commerce, *Public*

Utility Holding Companies, H.R. 5423, 74th Cong., 1st Sess., Part II, 1935, pp. 608 and 1147. See also testimony of S. R. Inch, president, Electric Bond & Share, pp. 1123 *et seq.*

[8] National Association of Railroad and Utilities Commissioners' suggestion that Section 204 be amended was made by General Solicitor John E. Benton before Senate Committee on Interstate Commerce, *Hearings on Public Utility Holding Company Act of 1935, S. 1725,* 74th Cong., 1st Sess., 1935, p. 751.

[9] Revenue Act of 1950 amended Internal Revenue Code of 1939, 130A by adding 64 Stat. 942, which was carried forward with modifications as Section 421 of the Internal Revenue Code of 1954. For details see U.S., Congress, Senate, Committee on Finance, *Stock Options— Hearings on S. 1625, a Bill to Amend the Internal Revenue Code of 1954 so as to Terminate the Special Tax Treatment Now Accorded Certain Employee Stock Options,* 87th Cong., 1st Sess., July 20, 21, 1961.

[10] Years in which stock option plans were inaugurated are from companies' annual reports to Federal Power Commission or Securities and Exchange Commission. Final approval of option plans by regulatory commissions was obtained in some instances a year or so after the dates listed.

[11] Securities and Exchange Commission File #70-3777, Middle South Utilities. Statement by Dean Erwin N. Griswold, Harvard Law School, before House Committee on Ways and Means, Dec. 7, 1959, appears as Appendix F to "Proposed Findings and Conclusions of the Division of Corporate Regulation," Securities and Exchange Commission, File #70-3777, May 16, 1960.

[12] Harvard's vote for Middle South's options was reported in a letter by Paul C. Cabot, Treasurer, for President and Fellows of Harvard College, to Vic Reinemer, Feb. 2, 1965.

[13] Securities and Exchange Commission File 70-3942, Ohio Edison.

[14] Securities and Exchange Commission Holding Company Act Release #14627, April 18, 1962, *re* approval of Central & Southwest's stock option plan.

[15] Federal Power Commission Docket #E-7046, Black Hills Power & Light. See especially Commissioner Howard Morgan's concurring opinion in "Memorandum Opinion and Order Denying in Part the Issuance of Common Stock, December 27, 1962"; testimony of Commission Staff Witness Walter H. Beidatsch during June 1963 hearing, Opinion #433; "Order Denying Authority for Issuance of Common Stock," June 30, 1964.

[16] Veto message of Governor John Bonner (D-Mont.) concerning H.B. 186, a bill to authorize the Public Service Commission of Montana to regulate and supervise the issuance of securities by public utilities

furnishing electric or gas service in Montana, appears in Montana, Legislature, 32d Sess., *House Journal,* Mar. 1, 1951, p. 638.

[17] Montana, Legislature, Senate, S.B. 186, an act to authorize the Public Service Commission of Montana to regulate and supervise the issuance of securities by public utilities furnishing electric or gas service in Montana, enacted Feb. 25, 1961.

[18] "Public Service Board Now Approves Issuance of Securities by Utilities," *Great Falls* (Mont.) *Tribune,* Nov. 10, 1961; "Montana Power Makes State Corporate Home," *Great Falls Tribune,* Dec. 1, 1961.

[19] Lack of Federal Power Commission jurisdiction over security issues of most companies was described by F.P.C. Chairman Joseph C. Swidler in June 24, 1964, and Mar. 4, 1965, letters to Senator Lee Metcalf and F.P.C. enclosure 11921 (1965).

[20] 1963 Form 10-K report of Central & Southwest Corporation to Securities and Exchange Commission; John C. Osborne, president, Central & Southwest, "Who Owns the Investor-Owned Electric Companies," Central & Southwest (pamphlet), Feb. 28, 1964.

[21] Letters by W. W. Lynch, president, Texas Power & Light, to S.E.C., May 6, 1964 (in files of S.E.C. section of ownership reports).

[22] Forrest McDonald, *Insull* (Chicago: University of Chicago Press, 1962), p. 113.

[23] National Association of Railroad and Utilities Commissioners, *NARUC Proceedings, 1963,* "Report of the Committee on Regulatory Procedure," 1963.

[24] Advertisement by Texas Power & Light in *Texas Town & City,* Nov. 1963.

[25] Capt. Douglas N. Jones, former Associate Professor of Economics, U.S. Air Force Academy, *New Concepts and Current Issues in Public Utility Regulation* (Denver: Peerless Publishing Company, 1963), pp. 62–63.

[26] Quotation from Franklin D. Roosevelt's Sept. 21, 1932, address in Portland, Oregon. A similar statement and an elaboration of Roosevelt's views on regulation appear in his *Looking Forward* (New York: The John Day Company, 1933), especially Chapter VIII, "The Power Issue."

PART III. HOW IT STAYS THERE: THE GENERATION, TRANSMISSION, AND DISTRIBUTION OF PROPAGANDA

Chapter 9. THE ADVERTISEMENTS—THE WORLD UPSIDE DOWN

(Pp. 92–113)

¹ Forrest McDonald, *Insull* (Chicago: University of Chicago Press, 1962), pp. 14, 162–87; U.S., Congress, Senate Document 92, *Utility Corporations,* 70th Cong., 1st Sess., 1928, especially Part 71A, Exhibits (Part 2).

² Arthur M. Schlesinger, Jr., *The Crisis of the Old Order* (Boston: Houghton Mifflin, 1957), pp. 121, 255; *Utility Corporations,* Exhibits (Part 2), pp. 123–4, "Speech by B. J. Mullaney—1921."

³ Floyd L. Carlisle, chairman, Niagara Hudson, quoted by William Mosher and Finla G. Crawford, *Public Utility Regulation* (New York: Harper & Bros., 1933), p. 549.

⁴ Replacement of National Electric Light Association by Edison Electric Institute from William A. Pendergast, *Public Utilities and the People* (New York: D. Appleton Century, 1933), pp. 39–40.

⁵ The advertised claim that electricity is "the biggest bargain in the family budget" has long been used by individual electric utilities. Typical of the widely advertised power industry claim that it is a tax-payer, and even the leading taxpayer, is the following ad, by Public Service Company of Colorado, in the Mar. 31, 1964, *Rocky Mountain News* (Denver):

> Most everybody pays taxes. And when it comes to paying their share of taxes, the investor-owned utility industry takes a back seat to no one. In fact, the industry is the nation's largest taxpayer. Public Service Co. is no different. As Colorado's largest taxpayer, we paid well over $25 million in taxes in 1963. . . .

The advertising slogan, "Your Tax-Paying (Not Tax-Eating) Electric Company," was stamped on a Feb. 9, 1965, letter to Vic Reinemer from Potomac Edison (Maryland). National advertisements by the power industry a few years ago were signed by "America's business-managed, tax-paying Electric Light and Power Companies." However, the industry no longer refers to itself as "tax-paying" in national ads. The signature changed to "Independent Electric Light and Power Companies," then to "Investor-Owned Electric Light and Power Companies" and, in 1966, to "The electric company people—the folks at your investor-owned electric light and power companies." (See, for example, *Look,* Sept. 20, 1966, p. 21; *Newsweek,* Aug. 29, 1966, p. 1.

[6] Ray Lyman Wilbur and Northcutt Ely, U.S., Congress, *The Hoover Dam Documents,* House Document 717, 80th Cong., 2d Sess., 1948. The story of Grand Coulee Dam is told by George Sundborg in *Hail Columbia* (New York: Macmillan, 1954). The record of power company opposition to Hungry Horse Dam appears in the hearings of the U.S. Congress, Senate and House, Interior Appropriations Subcommittees, 1947–50. Immediate and continuing need for power generated at Hungry Horse Dam has been regularly chronicled by Editor Mel Ruder in his *Hungry Horse News* (Columbia Falls, Mont.). Regarding the Hanford episode, see U.S., Congress, Joint Committee on Atomic Energy, *Utility Proposal for Powerplant Addition to Hanford New Production Reactor,* 87th Cong., 2d Sess., July 10–11, 1962; Vera Edinger, *The Hanford Story* (Seattle: Washington State Public Utility Association), Mar. 1964; Glenn C. Lee, publisher, *Tri-City Herald* (Pasco, Wash.), "The Hanford Story—1962," address before Bonneville Regional Advisory Council reprinted in *Public Power News* (published by Washington Public Utility Districts' Association), Oct. 1962, pp. 2–6.

[7] The utilities' claim that "they can supply all the additional electric power America will ever need" is widely used in national advertisements. See, for example, *Saturday Review,* May 25, 1963, p. 4.

[8] The advertisements depicting the I.O.U.s as sportsmen subjected to unfair competition have appeared in many national magazines, for example, *Saturday Evening Post,* July 27, 1957; *Life,* Aug. 19, 1957; *Look,* Sept. 17, 1957. United Utilities (Kansas) emblazoned "Free Enterprise" on the cover of its 1962 annual report to stockholders. The following example of the advertised claim that power companies are "free enterprise" appeared in the *Casselton* (N.D.) *Reporter,* Oct. 24, 1964, sponsored by Otter Tail Power (Minnesota):

Nikita doesn't like our way of doing business—and he hates what we stand for. We're the worst sort of business in Mr. K's eyes—an investor-owned, tax-paying, free enterprise industry. . . . Nikita hates us and every other free American enterprise. . . .

For many examples of the I.O.U.s' advertised inference that their competitors are socialistic see the *Saturday Evening Post,* 1950–1952.

[9] *Memphis Commercial Appeal* editorial quoted in a pamphlet, "The World's Tallest Dog," by Washington Public Utility Districts' Association, Seattle.

[10] For advertisements associating investor-owned utilities with patriotic symbols, see booklet collection of I.O.U. ads published by the *Saturday Evening Post.*

[11] Electric Companies Advertising Program, *The Public and You,* Jan. 1950.

[12] "FYI," bulletin, Bozell & Jacobs, May 31, 1950.

[13] National Association of Electric Companies, *National Association of Electric Companies, Goals and Objectives,* 1950.

[14] *Edison Electric Institute Bulletin,* July 1950, pp. 224, 237, 244.

[15] "Potomac Edison Produces Ad of Year," *Electrical World,* Jan. 16, 1950, pp. 46–47.

[16] The electric utilities ad, "A Socialistic U.S.A.," is reprinted in the Dec. 1955 issue of *Public Power,* p. 25, illustrating an article by Leland Olds, former chairman of the Federal Power Commission, "Power Trust Propaganda Techniques—How to Expose and Counteract Them."

[17] Results of Opinion Research Corporation poll reported in "Public Opinion," *Electrical World,* June 17, 1963, p. 84; "Public Opinion: Swinging to Investor Owned," *Electrical World,* June 24, 1963, pp. 39–42.

[18] Louis V. Sutton, president, Carolina Power & Light, quoted in *Public Utilities Fortnightly,* July 21, 1955, p. 126.

[19] John T. Flynn, *The Road Ahead* (New York: Devin-Adair, 1949), pp. 134–37.

[20] Elmer L. Lindseth, president, Cleveland Electric Illuminating, in company's annual report to stockholders, 1957.

[21] Ralph Elliott, "Washington News—New Public Power Lobby Launched with Wild Oratory Blasting Utility Industry," *Electric Light and Power,* June 1952, p. 206. Mr. Elliott was absolved by C. W. Leihy, publisher, *Electric Light and Power.* Clyde T. Ellis, general manager of the National Rural Electric Cooperative Association, threatened legal action against the magazine, after which Leihy wrote Ellis, on July 1, 1952:

... Believe me when I say that our Washington editor, Mr. Ralph Elliott, is an innocent bystander in this affair. His copy, submitted for the June issue, did not contain the offending phrase. That was added into his report by the green and inexperienced junior editor in Chicago, who apparently let personal emotionalism overbalance his perspective while adding a few words in order to "fill" the type page. His penance, among other things, will be to prepare an appropriate statement of correction for publication in the August issue. ...

[22] Clayton Rand, owner, The Dixie Press, Gulfport, Miss., and past president, National Editorial Association, "Spinning a Web," *Public Utilities Fortnightly,* May 23, 1963, pp. 38–41. The *Fortnightly* editors said, on page 3 of the May 23 issue, that the article drew a parallel "between the growth of the R.E.A. and the establishment of communism in the U.S.S.R."

[23] Edwin Vennard, managing director, Edison Electric Institute, quoted in *Public Utilities Fortnightly,* June 6, 1957, p. 809.

[24] Market performance of electric-utility stock in 1957 from *Moody's Handbook of Widely Held Common Stock* (2d ed.; New York: Moody's Investors Service, 1964).

[25] Statistics on utilities and other industries in 1957 from J. E. Corette, president, Montana Power, and president (in 1958), Edison Electric Institute, "Electric Power for a Strong America," speech at Edison Electric Institute convention, New Orleans, Apr. 1959, *Public Service Magazine*, May 1959, pp. 5–11.

[26] *Water Resources and Power,* A Report to the Congress by the Commission on Organization of the Executive Branch of the Government, Vols. I and II, June 1965.

[27] Admiral Ben Moreell, chairman of the board, Jones & Laughlin Steel Corporation, speech to Edison Electric Institute, reported in *Public Utilities Fortnightly,* July 3, 1958, pp. 48–9.

[28] "Cut Your Income Tax—*You* Decide How Much," full-page advertisements by *Human Events* in *Wall Street Journal,* Feb. 28, 1961, p. 17.

[29] "Government Always Shrinks a Dollar," full-page advertisement by Republic Steel in *Harper's,* Aug. 1957, p. 13.

[30] "The Electric Power Companies' Case for Public Confidence," advertisement by McGraw-Hill in *Wall Street Journal,* Mar. 16, 1954, p. 13.

[31] "The Real 'Give-Away,' " full-page advertisement by Guaranty Trust Company of New York in *Electrical World,* Sept. 17, 1956, p. 323. The same statement appeared in the Sept. 1956 issue of the bank's monthly publication, *Guaranty Survey.*

[32] Interlocks between Guaranty Trust and electric utilities from Representative Wright Patman (D-Tex.), "The J. P. Morgan-Guaranty Trust Merger Combines Two Financial Empires with Vast Influence in American Business," remarks in *Congressional Record,* Apr. 27, 1959, CV, Part 5, pp. 6850–54. Patman's data based on interlocks in 1956, the year in which Guaranty Trust ran the advertisement quoted above.

[33] Senator Estes Kefauver (D-Tenn.), "Internal Revenue Service Ruling on Private Power Company Advertising," Remarks in *Congressional Record,* Aug. 6, 1958, CIV, Part 6, Appendix, pp. A7047–8, and letter from Senator Kefauver to editors, Aug. 8, 1958.

[34] J. E. Corette, president, Montana Power, also then president, Edison Electric Institute, "Results of Complete Government Ownership and Control," speech before Rocky Mountain Electrical League, Jackson Hole, Wyo., *Public Service Magazine,* Dec. 1958, pp. 8–9.

[35] C. James Proud, president, Advertising Federation of America, and *Montana Standard* (Butte) quoted by Corette above.

[36] "Should the Power to Tax Include the Right to Censor Advertising?" editorial, *Saturday Evening Post,* June 21, 1958.

[37] Letters to Alex Radin, general manager, American Public Power Association, from C. James Proud, president, Advertising Federation of America, March 8, 1960, from Richard L. Scheidker, senior vice president, American Association of Advertising Agencies, March 21, 1960, and from Federal Trade Commission Chairman Earl W. Kintner, Mar. 22, 1960.

[38] Federal Power Commission docket E-6836. On Aug. 1, 1958, the Commission ordered electric utilities participating in the Electric Companies Advertising Program to show cause why a stated portion of their 1957 national advertising expenditures should not be reclassified as nonoperating expenses. A hearing was held on the matter and the F.P.C. order requiring reclassification was issued Aug. 17, 1960.

[39] U.S. Court of Appeals for the Fifth Circuit, #18667, Southwestern Electric Power *v.* Federal Power Commission; #18669, Alabama Power Company et al. *v.* Federal Power Commission; #18672, Arizona Public Service Company et al. *v.* Federal Power Commission, May 16, 1962.

[40] These and some other utility ads appear in the 1964 edition of Senator Ernest Gruening's *The Public Pays* (New York: Vanguard Press, 1931, 1964).

The advertisement that President Kennedy referred to as "particularly ugly" ("President's Remarks on T.V.A.," *Washington Post,* May 19, 1963, p. A8) was "Freedom Is Not Lost by Guns Alone," which appeared, for example, in *Saturday Review,* Apr. 20, 1963, p. 8. A similar ad, "How Is Freedom Lost?" in, for example, *Atlantic,* Sept. 1962, p. 9, and *Saturday Review,* Oct. 6, 1962, p. 2, was also sponsored nationally by the electric-power industry.

[41] *Rural Electric Fact Book* (Washington, D.C.: National Rural Electric Cooperative Association, 1965), p. 71.

[42] A. R. Watson, president, Southwestern Public Service, quoted in "Do Texans Overpay $84 Million a Year for Light and Power?" *Texas Observer,* June 12, 1964, p. 5.

[43] Kinsey Robinson, chairman, Washington Water Power, quoted in "Utilities Urged to Suport New Political Group," *Electrical World,* Oct. 14, 1963, p. 14. Robinson's option windfall was computed from his Form 4 report to Securities and Exchange Commission, concerning transaction of May 11, 1964.

[44] Investor-Owned Power Companies Prime Target of Socialist Planners," Edwin Vennard, managing director, Edison Electric Institute, *Manion Forum* (newsletter), Apr. 26, 1964 (also Manion Forum weekly broadcast #499).

[45] Recent use of "The Story of Ten Little Free Workers" advertise-

ment was reported in letter from Charles D. Lyon, president, Potomac Edison, to Vic Reinemer, Feb. 9, 1965; letter from Joseph C. Swidler, chairman, Federal Power Commission, and enclosure 94198 to Senator Metcalf, Feb. 1, 1965; F.P.C. correspondence files, Southern California Edison.

46 Detail on "Berlin Wall" ad of Florida electric utilities from F.P.C. advertising correspondence files.

47 Charles B. Jones, Leo Burnett Company executive, speech before Edison Electric Institute Sales Conference, Chicago, Apr. 8, 1964.

Chapter 10. THE CONGRESS—DON'T BETRAY THE SOURCE

(Pp. 114–130)

1 U.S., Congress, House, Select Committee on Lobbying Activities, *General Interim Report,* House Report 3138, 81st Cong., 2d Sess., 1950, p. 51.

2 All excerpts from "The Power Within" and introductory remarks by program chairman are from the *Project Action Manual,* produced by Varicom International, Boulder, Colo. The manual, including the script of the film, was placed in the *Congressional Record,* Jan. 8, 1964, CX, Part 1, pp. 30–56, by Senator Lee Metcalf. The script deletes the two maxims attributed to Lincoln which are heard at the film's conclusion.

3 "Film Urges Political Action," *Electrical World,* June 24, 1963, p. 14.

4 Utility officials' estimate of number of "grass roots" letters which could be generated by the film is from *Project: Action!,* a newsletter published by Varicom International, Boulder, Colo., Sept. 1963, p. 1.

5 Donald Bruce Johnson, *The Republican Party and Wendell Willkie* (Urbana, Ill.: University of Illinois Press, 1960). See also *Propaganda Analysis,* Oct. 15, 1940, p. 5.

6 Memorandum from Library of Congress to Senator Lee Metcalf, *Congressional Record,* March 18, 1964, CX, Part 4, pp. 5579–80; Al Toffler, "Lincoln Without Myths," *Coronet,* Feb. 1961, pp. 52–56.

7 Gerald L. Andrus, then president, New Orleans Public Service, now board chairman, Middle South Utilities, address before Junior Achievement banquet, New Orleans, May 10, 1962, *Public Service Magazine,* July 1962, pp. 17–21.

8 Use of "The Power Within" was reported in the Sept. and Oct. 1963 issues of *Project: Action!*

9 Use of "The Power Within" by National Tax Association and Sears, Roebuck episode from Mar. 6, Apr. 17, and June 12, 1964, issues of *The Rural Electric Minuteman* (Washington, D.C.: National Rural Electric Cooperative Association).

[10] U.S., Congress, Senate, Committee on Commerce, *Exemption of Certain Public Utilities from Federal Power Commission Jurisdiction,* 89th Cong., 1st Sess., May 12, 13, 14, and June 10, 1965.

[11] *We Believe, A Statement of the Position of Edison Electric Institute,* Edison Electric Institute, 1964, p. 3.

[12] Nat B. Knight, Jr., "Address by the President," National Association of Railroad and Utilities Commissioners, *Proceedings, 77th Annual Convention* (Honolulu, Dec. 2–5, 1964), p. 16.

[13] The minutes of the Miami meeting between officials of the National Association of Railroad and Utilities Commissioners and the National Association of Electric Companies were inserted by Senator Lee Metcalf in the *Congressional Record,* "NARUC 'Umpires' Join I.O.U. Ball Club," Apr. 30, 1965, CXI, pp. (Daily Record) 8749–50.

Chapter 11. THE PRESS—FREEDOM *FROM* INFORMATION

(Pp. 131–151)

[1] V. M. Newton, Jr., editor, *Tampa Tribune,* "Our Secret Government," speech before Arizona Newspaper Association, Tucson, Ariz., Jan. 14, 1961, published in *The Freeman,* May 1961, pp. 34–40.

[2] George D. Gentry, coordinator, Tampa Electric Speakers Bureau, "How to Organize and Operate a Speakers Bureau," speech before Sales, Advertising and Public Relations Section, Southeastern Electric Exchange, Williamsburg, Va., Nov. 12, 1963.

[3] "F.P.C. Publishes 'Statistics of Electric Utilities in the United States, Privately Owned' for 1963; Rate-of-Return Study of Major Utilities Included for First Time," Federal Power Commission press release, Mar. 30, 1965.

[4] "Electric Power Company Overcharges Documented by F.P.C.," inserted by Senator Lee Metcalf in *Congressional Record,* Apr. 7, 1965, CXI, pp. (Daily Record) 7029–31.

[5] Peter Bart, "How to Read Financial Pages Without Going Broke," *Harper's,* Aug. 1963, pp. 31–35; *Report of Special Study of Securities Markets of the Securities and Exchange Commission,* 88th Cong., 1st Sess., 1963, House Document 95 (five parts).

[6] Memorandum Prepared by the Division of Corporate Regulation, Securities and Exchange Commission, accompanying July 6, 1965, letter from S.E.C. Chairman Manuel F. Cohen to Senator Lee Metcalf; "Notice of Proposals for Revision of Form U5S and Adoption of Rule U-29," S.E.C. press release, Feb. 10, 1954; "Revision of Form U5S and Adoption of Rule U-29," S.E.C. press release, Mar. 29, 1954.

[7] Federal Power Commission Docket R-226, including Order 276, "Order Revising Account 426, Other Income Deductions, and Annual Report Forms," Dec. 18, 1963.

[8] U.S., Congress, Senate, Subcommittee on Antitrust and Monopoly of the Committee on the Judiciary, *Interim Report, Monopoly in the Power Industry,* 83d Cong., 2d Sess., 1955 (although hearings held in 1954), pp. 4, 45.

[9] "Things You Rarely Have to Think About: Sunlight, Air, Your Big Toe and Electricity," national advertisement by investor-owned electric light and power companies in, for example, *Look,* May 5, 1964, p. 119.

[10] *Sponsors of Investor-Owned Electric Light and Power Companies' Advertising—1964,* distributed by N. W. Ayer & Son.

[11] Quotations from and content analysis of Industrial News Review editorials are from the original editorials distributed by E. Hofer & Sons, Portland, Oregon, in the authors' files.

[12] *U.S. Newspapers Comment on Health Care for the Elderly,* American Medical Association, 1965.

[13] Ben H. Bagdikian, author and former newsman, described the U.S. Press Association in "Behold the Grass-Roots Press, Alas!" *Harper's,* Dec. 1964, pp. 103–104.

[14] Senator Ernest Gruening (D-Alaska) reported the Insullation of Industrial News Review in *The Public Pays,* published in 1931 when Gruening was editor of the *Portland* (Me.) *Evening News.* The book was enlarged and reissued (New York: Vanguard Press, 1964); Industrial News Review reference is pp. 189–97 of the 1964 edition. Details appear in U.S., Congress, Senate Document 92, *Utility Corporations,* 70th Cong., 1st Sess., 1928, Part 7, pp. 222–60.

[15] Recent electric-utility contributions to Industrial News Review from companies' annual reports (Form 1) to Federal Power Commission and letter responses from companies to F.P.C. requests for breakdown of unitemized expenditures.

[16] "FYI," Bulletin No. 12, distributed by Bozell & Jacobs and Central Surveys, May 1950.

[17] "Publishers Predict Goldwater Victory," *American Press,* Oct. 1964, p. 14.

[18] Correspondence file, Federal Power Commission–Montana Power.

[19] Gruening, *op. cit.,* pp. 165–7.

[20] Andrew Heiskell, board chairman, *Time,* and A. L. Cole, general manager, *Reader's Digest,* addresses before 29th annual convention of Edison Electric Institute, New York, June 7, 1961, *Edison Electric Institute Bulletin,* June 1961, p. 184 and pp. 246–8 respectively.

Saturday Evening Post comments are from the introduction to its pamphlet reprint of electric-utility advertising carried in the magazine.

Keith Wheeler, Henry Suydam, Norman Ritter, Bill Wise, and Howard Sochurek, "Now—See the Innards of a Fat Pig," *Life,* Aug. 16, 1963, pp. 20 *et seq.*

[21] Kenneth O. Gilmore and Eugene H. Methvin, "The R.E.A.—A Case Study of Bureaucracy Run Wild," *Reader's Digest,* Dec. 1963, pp. 81–87; Irving Kristol, "Why the Welfare State Doesn't Work," *Reader's Digest,* Nov. 1963, pp. 86–90 (condensed from *Harper's,* June 1963); Charles Stevenson, "The Real Truth about the Federal Budget," *Reader's Digest,* May 1963, pp. 49–51; O. K. Armstrong, "Should Those Co-ops Get Tax Privileges," *Reader's Digest,* Feb. 1962, pp. 69–72.

[22] Senator Hubert H. Humphrey (D-Minn.), "Unfair Attack on Cooperatives," *Congressional Record,* Mar. 16, 1962, CVIII, Part 4, pp. 4402–3.

[23] *Reader's Digest* attacks on the space program include Joe Alex Morris's "The Pork Barrel Goes into Orbit," Aug. 1964, pp. 87–92; Morris's "How Haste in Space Makes Waste," July 1964, pp. 82–87; Blake Clark's "A Job for the Next Congress: Stop the Race to the Moon," Jan. 1964, pp. 75–79; Frances Vivian Drake's "We're Running the Wrong Race with Russia," Aug. 1963, pp. 49–55; and Harland Manchester's "The Senseless Race to Put Man in Space," May 1961, pp. 64–67. The U.S. space effort was pictured as "a vital part of our defense" and one of the "real essentials" in the June 1962 issue, p. 24. However, this characterization of the space program appeared in one of the advertisements of the investor-owned electric light and power companies, from which the *Digest* receives approximately a quarter of a million dollars in advertising revenue annually. The advertisement, after extolling the space program (which provides good business for utilities that serve National Aeronautics and Space Administration facilities), went on to the industry's major point of agreement with the *Digest*—that investor-owned utilities should completely monopolize the industry—with these words:

There is no need to spend tax dollars to build more government power plants and lines . . . the investor-owned electric companies can supply all the additional electric power a growing America needs.

[24] "Anti-power Co-op Article Sent out with Meco Bills," *Gazette and Daily* (York, Pa.), Jan. 30, 1964.

Chapter 12. THE SCHOOLS—GUESS WHO TEACHER IS

(Pp. 152–164)

[1] John D. Garwood, dean of the faculty, Fort Hays Kansas State College, "Economic Education and the Economist," *Public Utilities Fortnightly,* Mar. 12, 1964, pp. 56–59; "Economic Education in the Schools," Report of the National Task Force on Economic Education,

Committee for Economic Development, Sept. 1961, pp. 8–10; "Economics in the Schools," A Report by a Special Textbook Study Committee of the Committee on Economic Education of the American Economic Association, *American Economic Review,* Mar. 1962, Vol. LIII, No. 1, Supplement.

[2] Paul A. Samuelson, professor of economics, Massachusetts Institute of Technology, *Economics, An Introductory Analysis* (6th ed.; New York: McGraw-Hill, 1964).

[3] Samuel Krislov, Michigan State University, and Lloyd D. Musolf, University of California (Davis), editors, *The Politics of Regulation* (Boston: Houghton Mifflin, 1964), p. ix.

[4] *Brookings Publications Checklist,* The Brookings Institution, July 1964; Richard Hellman, *Government Competition in the Electric Utility Industry of the United States.* A study at the Center for Advanced Study at Brookings, Washington, D.C., Aug. 1966.

[5] Robert W. Mayer, "The Decline of Academic Attention to Public Utility Economics," *Land Economics,* Nov. 1961, pp. 375–6.

[6] Garwood, " 'Public Utilities' Now Taught by Few Colleges," *Public Utilities Fortnightly,* Sept. 25, 1958, pp. 446–53.

[7] Letters from William S. Vickrey, chairman, department of economics, Columbia University, Jan. 27, 1965, and John F. Due, chairman, department of economics, University of Illinois, June 25, 1965, to Vic Reinemer; interviews with Texas University Professor Emeritus Robert Montgomery.

[8] Lawrence J. O'Connor, Jr., "Regulatory Accounting Coordination," *Public Utilities Fortnightly,* Mar. 18, 1965, p. 22.

[9] William J. Powell, technical assistant to the chief accountant, Federal Power Commission, "Regulatory Accountants on Trial," *The Federal Accountant,* Mar. 1964, pp. 74–87.

[10] Report of the Public Utilities Securities Committee, Investment Bankers Association of America, 1965 annual convention, Nov. 28–Dec. 3, 1965.

[11] *Consumers All, The Yearbook of Agriculture* (Washington, D.C.: U.S. Government Printing Office, 1965).

[12] U.S., Department of Commerce, "Do You Know Your Economic ABC's?" pamphlet (Washington, D.C.: U.S. Government Printing Office, 1963), p. 7.

[13] Richard Eells, adjunct professor in Business, and Clarence Walton, associate dean, both at Graduate School of Business, Columbia University, *Conceptual Foundations of Business* (Homewood, Ill.: Richard D. Irwin, Inc., 1961), pp. 468–72.

[14] Power-company contributions to economic-interest organizations are from recent annual reports (Form 1) from companies to the Federal Power Commission.

[15] Merryle Stanley Rukeyser, business consultant, writer, "What Education Should Business Support," *The Freeman*, Mar. 1961, p. 34.

[16] Ernest Gruening, *The Public Pays* (New York: Vanguard Press, 1964), pp. 82–84.

[17] Donald S. Kennedy, president, Oklahoma Gas & Electric, "The American Way to a Power-Full Future," *Public Utilities Fortnightly*, June 6, 1957, pp. 796–7.

[18] J. E. Corette, president, Montana Power, "Results of Complete Government Ownership and Control," *Public Service Magazine*, Dec. 1958, p. 9.

[19] J. E. Corette, president, Montana Power, "Electric Power for a Strong America," *Public Service Magazine*, May 1959, pp. 5–11.

[20] C. E. Wright, "Utility Company Starts Speakers Bureau," *Public Utilities Fortnightly*, Aug. 15, 1963, pp. 56–59.

Annual report to stockholders, Cleveland Electric Illuminating, 1963, Central Power & Light, 1963.

[21] "Columbia University 'Used' by Utility Propagandists," *Electric Consumers Information Committee Newsletter*, Oct. 12, 1962, pp. 2–4.

[22] Gruening, *op. cit.*, p. 64.

[23] Robb M. Winsborough, vice president, Middle West Service Company, "A Farm Family Visit to a Powerhouse," *Public Utilities Fortnightly*, June 8, 1961, pp. 810–17.

James H. Collins, "Rigging Your Own Quiz Programs," *Public Utilities Fortnightly*, Nov. 23, 1961, pp. 817–27.

[24] " 'Welfare State' Movie Probed," *Orlando* (Fla.) *Sentinel*, Oct. 24, 1964; "Utility Board Will Probe Disputed Film," *Tampa Tribune*, Oct. 24, 1964; Annual report to stockholders, Public Service Company of Oklahoma, 1962.

[25] Edwin Vennard, managing director, Edison Electric Institute, and Robb M. Winsborough, vice president, Middle West Service Company, *The American Economic System* (Chicago: Middle West Service Company, 1964).

Chapter 13.   LOOK, JANE, LOOK! SEE THE NICE LOW LIGHT BILL!
—The American Economic Foundation
(Pp. 165–179)

[1] Columbus & Southern Ohio letter of Nov. 19, 1964, reproduced and distributed by American Economic Foundation.

[2] "Hearst Loses Suit to Block Inquiry by Senate Group . . . Black Hears Crusaders, Senators Delve into the Radio Activities and Financing of That Organization," *New York Times*, Apr. 9, 1936, p. 1; U.S.,

Congress, Senate, Special Committee to Investigate Lobbying Activities, *Investigation of Lobbying Activities,* Testimony of Fred G. Clark, national commander of the Crusaders, 74th Cong., 2d Sess., Apr. 8, 1936, Part 5, pp. 1731 *et seq.*

³ Scope of American Economic Foundation activity from its 1965 pamphlet, "The Ten Pillars of Economic Wisdom," its monthly *The Economic Facts of Life,* and a flyer advertising the booklet "How We Live in America."

⁴ Kathryn Stewart, *Studies in How We Live* (Haverford, Pa.: Haverford House, 1963); Dr. Enos C. Perry, director, Bureau of Business Education, Chicago Board of Education, quoted in *Proceedings of Institute for Business Education and Secondary School Principals,* sponsored by American Economic Foundation, Connecticut Light & Power, Hartford Electric, United Illuminating, and Connecticut schools, May 2, 1963; *Destination: Burial?,* a staff paper of the American Economic Foundation, 1963.

⁵ Fred G. Clark, "The Socialistic Sixteenth—A National Cancer," *D.A.R. Magazine,* Jan. 1962, pp. 26 *et seq.*

⁶ *The Complete Set of Questions and Answers from the Directomat in the Hall of Free Enterprise at the New York World's Fair 1964–65,* American Economic Foundation, 1964.

⁷ Fred G. Clark, general chairman, American Economic Foundation, "Self-Government's Greatest Problem—Economic Illiteracy," *Public Service Magazine,* Mar. 1961, p. 18.

⁸ Brochure, John Birch Society, 1962; American Economic Foundation, "The Ten Pillars of Economic Wisdom" (pamphlet), 1965; "Responsible Leadership Through the John Birch Society" (pamphlet), John Birch Society, 395 Concord Ave., Belmont, Mass., n.d.; *American Opinion,* May 1966.

⁹ Letter from National Schools Committee to Vic Reinemer, Jan. 18, 1965.

¹⁰ Income of American Economic Foundation from its informational returns (Form 990-A) filed with Internal Revenue Service, and from reports to I.R.S. by the Donner Foundation (formerly Independence Foundation), Armco Foundation (Hook), Ada Hearne Foundation (Heinsohn), and Reader's Digest Foundation.

¹¹ "What Is the Heart of the American Idea?" advertisement on behalf of American Economic Foundation, *Coronet,* Aug. 1964, p. 3.

¹² Information on Christian Freedom Foundation from its literature (see, for example, *Christian Economics,* June 28, 1966), informational returns (Form 990-A) filed by Pew foundations with Internal Revenue Service; Ralph Lord Roy, *Apostles of Discord* (Boston: Beacon Press, 1953), pp. 294–99, 304, 328; Howard E. Kershner, "The Communist Takeover of America," address delivered at Harding College, Searcy,

Ark., Apr. 17, 1961; "Statement of Ownership and Circulation," *American Opinion,* Nov. 1963, p. 75.

13 Clark, "Self-Government's Greatest Problem . . . ," pp. 16–20.

14 Letter from Jack K. Busby, president, Pennsylvania Power & Light, to Senator Lee Metcalf, Dec. 10, 1964.

15 "Teachers Get New Look at Free Enterprise," *Montana Citizen* (published by Montana Chamber of Commerce), Sept. 10, 1964, p. 4.

16 Letter from J. J. Harrington, vice president, Montana Power, to Federal Power Commission, Nov. 6, 1964.

17 Letter from S. F. Leahy, vice president, Detroit Edison, to Fred G. Clark, chairman, American Economic Foundation, Apr. 11, 1963, distributed by A.E.F.

18 Data on power-company contributions to American Economic Foundation from companies' annual (Form 1) reports to Federal Power Commission and F.P.C. correspondence files, and from American Economic Foundation's annual (Form 990-A) reports to Internal Revenue Service.

19 The Internal Revenue Service decision against publicizing contributors and amounts contributed to a tax-exempt organization is based upon Sections 6033 (b) and 6104 of the Internal Revenue Code. Section 6033 (b) (8) refers to publicizing "the *total* of contributions and gifts received by it during the year." The accompanying House committee report (House Report 775, 85th Cong.) said, in explanation of the public availability of the information on contributions to tax-exempt organizations:

It should be noted that this refers merely to the total contributions and gifts received. Thus, it will not be necessary to submit lists of contributions made by individual contributors. (U.S., Congress, House, Ways and Means Committee, *Technical Amendments Act of 1957,* 85th Congr., 1st Sess., House Report 775, pp. 41–43.)

Chapter 14. GET THE GOVERNMENT OUT OF GOVERNMENT
—The Foundation for Economic Education

(Pp. 179–191)

1 Letter from Leonard E. Read, president, Foundation for Economic Education, to W. C. Mullendore, president, Southern California Edison, U.S., Congress, House Select Committee on Lobbying Activities, *Lobbying, Direct and Indirect,* 81st Cong., 2d Sess., 1950, Part 8, pp. 58–59.

2 The hearing cited above, at which FEE President Read testified, and FEE correspondence and publications that were placed in the

hearing record are the sources for information on the foundation's early years. Contributions to and purchases from FEE and other organizations, by company, are found in the committee's subsequent report, U.S., Congress, House Select Committee on Lobbying Activities, *Expenditures by Corporations to Influence Legislation*, 81st Cong., 2d Sess., 1950, House Report 3137.

[3] Leonard E. Read, "Activities at FEE," brochure, Foundation for Economic Education, 1964.

[4] Leonard E. Read, "The Market Is a Computer," *The Freeman*, Mar. 1964, pp. 44–52.

[5] Leonard E. Read, "The Case for the Free Market in Education," *The Freeman*, Sept. 1964, pp. 10–20.

[6] Admiral Ben Moreell, "Adult Delinquency," *The Freeman*, July 1960, pp. 3–12; Leonard E. Read, "Kakistocracy," *The Freeman*, August 1963, pp. 19–27; John Chamberlain, "Overlooked Taxes—And Principles," *The Freeman*, Jan. 1964, pp. 60–63.

[7] John C. Sparks, "Zoned Or Owned?" *The Freeman*, June 1964, pp. 3–14.

[8] John C. Sparks, "The Highway Dilemma," *The Freeman*, Aug. 1961, pp. 14–18.

[9] Leonard E. Read, " 'Business Is Entitled to a Fair Profit,' " *The Freeman*, Apr. 1963, pp. 38–40.

[10] Paul L. Poirot, "The War on Poverty," *The Freeman*, July 1964, p. 46.

[11] Ronald H. Coase, professor of economics, University of Virginia, "Why Not Use the Pricing System in the Broadcasting Industry?" *The Freeman*, July 1961, pp. 52–57.

[12] Melvin D. Barger, "Let the People Own the Airwaves," *The Freeman*, June 1962, pp. 3–15.

[13] Melvin D. Barger, "Could A.T.&T. Run the Post Office?" *The Freeman*, Oct. 1962, pp. 22–31.

[14] John Chamberlain, "A Reviewer's Notebook," *The Freeman*, Dec. 1956, pp. 55–59.

[15] Leonard E. Read, "Violence as a Way of Life," *The Freeman*, Feb. 1962, pp. 18–27.

[16] Paul L. Poirot, "$48,000," *The Freeman*, Feb. 1965, pp. 44–45.

[17] Dean Russell, "The T.V.A. Idea," Foundation for Economic Education, 1949.

[18] Fred Rogers Fairchild, Knox Professor Emeritus of economics, Yale, and Thomas J. Shelly, former economics teacher, Yonkers (N.Y.) High School, *Understanding Our Free Economy* (3d ed.; Princeton: D. Van Nostrand, 1962).

[19] Thomas J. Shelly, "High School Economics," *The Freeman*, Feb. 1956, pp. 29–31.

20 "A Literature of Freedom," Foundation for Economic Education book order form distributed in 1964; "Approved" (book) list, *Bulletin, John Birch Society*, Apr. 1962.

21 Dr. Hans F. Sennholz, professor of economics, Grove City College (Pa.), "Volunteers for the Peace Corps," *The Freeman*, Sept. 1961, pp. 38–43.

22 John Birch Society affiliations of FEE trustees from Society letterheads in 1965 and from 1962 listing of endorsers published by the Society. In July 1966 the Society advised the Library of Congress that it had not since listed its committee of endorsers. See also "Responsible Leadership Through the John Birch Society" (brochure), n.d., John Birch Society, with sketches of Founder Robert Welch and the 30-man national council, described as "the top advisory body in matters of organization and policy."

23 Power-company donations to Foundation for Economic Education during its early years appear in the hearings and report of the House Select Committee on Lobbying Activities referred to in note 2 above. Contributions in fiscal 1964 are from FEE's report to Internal Revenue Service, Form 990-A, "Return of Organization Exempt from Income Tax."

Chapter 15. HOW THE OLD GRADS STRUNG ANOTHER
TRANSMISSION LINE
—The Intercollegiate Society of Individualists

(Pp. 191–194)

1 M. Stanton Evans, *Revolt on the Campus* (Chicago: Henry Regnery, 1961), pp. 5–7, 31–32, 60, 63–65; *Human Events*, Apr. 21, 1961.

2 Young Americans for Freedom newsletter, Feb. 16, 1962; 1962 listing by John Birch Society.

3 U.S., Congress, House, Committee on Interstate and Foreign Commerce, *Public Utility Holding Companies*, H.R. 5423, 74th Cong., 1st Sess., 1935. Also *Congressional Record*, June 28, 1935, pp. 10358–9; Aug. 15, 1935, pp. 13275–7; Aug. 26, 1935, pp. (Appendix) 15112–3. The first two *Record* references carry speeches on Congressman Pettingill's role in the holding company fight by a fellow member of the House Interstate and Foreign Commerce Committee, Representative Edward S. Eicher of Iowa. The third *Congressional Record* reference carries an exchange of correspondence between Pettingill and Eicher.

4 Annual reports (Form 990-A) by Intercollegiate Society of Individualists to Internal Revenue Service.

Chapter 16. A MULTI-WATT GENERATOR
—The National Education Program at Harding College

(Pp. 194–201)

[1] Dr. George S. Benson, president (until 1965) of Harding College and still president of the National Education Program, quoted by Cabell Phillips, "Wide Anti-Red Drive Directed from Small Town in Arkansas," *New York Times,* May 18, 1961, p. 26.

[2] Middle South Services quoted in "Can Private Enterprise Survive in America," the National Education Program, 1965.

[3] "Thunder on the Far Right," *Newsweek,* Dec. 4, 1961, p. 20.

[4] Phillips, *op. cit.*

[5] "Direct Tax Urged on All Incomes," *New York Times,* Aug. 22, 1941, p. 9.

[6] Richard Dudman, *Men of the Far Right* (New York: Pyramid Books, 1962), p. 100; Hilger v. Harding College, Inc., 331 S.W. 2d 851.

[7] *American Opinion,* May 1966; *Freedom Forum Facts,* National Education Program, n.d.; "Responsible Leadership Through the John Birch Society" (pamphlet), John Birch Society, n.d.

[8] *National Program Letter,* National Education Program, Apr. 1960.

[9] *Bulletin,* John Birch Society, May 1960, pp. 3–5.

[10] *Ibid.,* April 1961, p. 2.

[11] Phillips, *op. cit.*

[12] Purchase or use of the film, *Communism on the Map,* by power companies from "Communism on the Map," a brochure by National Education Program; George D. Gentry, coordinator, Tampa Electric Speakers Bureau, "How to Organize and Operate a Speakers Bureau," speech before Sales, Advertising and Public Relations Section, Southeastern Electric Exchange, Williamsburg, Va., Nov. 12, 1963; "P.G.&E. Answers Teacher's Charges on Ad Expenses," *Electrical World,* Aug. 19, 1963, p. 18; Alan F. Westin, associate professor of public law and government, Columbia University, "Anti-Communism and the Corporations," *Commentary,* Dec. 1963, pp. 479–87.

[13] Donations by utilities to National Education Program or Harding College from the companies' annual (Form 1) reports to Federal Power Commission and F.P.C. correspondence files.

[14] Benson, "Workers Reject 'Public' Power," *Public Service Magazine,* 1956, pp. 20–21.

[15] Participation of power companies and other organizations in Freedom Forums from *Freedom Forum Facts.*

Chapter 17. HOW TO FIND REDS UNDER EVERY BED
—The Southern States Industrial Council

(Pp. 201–209)

¹ "A Declaration of Policy," board of directors, Southern States Industrial Council, adopted at annual meeting, Ponte Vedra Inn, Ponte Vedra, Fla., May 21–23, 1962, and reaffirmed at The Homestead, Hot Spring, Va., May 20–22, 1963.

² Howard A. Rusk, M.D., "Hoover and the U.N.," *New York Times,* Aug. 9, 1964, p. 79; Mrs. Virginia M. Gray, executive secretary, Citizens Committee for UNICEF, statement before House Committee on Foreign Affairs, Mar. 9, 1965; "Foreign Assistance Act of 1965," Part IV, pp. 561–72; Representative Walter H. Judd, "The Facts about the United Nations Children's Fund," *Congressional Record,* Aug. 14, 1962, CVIII, Part 12, pp. 16532–34; *UNICEF Facts and Fallacies,* United States Committee for UNICEF, 1964.

³ "Says South Clings to Moral Values," *New York Times,* April 30, 1935; Southern States Industrial Council pamphlets; Tyre Taylor, general counsel, Southern States Industrial Council, statement before House Ways and Means Committee, *President's 1963 Tax Message,* Part V, Mar. 19, 1963, pp. 2712–16.

⁴ "The Civil Rights Bill," statement adopted by the board of directors of the Southern States Industrial Council on May 22, 1964, at its annual meeting.

⁵ Thurman Sensing, executive vice president, Southern States Industrial Council, "Conservatism Is Patriotism," pamphlet, Southern States Industrial Council.

⁶ Luther J. Carter, "A 'Voice' Guides Conservative South," Norfolk *Virginian-Pilot,* Aug. 2, 1964, p. B1.

⁷ W. Brooke Graves, *American Intergovernmental Relations* (New York: Scribner's, 1964), "One Hundred and Eighty-Five Years of Federal Aid to Education, Major Educational Enactments" (table), pp. 510–11; *It's Older than the Constitution,* National Education Association, Aug. 1957.

⁸ Contributions to Southern States Industrial Council from reports to Secretary of the Senate in compliance with Regulation of Lobbying Act, P.L. 79–601.

⁹ Annual reports (Form 1) from Idaho Power to Federal Power Commission, 1953–62.

¹⁰ U.S., Congress, House, Select Committee on Lobbying Activities, *Expenditures by Corporations to Influence Legislation,* 81st Cong., 2d Sess., 1950, House Report 3137, p. 421.

Chapter 18. BOOK REVIEWS FOR THE BIRCHERS
—America's Future

(Pp. 210–220)

[1] U.S., Congress, House, Select Committee on Lobbying Activities, *General Interim Report*, 81st Cong., 2d Sess., 1950, House Report 3138, pp. 50–51.

[2] *What America's Future Does to Keep Free Enterprise and Constitutional Government Alive and Healthy for America*, America's Future, Inc., n.d., distributed in 1964.

[3] *Readings in Liberty*, America's Future, Inc., n.d., distributed in 1965.

[4] Rosalie M. Gordon, *Nine Men Against America* (New York: Devin-Adair, 1958).

[5] Ted Schafers, "Welch Defends Birch Society Ideals," *St. Louis Globe-Democrat*, Jan. 21, 1963, p. 3A.

[6] Dr. E. Merrill Root, *Brainwashing in the High Schools* (New York: Devin-Adair, 1958) and *Collectivism on the Campus* (New York: Devin-Adair, 1955), *American Opinion*, May 1966.

[7] *Dynamic Programs Upholding Free Enterprise and Constitutional Government*, America's Future, Inc., n.d., distributed in 1964; *The Textbook Evaluation Committee of America's Future, Inc.*, America's Future, Inc., n.d.; "FYI," Bulletin No. 12, Bozell & Jacobs, Inc., and Central Surveys, Inc., May 31, 1950; John Birch Society brochure, 1962; *White Book*, John Birch Society, 1961; *Educational Reviewer*, July 15, 1949; "Speakers Rap 'Collectivism' in Education," *Omaha Evening World-Herald*, Oct. 1, 1953, p. 1; masthead, *American Opinion*.

[8] Harry and Bonaro Overstreet, *The Strange Tactics of Extremism* (New York: W. W. Norton, 1964), esp. Chapter 17, "Four Targets"; Jack Nelson and Gene Roberts, Jr., *The Censors and the Schools* (Boston: Little, Brown, 1963); Donald Janson and Bernard Eismann, *The Far Right* (New York: McGraw-Hill, 1963); Mary Anne Raywid, *The Ax-Grinders* (New York: Macmillan, 1962); *On Target* (published by Minutemen), Sept. 1, 1965.

[9] U.S., Congress, House, Select Committee on Lobbying Activities, *General Interim Report*.

[10] U.S., Congress, House, Select Committee on Lobbying Activities, *Expenditures by Corporations to Influence Legislation*, 81st Cong., 2d Sess., 1950, House Report 3137.

[11] U.S., Congress, House, Select Committee on Lobbying Activities, *Lobbying, Direct and Indirect—Committee for Constitutional Government*, Part V, 81st Cong., 2d Sess., June 27, 28, 29, and Aug. 25, 1950.

[12] Annual reports (Form 1) of power companies to Federal Power Commission.

[13] Forster and Epstein, *Danger on the Right,* p. 12.

Chapter 19. GODFATHERS, RELATIVES, AND THE
ILL-BEGOTTEN

(Pp. 220–226)

[1] Southern States Industrial Council brochure and letterhead, 1964; Ernest Gruening, *The Public Pays* (New York: Vanguard, 1931, 1964), pp. 217–8 (1964 edition); U.S., Congress, Senate Document 92, *Utility Corporations,* 70th Cong., 1st Sess., 1928, Part 71A, pp. 92, 98, 100–2, 378–9.

[2] U.S., Congress, House, Select Committee on Lobbying Activities, *Expenditures by Corporations to Influence Legislation,* 81st Cong., 2d Sess., 1950, House Report 3137.

[3] Federal Power Commission correspondence files re Florida Power & Light.

[4] Gerald L. Andrus, then president, New Orleans Public Service, now board chairman, Middle South Utilities, "Future Unlimited," an address before Junior Achievement banquet, May 10, 1962, New Orleans, *Public Service Magazine,* July 1962, pp. 17–21; editorial paragraph, *loc. cit.,* June 1962, p. 7; "The Southwestern Power Administration: A Case History in Plunder by Bureaucrats," *loc. cit.,* Apr. 1964, p. 23; "Monopolies, Corporations and the Government," *loc. cit.,* Jan. 1963, pp. 21–4; "How Does One Measure a Yardstick?" *loc. cit.,* Sept. 1964, p. 15; "A Convincing Experience in Municipal Ownership of Electric System," *loc. cit.,* Apr. 1963, p. 29–30.

[5] Sterling Starbuck, "Education Policy Makers Urge Marxian Teaching in Schools," *Public Service Magazine,* Dec. 1953, pp. 6–8.

[6] "Initial List of Approved Books," "Recommended Periodicals," *Bulletin,* John Birch Society, Apr. 1962, pp. 21–32.

[7] *Bulletin,* John Birch Society, May 1961, pp. 23–4.

[8] Barry Goldwater, then U.S. Senator from Arizona, "The American Way in Tomorrow's World," condensation of address before 27th annual convention, Edison Electric Institute, New Orleans, Apr. 1959, *Public Service Magazine,* May 1959, pp. 13–17.

[9] Dan Thomasson, "Sale of Political Books Hit by Some G.O.P. Heads," *Rocky Mountain News* (Denver), Sept. 14, 1964, p. 14.

[10] *Bulletin,* John Birch Society, January 1965; "Recommended Election-Year Reading," *Southern States Industrial Council Bulletin,* Aug. 1, 1964; form letter (n.d.) distributed by America's Future, Inc.

PART IV. WHAT TO DO ABOUT IT

Chapter 20. REGULATION

(Pp. 227–236)

1 Re General Telephone Co. of Florida (1959) 29 PUR (3rd) 29, Florida Public Service Commission.

2 Paul J. Garfield, Ph.D., and Wallace F. Lovejoy, Ph.D., *Public Utility Economics* (Englewood Cliffs, N.J.: Prentice-Hall, 1964), pp. 264–66.

3 U.S., Congress, Senate, Appropriations Subcommittee on Independent Offices, *Independent Offices Appropriations, 1966,* May 17, 1965, testimony of Joseph C. Swidler, chairman, Federal Power Commission, pp. 373 *et seq.*

4 John R. Barrett, city attorney, Miami, "Municipal Participation in Public Utility Rate Hearings," remarks before 39th annual convention, Florida League of Municipalities, Miami, Oct. 25, 1965; Maurice Te Paske, mayor, Sioux Center, Iowa, quoted in "Help Other Cities Establish Municipal Systems, Iowa Mayor Urges," *APPA Weekly Newsletter,* published by American Public Power Association, Sept. 24, 1965.

5 Dr. John J. Reid, chairman, Massachusetts Council, quoted in "Massachusetts May Create Commission to Study Power Rates," *APPA Weekly Newsletter,* Nov. 19, 1965, p. 7.

6 Davis A. Kosh, public-utility consultant, "Uncle Sam—Biggest Utility Customer," *Public Utilities Fortnightly,* July 21, 1955, pp. 84–94.

7 U.S., Congress, House, *1964 Annual Report, Federal Power Commission,* 89th Cong., 1st Sess., House, Doc. 17, pp. 121–22.

8 *Empire Trust Letter,* Sept. 1965, p. 1.

9 "Survey of Utility Losses Due to Bad Handwriting," *Public Utilities Fortnightly,* July 21, 1955, pp. 127–28.

10 "Computer Use Grows in Electric Utility Industry," *Public Utilities Fortnightly,* Jan. 21, 1965; "If Industry Computers Spoke the Same Language," *Electrical World,* June 1, 1964, p. 7; Francis X. Welch, editor, *Public Utilities Fortnightly,* "Computer Information Expands," *Public Utilities Fortnightly,* Jan. 21, 1965, p. 6; "Service Bureaus Offer Utilities Computer Use," *Public Power,* Nov. 1964, p. 11; Wayne Hall, manager of public operation, Midwest region, International Business Machines, "Putting the INFORM in INFORMation," *Public Power,* Nov. 1964, pp. 9–10.

11 Frank Twohy, vice president, Wainwright and Ramsey, Inc., "The Accountant and E.D.P.," *Public Power,* Apr. 1965, pp. 29 *et seq.*

[12] "F.C.C. Recommends Computer Use in Records Maintenance," *Public Utilities Fortnightly,* June 18, 1964, pp. 43–44.

[13] Francis X. Welch, editor, "Regulating Utility Competition," *Public Utilities Fortnightly,* Jan. 16, 1964, pp. 6–7.

[14] The company with a 6.91% rate of return and 20.83% return on common stock (in 1963) is Indiana-Michigan Electric, a subsidiary of American Electric Power. See Appendix C, pp. 260–269, for similar data on other companies.

[15] William B. Heberton, senior analyst, Drexel and Company, "Stock Purchase Plan for Customers," *Public Utilities Fortnightly,* Aug. 1, 1963, pp. 24–9; William H. Dinsmore, "Dear Stockholders, Everything Looks Rosy . . . ," *Harper's,* Mar. 1965, pp. 134–35. For details on how Samuel Insull, utility leader during the early 20th century, introduced customer stock ownership as a public-relations device, see Forrest McDonald, *Insull* (Chicago: University of Chicago Press, 1962), pp. 203–205.

[16] *Bluefield Waterworks & Improvement Co.* v. *Public Service Commission of West Virginia,* 262 U.S., 679, 692 (1923); *Re Hope Natural Gas Co.,* 44 PUR (NS) 1, 24 (1942).

[17] Paul J. Garfield, Ph.D., and Wallace F. Lovejoy, Ph.D., *Public Utility Economics* (Englewood Cliffs, N.J.: Prentice-Hall, 1964), pp. 73, 118–9.

Chapter 21. COMPETITION

(Pp. 237–252)

[1] Hans H. Landsberg, Leonard L. Fischman, and Joseph L. Fisher, *Resources in America's Future* (Baltimore: Johns Hopkins Press, 1963), p. 189.

[2] "In 1970: Six Million Electrically Heated Homes," *Electrical World,* Nov. 18, 1963, pp. 88–94; Donald C. Cook, president, American Electric Power, quoted in "E.E.I. Convention," *Public Utilities Fortnightly,* July 4, 1963, p. 59.

[3] M. L. Feldman, General Electric official, "Urban Transportation Alternatives," a paper presented at Urban Transportation Symposium, Stanford Research Institute, Menlo Park, Calif., May 27, 1964; Howard Simons, "New Idea Would Put Americans in 'Go-Carts,' " *Washington Post,* Feb. 2, 1965, p. A2.

[4] *Restoring the Quality of our Environment,* report of the Environmental Pollution Panel, President's Science Advisory Committee, Nov. 1965; Howard Simons, "Report to L.B.J. Urges Taxing All Polluters," *Washington Post,* Nov. 7, 1965, pp. 1 *et seq.*

[5] "Fight Water with Water, Assertions with Facts," editorial, *Electrical World,* June 22, 1964, p. 5; "The Quest for Water," *Agriculture and Livestock,* monthly publication of Valley National Bank of Arizona, reprinted in *Congressional Record,* Jan. 14, 1965, CXI, Part 1, Appendix, pp. A141–2.

[6] Albert W. Stone, editor, *Is a Preference among Distributors of Federal Power Justified?,* Proceedings of the First Annual Water Resources Conference, University of Montana, Missoula, Mont., July 20–21, 1956.

[7] Charles R. Ross, member, Federal Power Commission, statement in support of proposed bill (draft B) concerning F.P.C. jurisdiction over extra-high-voltage transmission lines, to Senate Commerce Committee, Apr. 16, 1965.

[8] Representative John Moss (D-Calif.), "Repeal the Keating Proviso," *Public Power,* Mar. 1965, pp. 17 *et seq.*

[9] Rufus Terral, "Struggle for Power," series of three articles, *St. Louis Post-Dispatch,* Feb. 24–26, 1964; "Our Stakes in Pooled Power," editorial, *St. Louis Post-Dispatch,* Feb. 28, 1964; Senator Lee Metcalf, "Mid-Continent Area Plans," speech including documents relating to origin and goals of Mid-Continent Area Power Planners (MAPP), *Congressional Record,* Aug. 20, 1963, Vol. CIX, Part 11, pp. 15397–15409.

[10] Robert O. Marritz, assistant engineer-counsel, National Rural Electric Cooperative Association, "Electric Power Pools and the Anti-Trust Laws," monograph.

[11] Examples of territorial disputes obtained from reports to Congress by the Rural Electrification Administration and from *Rural Electrification* and *Rural Electric Minuteman,* both published by the National Rural Electric Cooperative Association.

[12] Benjamin Friedman, mayor, Taunton, Mass., "Importance of a Municipal Power Plant in Your Community," address, Oct. 14, 1964, before Holyoke (Mass.) Gas and Electric Guild.

[13] Mark R. Anson, "They're Sorry They Sold," *Public Power,* Nov. 1965, pp. 12 *et seq.*

[14] Leland Olds, former chairman, Federal Power Commission, "The Public Power Issue in 1956," address at Colby College, Waterville, Me., Apr. 26, 1956; Georgia Power agreement from the company's Form 1 report to Federal Power Commission, 1962.

[15] Aubrey J. Wagner, chairman of the board, Tennessee Valley Authority, "The T.V.A. Experiment—Past, Present and Future," address at Littauer Center of Public Administration, Harvard University, Dec. 8, 1965; Wagner, "Public Power: In the American Tradition," address to Electric League of Chattanooga, Tenn., May 19, 1964; *T.V.A.'s Influence on Electric Rates,* Tennessee Valley Authority, Mar. 1965.

[16] Lawrence Howard, president, Franklin Power & Light, Franklin, Tenn., signed editorial reprinted in *Lewistown* (Mont.) *Daily News,* Jan. 31, 1964.

Chapter 22. INFORMATION

(Pp. 252–254)

[1] Willard Clopton, "P.U.C. Hearing Invites 86 Groups; One Appears," *Washington Post,* Apr. 30, 1964, p. D17.

INDEX